Practical Data Mining Techniques and Applications

Data mining techniques and algorithms are extensively used to build real-world applications. A practical approach can be applied to data mining techniques to build applications. Once deployed, an application enables the developers to work on the users' goals and mold the algorithms with respect to users' perspectives.

Practical Data Mining Techniques and Applications focuses on various concepts related to data mining and how these techniques can be used to develop and deploy applications. The book provides a systematic composition of fundamental concepts of data mining blended with practical applications. The aim of this book is to provide access to practical data mining applications and techniques to help readers gain an understanding of data mining in practice. Readers also learn how relevant techniques and algorithms are applied to solve problems and to provide solutions to real-world applications in different domains. This book can help academicians to extend their knowledge of the field as well as their understanding of applications based on different techniques to gain greater insight. It can also help researchers with real-world applications by diving deeper into the domain. Computing science students, application developers, and business professionals may also benefit from this examination of applied data science techniques.

By highlighting an overall picture of the field, introducing various mining techniques, and focusing on different applications and research directions using these methods, this book can motivate discussions among academics, researchers, professionals, and students to exchange and develop their views regarding the dynamic field that is data mining.

Practical Data Mining Techniques and Applications

Edited by
Dr. Ketan Shah
Dr. Neepa Shah
Dr. Vinaya Sawant
Dr. Neeraj Parolia

CRC Press
Taylor & Francis Group

AN AUERBACH BOOK

First edition published 2023
by CRC Press
6000 Broken Sound Parkway NW, Suite 300, Boca Raton, FL 33487-2742

and by CRC Press
4 Park Square, Milton Park, Abingdon, Oxon, OX14 4RN

CRC Press is an imprint of Taylor & Francis Group, LLC

ISBN: 978-1-032-23267-6 (hbk)
ISBN: 978-1-032-48677-2 (pbk)
ISBN: 978-1-003-39022-0 (ebk)

DOI: 10.1201/9781003390220

Typeset in Adobe Garamond Pro
by codeMantra

Contents

Preface

The computerization has substantially enhanced our capabilities for both generating and collecting data from diverse sources. This tremendous and explosive growth in the data has generated an urgent requirement for new methods and software tools that can brilliantly help in converting this huge dataset into useful information and knowledge. This demand has given rise to promising field in computer science known as data mining. Data mining, which is also known as Knowledge Discovery in Databases (KDD), is the automated retrieval of hidden patterns representing knowledge. This can be either captured from a large database, or data warehouses, or the Web. It is a multidisciplinary field and thus involves work from different areas like statistics, machine learning, pattern recognition, database technology, information retrieval, network science, knowledge-based systems, artificial intelligence, high-performance computing, and data visualization.

Data mining techniques and algorithms can be extensively used to build real-world applications. A practical approach can be applied to data mining techniques to build these applications. An application once deployed enables the developers to work on the users' goals and mold the algorithms with respect to users' perspectives.

This book majorly focuses on various concepts related to data mining and how these techniques can be used to develop and deploy applications. The book provides systematic composition of fundamental concepts of data mining blended with practical applications. The aim of this book is providing access to a number of practical applications of data mining along with the techniques used. This will help readers to gain the understanding of data mining techniques and how relevant techniques, or algorithms, are applied to solve the problem or provide the solution to real-world applications in different domains. This book will help academicians to extend their knowledge in the field of data mining and understanding applications based on different techniques will give a deep insight of the topic. This will also help researchers to work toward these real-world applications and dwell deeper into it.

It is also useful for computing science students, application developers, and business professionals, as well as researchers involved in any of the disciplines previously listed. This book highlights an overall picture of the field, introducing various mining techniques and then focusing on different applications and research directions using these methods. We hope that this book will motivate people with different backgrounds and expertise to exchange their views regarding data mining. This in turn will be the contribution toward this dynamic field.

This book is not intended as an introduction to statistics, machine learning, database systems, or other such areas.

Organization of the Book

The book chapters deal with the applications that are implemented using data mining techniques. The applications are not just restricted to classic data mining techniques such as clustering, classification, and rule mining. These applications are also implemented in the domains of machine learning, image mining, human mobility mining, distributed mining, sensor data mining, medical data mining, etc. The chapters identified talk about the problem statement in the respective domain, its implementation using data mining algorithms and applications based on the applied data mining.

Chapter 1 introduces the multidisciplinary field of data mining. Chapter 2 focuses on the application of classification; Chapter 3 describes the application of neural networks titled Near Human-Level Style Transfer. A research work on document clustering is presented in Chapter 4. An application of machine learning in the field of medical science is described in Chapter 5. Chapter 6 also deals with an application of Federated Machine Learning. Chapter 7 specifically focuses on medical data mining. A distinctive application of Human Mobility Data Mining is well attended in Chapter 8. A very popular application market basket analysis using Association Rule Mining can also be handled using distributed data mining and that is presented in Chapter 9. In the era of security, Chapter 10 deals with the intrusion detection using data mining. Today's world deals with the data from sensors and to handle the data mining in IoT domain, Chapter 11 focuses on a smart application of cradle for infant soothing and monitoring. Chapter 12 is an example of pattern mining where the focus of the application is recognizing word-level patterns in Devanagari text. Chapter 13 concentrates on the interesting applications of image mining in the form of Wall Paint Visualizer. Chapter 14 illustrates an artificial intelligence based clothing fashion stylist.

Acknowledgments

This book is the result of a conversation between best friends thinking and discussing many times the research work in data mining and looking forward for young generations to explore more in this domain. It took an immense amount of time and work, and it would have not been possible without the invaluable contributions of incredibly thoughtful and supportive people. Writing a book is harder than we thought and more rewarding than we could have imagined.

Writing book reviews is tough. It doesn't matter whether it is a couple of lines and a rating, or a well-thought-out essay, it takes effort for a reviewer to translate all the emotions and experiences they've just felt and translate it into something concise, considered, and heartfelt. We wanted to take a moment to say a special "thank you" to several people who took the time to write extended reviews. We greatly appreciate your time and feedback.

We would like to thank God Almighty for giving us the strength, knowledge, ability, and opportunity to embark on this book and to persevere and complete it satisfactorily. Without his blessings, this achievement would not have been possible. Great thanks to all our family members who have always been our backbone for support and encouragement in the form of blessings and understanding.

Last, but not least, we would like to thank all the people who have directly or indirectly helped us.

Dr. Ketan Shah   **Dr. Neepa Shah**   **Dr. Vinaya Sawant**   **Dr. Neeraj Parolia**

Contributors

Vrutik Adani
Department of Information
  Technology
St. Francis Institute of Technology
Mumbai, Maharashtra, India

Aditya Adhduk
Department of Information
  Technology
Dwarkadas J. Sanghvi College of
  Engineering
Mumbai, Maharashtra, India

Harshil Suresh Bhorawat
Department of Information
  Technology
Dwarkadas J. Sanghvi College of
  Engineering
Mumbai, Maharashtra, India

Jeff Conlin
William Allen White School
  of Journalism and Mass
  Communications
University of Kansas
Kansas City, Kansas, USA

Beryl Coutinho
Department of Information
  Technology
St. Francis Institute of Technology
Mumbai, Maharashtra, India

Martin Devasia
Department of Information
  Technology
St. Francis Institute of Technology
Mumbai, Maharashtra, India

Pratiti Diddi
Department of communication
George Mason University
Fairfax, Virginia, USA

Princy Doshi
Department of Information
  Technology
Dwarkadas J. Sanghvi College of
  Engineering
Mumbai, Maharashtra, India

Jenslee Dsouza
Department of Information
  Technology
St. Francis Institute of Technology
Mumbai, Maharashtra, India

Cyrus Ferreira
Department of Information
  Technology
St. Francis Institute of Technology
Mumbai, Maharashtra, India

Vaishali Jadhav
Department of Information
  Technology
St. Francis Institute of Technology
Mumbai, Maharashtra, India

Chirag Jagad
Department of Information
  Technology
Dwarkadas J. Sanghvi College of
  Engineering
Mumbai, Maharashtra, India

Chirag Jain
Department of Information
  Technology
Dwarkadas J. Sanghvi College of
  Engineering
Mumbai, Maharashtra, India

Neha Katre
Department of Information
  Technology
Dwarkadas J. Sanghvi College of
  Engineering
Mumbai, Maharashtra, India

Shreya Kulkarni
Department of Information
  Technology
Dwarkadas J. Sanghvi College of
  Engineering
Mumbai, Maharashtra, India

Chaitanya Kumbar
Department of Information
  Technology
Dwarkadas J. Sanghvi College of
  Engineering
Mumbai, Maharashtra, India

Sushma Kumble
Department of Mass Communication
Towson University
Towson, Maryland, USA

Sahil Lunawat
Department of Information
  Technology
Dwarkadas J. Sanghvi College of
  Engineering
Mumbai, Maharashtra, India

Sunita Mahajan
Institute of Computer Science
M.E.T., Bandra (west)
Mumbai, Maharashtra, India

Shikha Mehta
Department of Information
  Technology
Dwarkadas J. Sanghvi College of
  Engineering
Mumbai, Maharashtra, India

Sheldon Moonjelil
Department of Information
  Technology
St. Francis Institute of Technology
Mumbai, Maharashtra, India

Om Naik
Department of Information
  Technology
Dwarkadas J. Sanghvi College of
  Engineering
Mumbai, Maharashtra, India

Neeraj Parolia
Business Analytics and Technology
  Management Department
Towson University
Townson, Maryland, USA

Leander Pereira
Department of Information
   Technology
St. Francis Institute of Technology
Mumbai, Maharashtra, India

Rahul Pereira
Department of Information
   Technology
St. Francis Institute of Technology
Mumbai, Maharashtra, India

Jayashree Rajesh Prasad
Department of Computer Science &
   Engineering
MIT Art, Design, and Technology
   University
Pune, Maharashtra, India

Rajesh Shardanand Prasad
MIT Art, Design, and Technology
   University
Pune, Maharashtra, India

Jainam Rambhia
Department of Information
   Technology
Dwarkadas J. Sanghvi College of
   Engineering
Mumbai, Maharashtra, India

Nihar M Ranjan
Department of Information
   Technology
Rajarshi Shahu College of Engineering
Pune, Maharashtra, India

Sannidhi Rao
Department of Information
   Technology
Dwarkadas J. Sanghvi College of
   Engineering
Mumbai, Maharashtra, India

Pavan Raval
Department of Information
   Technology
St. Francis Institute of Technology
Mumbai, Maharashtra, India

Lissa Rodrigues
Department of Information
   Technology
St. Francis Institute of Technology
Mumbai, Maharashtra, India

Aakash Sangani
Department of Information
   Technology
Dwarkadas J. Sanghvi College of
   Engineering
Mumbai, Maharashtra, India

Ritik Sanghvi
Department of Information
   Technology
Dwarkadas J. Sanghvi College of
   Engineering
Mumbai, Maharashtra, India

Hritik Ganesh Sawant
Department of Information
   Technology
Dwarkadas J. Sanghvi College of
   Engineering
Mumbai, Maharashtra, India

Vinaya Sawant
Department of Information
   Technology
Dwarkadas J. Sanghvi College of
   Engineering
Mumbai, Maharashtra, India

Ketan Shah
Department of Information
  Technology
Mukesh Patel School of Technology
  Management and Engineering,
  NMIMS
Mumbai, Maharashtra, India

Neepa Shah
Department of Information
  Technology
Dwarkadas J. Sanghvi College of
  Engineering
Mumbai, Maharashtra, India

Raj Shah
Department of Information
  Technology
St. Francis Institute of Technology
Mumbai, Maharashtra, India

Rutwik Shailesh Shah
Department of Information
  Technology
Dwarkadas J. Sanghvi College of
  Engineering
Mumbai, Maharashtra, India

Sakshi Shetty
Department of Information
  Technology
St. Francis Institute of Technology
Mumbai, Maharashtra, India

Dhrumil Thakore
Department of Information
  Technology
Dwarkadas J. Sanghvi College of
  Engineering
Mumbai, Maharashtra, India

Bhoomika Valani
Department of Information
  Technology
Dwarkadas J. Sanghvi College of
  Engineering
Mumbai, Maharashtra, India

Shivam Vora
Department of Information
  Technology
Dwarkadas J. Sanghvi College of
  Engineering
Mumbai, Maharashtra, India

Chapter 1

Introduction to Data Mining

Neepa Shah
Dwarkadas J. Sanghvi College of Engineering

Ketan Shah
MPSTME Mumbai, NMIMS University

Contents

The data is everywhere now, growing rapidly at an express rate. We are deluged by data – scientific data, medical data, demographic data, financial data, and marketing data as storage is inexpensive and getting even less so, as are data sensors. This is simply because collection and storage of data is easier than ever before.

Every enterprise benefits from collecting and analysing its data. For instance, hospitals can use this analysis in spotting trends and anomalies in patient records, and search engines can do perform better page ranking and advertisement placement. Besides these, intrusion detection in cybersecurity and computer networks; keeping track of the energy consumption of household appliances; pattern analysis in bioinformatics and pharmaceutical data; financial and business intelligence data; and spotting trends in blogs, Twitter, and other social networking sites are few more examples.

The major issue is that people have no time to look at this data. Thus, this raw and huge data needs to be processed intelligently to extract the meaningful information and apply it to develop real-world applications in the domain of Finance,

DOI: 10.1201/9781003390220-1

1

Healthcare, Education System, Retail, Sensor Networks, etc. For instance, for a marketing manager, a simple listing of marketing contacts is not at all useful; he would rather prefer a detailed information about all past purchases of various customers as well as predictions of their future purchases. Thus, analysing this large amount of data is a prime necessity. So, the problem now shifts to efficient analysis of the data [1]. We must not just find ways to automatically analyse the data, but also to automatically classify it, summarize it, discover, and characterize trends in it, and flag anomalies. Simple structured/query language queries are not adequate to support these increased demands for information. This is where data mining comes into picture.

Data mining is often defined as finding hidden and useful information in a database. It is a process of extracting and discovering patterns in large datasets involving methods at the intersection of machine learning, statistics, and database systems [1].

Alternatively, it has been called exploratory data analysis, data-driven discovery, and deductive learning [2]. Data mining is the process of extraction of the inherent/hidden but unknown and helpful information from the unstructured data [3]. The main functionality of data mining process is to read the dataset, extract useful information, and convert it into a structure that is easily understandable and can be used further for various applications. This is one of the most upcoming and fully evolving areas of the database research community. Researchers in areas include studies and contributions of various domains like statistics, visualization, artificial intelligence, and machine learning, to list a few. The field has matured with many new and improved algorithms and has broadened to include many more datatypes: streams, sequences, graphs, time-series, geospatial, audio, images, and video [1].

Traditional database queries make use of Structured Query Language (SQL) to access the data from the database. After executing the query correctly, the result is the required data extracted from the original database. The way to extract data using data mining techniques differs from traditional database access. The concept of data mining can be implemented using many different algorithms that have functionality to accomplish the task. Many different algorithms are used to execute and accomplish the data mining tasks. Depending upon the characteristics of data, the data mining algorithms need to follow the model describing the data mining tasks. Data mining models can be classified as predictive models or descriptive models. Data mining tasks are grouped according to these models.

A predictive model predicts the data value based on the results obtained from the previous steps or using the historical data. Predictive model makes use of historical data. The various techniques that come under predictive modelling are classification, regression, time-series analysis, and prediction. Another model called 'descriptive model' is used to identify various patterns or relationships within the data. A descriptive model does not perform any kind of prediction, but instead tries to explore the data and examine its properties. A descriptive model identifies different patterns and the relationship between them [2].

Below we highlight very challenging and upcoming areas of research and applications of data mining domain.

Classification	Classification is a supervised learning approach in which the algorithm reads the input data that has predefined classes and then uses this learning to classify new observations [1,2]. The different types of classification algorithms are Logistic Regression, Naive Bayes Classifier, Nearest Neighbour, Support Vector Machines, Decision Trees, and Random Forest. Some practical examples of classification problems are speech recognition, handwriting recognition, biometric identification, document classification, etc.
Neural networks	Neural networks help to cluster and classify the input dataset. They are like a layer of clustering and classification above the data that is stored and managed. They are used to group unlabelled data as per the similarities among the example inputs. At the same time, they can also classify data when they have a labelled dataset to train on. Neural networks can adapt to changing input; so, the network generates the best possible result without needing to redesign the output criteria [1,2]. The three important types of neural networks that form the basis for most pre-trained models are artificial neural networks (ANN), convolution neural networks (CNN), and recurrent neural networks (RNN).
Document clustering	Document clustering is a topic under data clustering in a narrower aspect and data mining in a broader aspect. It includes concepts combined from the information retrieval, natural language processing, and machine learning domains. In document clustering, the documents are organized into different groups, which are known as 'clusters'. The documents in each cluster exhibit some common properties as per the similarity measure. For effective navigation, summarization, and organization of the huge information, the document clustering algorithm must be efficient. A good clustering algorithm should have good quality. It should also be scalable and less time-consuming.

Data mining and Machine learning	'Data mining' is the term coined before machine learning, though there is a blurred line between the usage of these two terms as both of them work on data. Data mining is designed to extract the rules from large quantities of data, while machine learning trains the data and comprehends the given parameters.
Medical data mining	Data mining has gained importance in the domain of healthcare tremendously. As compared to earlier systems, where data is maintained manually, nowadays EHR (electronic health record) maintains health-related data securely and the required information can be extracted using data mining algorithms.
Human mobility data mining	Over the past years, a fast-growing number of projects and applications have demonstrated the potential of using various types of big data sources such as mobile phone, social media, or satellite data. This helps to improve the understanding of phenomena related to global migration and human mobility [4]. The applications involve mobile call details, social media usage data, spatial data, satellite imagery, etc.
Distributed data mining	The data that is available today is humongous and highly difficult to extract the useful information from a centralized repository. The major advantage of a distributed system is that it allows data to spread across multiple geographical locations and specialized distributed data mining algorithms retrieve the information aiming for minimum execution time and less message communication overhead.
Intrusion detection Using data mining	Intrusion detection is the act of detecting actions that attempt to compromise the confidentiality, integrity, or availability of a resource [5]. The research in developing general and systematic methods and applications based on it are evolving. The major focus of integration of these two domains is application of data mining techniques to discover consistent and useful patterns of system features that describe programme and user behaviour and use the set of relevant system features to compute classifiers that can recognize anomalies and known intrusions.

Sensor data mining	In the era of Internet of Things (IoT), sensor data is the one that replaces artificially compiled data. How to extract valuable knowledge and patterns from a large amount of data generated by sensors is a challenging research topic [6]. This is another upcoming research domain of applied data mining techniques on wireless sensor networks. The various existing techniques have focused on clustering, association rules, frequent patterns, sequential patterns, and classification for sensor data. However, the design and deployment of sensor networks creates unique research challenges due to their large size (up to thousands of sensor nodes), random deployment, and communication environment.
Pattern mining	One of the major fields of data mining is to analyse the patterns in the data, and based on that, further analysis can be done for decision making in an organization. In a given set of transactions, pattern mining's aim is to find the rules that enable us to speculate a certain item based on the happening of other items in the transaction. The focus of this applied data mining techniques is in the effective identification of the desired patterns.
Image mining	Image mining deals with the extraction of implicit knowledge, image data relationship, or patterns that are extracted using image processing techniques [7]. The focus of image mining is the extraction of patterns from a large collection of images and understanding or extracting specific features from an image. The applications that deal with the concept of image processing implemented using data mining techniques is one of the trending research domains.

References

1. Jiawei, H. and Kamber, M. 2001. *Data Mining: Concepts and Techniques*. San Francisco: Morgan Kaufmann.
2. Dunham Margaret, H. 2003. *Data Mining Introductory and Advanced Topics*. Upper Saddle River, NJ: Prentice Hall/Pearson Education.
3. Witten, I. H., Frank, E., Hall, M. A. and Pal, C. J. 2017. *Data Mining: Practical Machine Learning Tools and Techniques*. Cambridge, MA: Morgan Kaufmann Publisher.
4. Big Data, Migration and Human Mobility. Available at https://www.migrationdata-portal.org/themes/big-data-migration-and-human-mobility, visited on 5th January 2022.

5. Jagjeet Jakhar, Vinay Kumar and Vinod Kumar. 2013. Intrusion detection using data mining techniques: A study through different approach. *International Journal of Applied Science & Technology Research Excellence*, 3(4). ISSN NO. 2250-2718(Print), 2250—2726 (Online).
6. Yin, Y., Long, L. and Deng, X. 2020. Dynamic data mining of sensor data. *IEEE Access*, 8, 41637–41648. DOI: 10.1109/ACCESS.2020.2976699.
7. Yousofi, Mohammad Hadi, Esmaeili, Mahdi, Sharifian, Majide Sadat. 2016. A study on image mining; Its importance and challenges. *American Journal of Software Engineering and Applications, Special Issue: Academic Research for Multidisciplinary*, 5(3–1), 5–9. DOI: 10.11648/j.ajsea.s.2016050301.12.

Chapter 2

Review of Latent Dirichlet Allocation to Understand Motivations to Share Conspiracy Theory: A Case Study of "Plandemic" during COVID-19

Sushma Kumble
Towson University

Pratiti Diddi
George Mason University

Jeff Conlin
University of Kansas

DOI: 10.1201/9781003390220-2

Contents

During the global COVID-19 pandemic, a trove of anti-science rhetoric emerged in the form of misinformation and conspiracy theories. In fact, the prevalence of "infodemic" or an overabundance of information that can or cannot be verified on social media platforms alarmed the World Health Organization (Tangcharoensathien et al, 2020). One such source of circulating disinformation was a highly watched 26-minute online documentary called "Plandemic" that was disseminated on social media platforms, including YouTube, Facebook, Vimeo, and Twitter between May 6 and 11, 2020 (Andrews, 2020; Frenkel et al., 2020). The video contained conspiracy theories that aligned with the film's blended name—that the global coronavirus (COVID-19) pandemic was planned by a small group of high-profile individuals. Dr. Anthony S. Fauci, director of the U.S. National Institute of Allergy and Infectious Diseases, Bill Gates, Microsoft founder-billionaire, and other elites were cast as villains behind the spread of the virus in order to profit financially by introducing a cure. On the opposite side, Dr. Judy Mikovits, a discredited molecular biologist, was framed as one of the film's heroes after claiming that Fauci stole her past work and was trying to discredit the president of the United States and hurt its citizens (Shepherd, 2020). Mikovits also contended that COVID-19 did not cause widespread deaths, and that face masks intended to slow its contagion instead contributed to spreading the disease. The video was eventually removed or tagged by all of the social media platforms for spreading false information, but not before being republished and shared among millions of users (Andrews, 2020).

Prior research indicates that social media is one of the largest mediums for conspiracy theories and misinformation dissemination (Enders et al., 2021). Studies have also begun to consider the extent of rumors and conspiracy theories surrounding the global COVID-19 pandemic on platforms such as Twitter, YouTube, Facebook, Google, Google Fact Check, and Parler (Baines et al., 2021; Islam et al., 2021). Islam et al. (2021) conducted a mixed-methods study to examine COVID-19 vaccine-related rumors and conspiracy theories that were circulated during the first 11 months of 2020 across 52 countries. Results included 637 total items with 59 items categorized as conspiracy theories, and 97% (57) of them contained false information. Some of the theories, for example, touted the COVID-19 vaccine's ability to monitor and manipulate vaccine recipients for global domination. Conspiracy theorists also made reference to microchips transmitting biometric data after vaccines were administered, and corporations sending signals through 5G networks to the chips—all to control people. While it is not always easy to correct or challenge misinformation (Chan et al., 2017), preventing misinformation from snowballing in social media can only occur through detection. Given the vast volume of data that is generated on social media platforms, performing manual content analyses for detection and prevention is usually not possible. The central aim of this chapter, therefore, is to understand how to identify and classify social media messages according to how users express their conspiracy theory beliefs on Twitter using unsupervised machine learning. Before describing unsupervised machine learning and why the technique is suitable for the research question, this chapter initially examines previous literature about conspiracy theories and the motives behind why people are drawn to them.

2.1 Literature Review

2.1.1 Conspiracy Theories

Conspiracy theories are often disseminated through disinformation and can be defined as an individual or group's feelings that occur when responsibility for a social or political event is attributed to the actions of a manipulative, malevolent group (Douglas et al., 2019; Warner & Neville-Shepard, 2014). Individuals are attracted to conspiracy theories to fulfill specific epistemic, existential, and social motives (Douglas et al., 2017, 2019).

Epistemic motives represent a desire for understanding, for accuracy, and for certainty. These motives may be related to the need to make sense of complex problems with simplified solutions (Hollander, 2018). Existential motives comprise a need for control and for security. From an existential point of view, Douglas and colleagues (2017, 2019) suggest that anxiety, insecure attachment styles, feelings of powerlessness, lack of control, unrest, and the belief that the economy is worsening may contribute to conspiracy beliefs. Social motives include a desire to belong and to maintain a positive self or group image. By blaming powerful elites who cause misfortune to others, individuals present themselves and their fellow group members as harmed. Together these three motives form a taxonomy of reasons for believing in conspiracies and for systematically identifying observable conspiracy beliefs in communication, and between senders and receivers of related disinformation.

2.1.2 Measuring Conspiracy Theories Beliefs

Researchers have introduced and validated a generic scale as an index of conspiracy beliefs (Brotherton et al., 2013). Facets of these beliefs include beliefs in recurring government malfeasance such as secretly killing innocent civilians; knowledge of extraterrestrial, alien, and unidentified flying objects that are kept secret from the public; coordination of small groups to wield malevolent power and manipulate world events; threats to personal well-being and the spread of viruses and diseases from the efforts of an organization; and control of information by groups of scientists to deceive the public. In relation to observational studies, communication and psychology scholars have detected vaccine-relevant conspiracy theories by identifying manifest content that attributes responsibility to get vaccinated as "part of a hidden and malicious plot by a greater organization" (McClaran & Rhodes, 2021, p. 4); as "government/companies/doctors are only out to make money on the vaccine," and "vaccine is a hoax" (Briones et al., 2011; Kata, 2010; Madden et al., 2012). However, there is a dearth of studies that have considered identifying and analyzing manifest conspiracy belief motives found in communication messages on social media platforms.

2.1.3 Textual Analysis and Text Mining

Traditionally, when studying text-based communication, content analysis has been a popular method of choice for media studies (Riffe et al., 2014). Typically, human coders are trained to manually identify and systematically evaluate and categorize (code) the text and make meaningful inferences (Riffe et al., 2014). However, the vast number of messages and other forms of content from millions of users yield an exponential volume of information and sources. Manually coding content is often time-consuming, expensive to compensate coders, and focused on a sample that is drawn from the larger population of data, which are methodological characteristics that are not always realistic with large social media datasets. However, where manual content analysis can be impractical, machine learning techniques can be time-efficient, inexpensive, and capable of analyzing themes behind the vast array of textual information.

Machine learning is a subdiscipline of information sciences, wherein machines are taught to replicate human intelligence by learning and recognizing the patterns in the environment where it is present (El Naqa & Murphy, 2015). Within the context of communication, machines can automate content analysis and help understand the content better. One powerful text mining machine learning analysis is topic modeling, which can help with automated content analysis. This method uses natural language processing (NLP) to identify topics within a set of documents (Jelodar et al., 2018). Text mining via machine learning can be either supervised or unsupervised, which can be considered deductive and inductive approaches. Supervised machine learning techniques initially rely on hand-coding a subset of content, that is informed through a theoretical model. Subsequently, the machine is taught to recognize the codes in a large dataset (Boumans, & Trilling, 2016). The benefit of supervised topic modeling is that the method can perform fine-grain analysis of the text. However, supervised topic modeling still requires human coders to develop a codebook for the categorization of operationalized variables and several rounds of coding a subset of the data. Alternatively, unsupervised approaches are inductive by definition, as they do not require the researcher to select significant subjects prior to developing classifiers or categories (Boumans, & Trilling, 2016). Unlike traditional research, deductive and inductive methods, such as supervised and unsupervised machine learning, can be complementary ways to test and build social science theoretical propositions and answer research questions.

As previously stated, the main goal of this chapter is to deduce the manifest or observable motivations behind a conspiracy theory in social media (specifically in tweets). Since the topics were not specified in advance and there was no guarantee that psychological motives identified in the literature would be manifested in tweets and align with how researchers typically categorize content, an unsupervised machine learning technique was selected to explore the dataset. Latent Dirichlet Allocation (LDA) is the method that was selected to conduct unsupervised topic modeling on the dataset (LDA; Blei et al., 2003; Blei, 2012). LDA is a probabilistic approach that uses a Bayesian statistics framework to identify key themes or patterns in text (tweets in this case) in a quick and efficient manner (Maier et al., 2018). There are three important concepts in understanding word grouping and topic identifications for LDA (Maier et al., 2018) as explained in Figure 2.1. The first term is called the *corpus*, which refers to the entire textual dataset. Within the corpus are *documents*, and within each document, there are several words called *terms* (Maier et al., 2018). LDA employs a *bag of words method*, viewing each topic as a grouping of terms or words within the textual document wherein it is assumed that the corpus has a collection of topics, each of which contains a distribution of words that occur together (Blei et al., 2003). In recent years, LDA has been used in several studies to identify themes or patterns from Twitter data (for example, Negara & Triadi, 2021; Zhou et al., 2021; Xue et al., 2020).

Previous research in the area of information technology has suggested that machine learning approaches can be useful in the detection of health-related disinformation conspiracy theories (Choudrie et al., 2020; Wang et al., 2019). However, previous studies have not examined whether unsupervised topic modeling can be

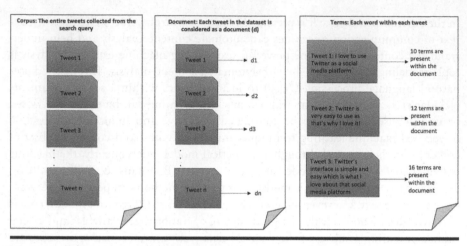

Figure 2.1   Illustrations of key LDA terms.

used to recognize and classify the stated conspiracy theory motives of users who spread disinformation. Stated motives represent a way to classify components of conspiracy theories and therefore provide guidance for detecting different levels of support for a particular theory. Understanding this information could help establish specific parameters for detecting conspiracy theories related to COVID-19 in order to correct misinformation and combat the spread.

In addition to computational LDA analysis, the study also employs a manual strategy of thematic analysis. The goal is to use the computational unsupervised procedure of LDA to reduce and organize the digital discourse and sequentially employ the manual and context-informed classification of data by human coders (Baden et al., 2020). The current study thus utilized the sequential hybrid approach of Latent Dirichlet Allocation (LDA; Blei, 2012) and thematic analysis to identify thematic patterns of conspiracy theory motives within the Twitter dataset. The method was employed to answer the study's main research question, which follows:

> *RQ1. Using unsupervised LDA and thematic analysis, what are the predominant observable conspiracy theory motives that emerge through analysis of Plandemic tweets?*

2.2 Methods

2.2.1 Data Collection

Data were retrieved between May 6 and 12, 2020 using Python, an open-source programming language using the search query "Plandemic." This timeline was selected as this was the period when the documentary was released and the peak time when tweets about the documentary occurred. A total of 18,248 English language tweets were retrieved from the query. After cleaning for duplicates, the dataset contained 16,463 tweets. Since the data were collected after May 12, some tweets could not be retrieved due to removal by Twitter as the platform had begun to eliminate tweets that were trying to spread the misinformation/conspiracy theory.

2.2.2 Executing Latent Dirichlet Allocation

After gathering the data, the LDA analysis was used. In order to conduct the LDA analysis, we used a combination of Gensim library (Řehůřek, & Sojka, 2011) and Natural Language Toolkit (NLTK; Loper & Bird, 2002) library. Initially, duplicate tweets were identified and removed using a custom code in Python. Since machine learning models cannot comprehend raw text, there are several steps taken to convert tweets into numeric data that can be used to train the model. Figure 2.2 describes the LDA procedures and explains the importance of each.

2.2.2.1 Dataset Cleaning

The first step is to clean the dataset. Cleaning of the data is essential to remove any duplicates, which are purely a result of the collection process. Additionally, the collection process may introduce blank or empty lines, which need to be eliminated.

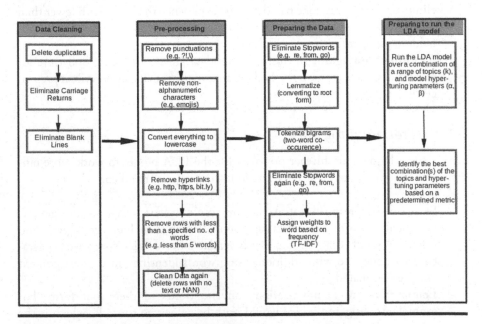

Figure 2.2   Flowchart of LDA methodology.

Each tweet may also contain separate lines or a carriage return, which are also removed to reduce ambiguity for the program while processing.

2.2.2.2 Dataset Preprocessing

Once the dataset is cleaned, the data needs to be preprocessed. The preprocessing step is performed to remove any characters or features that do not play any role in determining the topics of analysis. Preprocessing is performed by taking the following steps where the ordering of the steps is important since we are working with unstructured textual data along with specific theories and themes. The steps outlined below were performed on the Gensim library on Python (Řehůřek & Sojka, 2011).

1. **Removing the punctuation marks:** Punctuation marks or symbols do not contribute to the topic determination, as the program uses a bag of words approach and is looking for a combination of words for topic associations.
2. **Removal of non-alpha-numeric characters:** This step is mainly performed to eliminate emoticons and any residual introduction of non-English language characters within the text.
3. **Converting to lowercase:** The entire text is converted to lowercase in order for every word to be treated as the same irrespective of any uppercase letters.
4. **Removing hyperlinks:** Hyperlinks do not contribute to topic identification or associations and therefore are eliminated.
5. **Removing rows based on length:** Tweet text with less than five words is eliminated. This was done based on past experience that texts with fewer than five words do not contribute to the content analysis and were generally difficult to associate with a specific topic.
6. **Cleaning data again:** In this step, the data are scanned a second time for blank rows that may have resulted because of the previously described preprocessing steps.

2.2.2.3 Preparing the Data

In this step, the data are further prepared for the LDA model to work more efficiently. In order to prepare the data, the following steps were taken:

1. **Stop words removal:** Stop words are common words that are too generic to contribute to topic associations. Some examples include "go," "get," and "from." A set of common stop words available in the NLTK stop words database are appended with additional stop words identified in the text context and are eliminated.
2. **Lemmatization:** Lemmatization converts words to their root form. For example, trading and traded would both be converted to trade, which is the base form of those words.

3. **Tokenization:** Tokenization converts the text into smaller pieces or "tokens." These may include words, or two-word co-occurrences, called "bigrams." The package *TweetTokinizer* on NLTK was used to perform this step.
4. **Stop word removal:** The stop word removal step was run again, to eliminate any stop words that may have resulted from the lemmatization step.
5. **Relative pruning:** Relative pruning is performed by removing words that appeared frequently (over 90%) or infrequently (less than 5% of the time). This process improves the performance of the model (Maier et al., 2018).
6. **TF-IDF:** The term "frequency-inverse document frequency" (TF-IDF) step assigns a weightage to each token based on the frequency of its appearance. This helps identify the importance of each of these tokens within the dataset.

2.2.2.4 Determining Topics and Corresponding Tweets for the LDA Model

Recall that LDA assumes that each document for analysis has a set of topics. However, there is no ideal way of determining the optimal number of topics present in a corpus. As a solution, Maier et al. (2018) suggest running multiple models by systematically varying the model parameters to determine an appropriate number of topics. The main input to the LDA model is the number of topics (k). However, the model also includes hypertuning parameters (α and β). Different combinations of these parameters can lead to different topic distributions. Therefore, for the model tuning process for the current study, the coherence score evaluation was performed for each combination of k (within a specific range) and the hypertuning parameters α and β (range of 0–1).

Subsequently, a performance model with LDA was run over a range of topics from 1 to 15, labeled k, with α (topic density within the tweets) and β (the word density within a topic) values ranging from 0.01 to 1.0. Given that the dataset was relatively smaller, we felt that up to 15 topics was a good number to run our tuning run (if you have millions of tweets in your dataset, a higher number might be good depending on the topic). We ran 600 different models varying the α, and β to each of the values of k for the purpose of training the model and determining the optimal number of topics that can emerge from the corpus. A coherence value measure labeled Cv, developed by Röder et al. (2015), was employed as the metric for model parameter evaluation and was calculated for each trial run. Coherence scores are calculated to estimate how well the topics generated by the model can be interpreted by a person. In other words, coherence scores are a measure of semantic similarity between the most strongly associated words for each topic. A higher coherence score would indicate a more "coherent" topic or theme from the top few words for each topic. The measure employed in this study is the C_V score, as it is one of the most commonly used metrics. It calculates the score for co-occurring words using normalized pointwise mutual information (NPMI) and cosine similarity (Röder et al., 2015). The Cv values for each combination of the model parameters were calculated, tabulated, and reviewed. Finally, the selection of the model was based on Cv≥95% of max Cv and a combination of k, α, and β that corresponded to that model and was used to run the final LDA model.

Apart from calculating the Cv values, we also employed data visualization techniques to determine the optimal number of topics. Two main techniques are employed for the visualization and comprehension of the results: Word Clouds and pyLDAvis. Word Cloud is a visual representation of a collection of the salient words within each topic where the words are presented in different font sizes. The font sizes indicate the relative weight of that word within each topic. For example, a prominent word within a topic would have a larger font size and bolder shading within the cluster of words and a relatively unimportant word would have a small size. Word Clouds provide an idea of the topic at a glance, particularly when the topics are distinct. pyLDAvis is among the most popular visualization techniques employed for LDA studies (Sievert et al., 2014). The technique provides an interactive web-based visualization tool that shows the output of the LDA model at a glance. It also provides further tools for customizing the visual presentation as well as for probing the results for more nuanced analyses. The typical output from the method consists of two parts on the left-hand and right-hand sides of the page. On the left, the topics are represented visually as a cluster of circles, one circle for each topic. The size of the circle represents the weight or prominence of that topic within the entire dataset. The distance between the centers of any two circles indicates the similarity between the topics. For example, if two circles have a significant region of intersection, this output suggests that the two topics are very similar to each other. On the right, the top N words (where N can be specified) are presented as a bar chart. By clicking on a particular topic circle on the left, the words that correspond to that specific topic can be observed. Therefore, this comprehensive display provides a quick but comprehensive way to understand the topic distribution as well as the word distribution within each topic.

Finally, once the topic numbers are determined, the final step for the LDA model is to determine which tweets are associated with the topic. We accomplished this procedure by utilizing Genism's feature vectors (Řehůřek & Sojka, 2011). The feature vector classification assigns a probabilistic ratio to each tweet based on the word weight and the subject number.

2.2.3 Thematic Analysis

After the LDA model identified the specific number of topics and associated each tweet with a certain topic, determining the labels for each of the topics is crucial in understanding the underlying themes of the tweets. This entails human interpretations of topics. For that, the study employed a thematic analysis (Braun & Clark, 2006) to develop subject labels for each topic generated by the LDA model. We specifically employed a deductive thematic analysis, which is driven by the specific research questions and the study's theoretical framework

(Braun & Clark, 2006). Based on the descriptive conspiracy taxonomies guided by literature from Douglas et al. (2017, 2019), the top-down approach aimed to identify the predominant and observable conspiracy motives in the Plandemic tweets. Braun and Clark (2006) recommend six stages in order to produce themes. While we move from one step to another, often the steps are not very linear, and they operate simultaneously.

The initial stage is to become acquainted with the data. We performed a review of the most frequently used terms connected with each topic in this step. For example, the LDA analysis generated a list of keywords for Topic 1 (e.g., fake, bullshit, narrative, news, fact). At this stage, we looked at these keywords and took notes of early impressions to understand the logic that determined for these keywords to appear together.

Following that, the next second step involved developing initial codes based on the assessment of the data. Two of the study authors randomly select and read between 100 and 150 tweets from each topic generated by the LDA algorithm during this step. We focused on generating an initial/basic list of thoughts and ideas on what is in the tweets, what is intriguing about them, and how they are potentially relevant to our research questions. For example, while reading one of the tweets in Topic 1 such as "*Fake deaths, fake nurses, fake doctors, fake science, fake patients, fake testing, fake treatments, fake vaccine, fake news = fake pandemic. Only #COVIDIOTS still buy the lies #TheGreatAwakening #LockdownIreland #Plandemic #ArrestBillGates2020 #arrestBarackObama*" we highlighted the important sections of the content and came up with initial shorthand labels and codes such as "hoax" and "non-existent" that could describe the specific characteristic of the content in relation to the overall theoretical framework of conspiracy theories. Here, codes like "hoax" and "non-existent" described the idea that tweets in Topic 1 indicated that the pandemic was fake and it was not actually happening.

Next, at the third stage, we sorted and combined the list of codes identified across the dataset, followed by searching for recurring potential overarching themes in the data. We explored categorization further in this stage, comparing our notes, tweets, and frequently recurring words to aid in the search for topic labels for the themes created by the LDA algorithm. Codes, patterns, and different levels of themes (e.g., overarching and subthemes) were all interconnected at this point to understand how they were connected to create meaning within the data. For example, at this stage, different relevant codes for Topic 1 like "fake," "hoax," and "low trust" were combined to form a theme. We decided that an overall code "expressing distrust in the official news or information about plandemic" made sense as a theme.

The fourth stage entails an examination of potential themes. This is a recursive stage wherein the identified themes are first reviewed in relation to the coded data extracts and then to see if they make a meaningful connection to the overall dataset. The focus is on the refinement of the themes wherein researchers either expand the boundaries of themes or split them to create additional themes or collapse similar potential themes or even discard the themes that do not effectively capture the most important elements/aspects of data anymore.

The fifth step entails naming the themes associated with each topic. After reviewing and refining the potential themes, at the fifth stage, each theme was assigned a working title or name based on the unique story and narrative it was telling in relation to overarching patterns of the data and in relation to research questions of the study. For example, as Table 2.2 indicates later, some of the codes for Topic 1 and Topic 2 could be collapsed and clustered under the unifying potential dimensions of "distrust in authorities," "finding patterns," and "desire for understanding for accuracy," which in turn generated a bigger cohesive theme of epistemic motives. As shown in the table, some of the prominent themes that emerged in the dataset regarding conspiracy motives were existential motives, social motives, and epistemic motives.

The last stage of the six-step thematic analysis is to write up the analysis wherein the goal is to explain all themes in turn with relevant examples and how each theme answered the research question(s) at hand. This is the stage wherein the results of the study are written, and this section is explained under the results section of this chapter.

2.3 Results

2.3.1 Results from LDA Tuning Run

As indicated, we performed an LDA tuning run to determine the optimal number of topics for the present dataset. The results from the tuning analysis are presented in Figure 2.3. The results indicated that the optimal number of topics were 9 and 15. The LDA models that ran on the topics were visualized using pyLDAVis visualization package. The results indicated that the model with 14 topics had a lot of clusters and did not have a good inter-topic distance. On the other hand, Topic 9 had a better inter-topic distance and few clusters. Figure 2.4 compares the inter-topic visualization for both topics. Finally, we took a closer look at the model with nine topics and found that it was a good fit for answering the research question posed in this chapter. Hence, we selected a model with nine topics.

Based on the bigram words generated by the unsupervised model, Table 2.1 presents the top keywords generated by the model.

2.3.2 Results from Thematic Analysis

As explained in the methods section, after the emergence of the topics from the LDA approach, we employed the six-step deductive thematic analysis to search for stated/ observable conspiracy motives in the "Plandemic" tweets. Following our research question and theoretical framework of conspiracy motives, the emergent themes

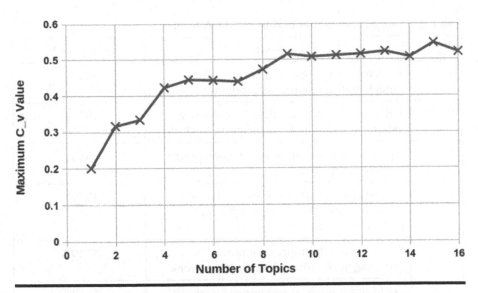

Figure 2.3 Coherence values of different K selected in the tuning LDA run.

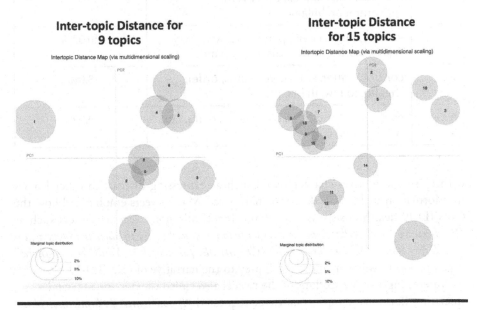

Figure 2.4 PyLDAVis topic visualization for Topics 9 and 15.

focused on identifying three different types of conspiracy motives: epistemic, existential, and social motives. All the themes that were not conspiracy-related were assigned to the non-conspiracy motives category.

Results indicated that Topic 1 had observable epistemic conspiracy motives. Some of the common labels observed during thematic analysis that were consistent

Table 2.1   Keywords Generated by the LDA Model

Topic	Keywords	Percentage of Tweets
1	fake, fact, news, research, look, science, much, bullshit, narrative, medium	13.2%
2	video, com, watch, youtube, covid, www, share, documentary, coronavirus, bitchute	19.2%
3	bill_gate, news, warn, lose, let, com, power, million, mind, hide	6.05%
4	obamagate, fauci, truth, qanon, expose, realdonaldtrump, firefauci, mikovit, fakenews, treason	10.09%
5	life, destroy, let, trump, economy, obamagate, country, election, state, week	12.19%
6	covid, scamdemic, coronavirus, lockdown, agenda, coronahoax, test, event, government, billgate	10.82%
7	vaccine, mask, covid, pandemic, wwg_wga, virus, work, coronavirus, plan, stand	10.92%
8	control, twitter, stop, com, status, order, health, follow, thank, global	8.0%
9	covid, death, number, die, year, bad, flu, talk, wrong, cause	9.39%

with epistemic motives characteristics such as expressing distrust in official news of information included "fake" and "narrative." Many tweets emphasized how the COVID-19 health crisis was a hoax and practically non-existent. Tweets such as *"I've been won over. #Plandemic makes sense to me now. Shelter in place is a hoax and it goes deeper than #DrFauci or #5G or #Chemtrails. Just watch it. You'll be convinced"* urged people to wake up and not fall prey to the narrative of COVID-19.

Interestingly, some sections of the tweets also called the documentary fake and spreading lies. For example, one tweet requested *"If you watch #Plandemic, please don't share it. This 'documentary' is dangerous and incorrect. COVID-19 is real, and it is not part of any plan. Don't be part of the problem. Look for information about the people behind it and don't accept anything on it as fact. #PlandemicIsFalse."* Another tweet addressed: *"Nope, there's no "#plandemic...#viruses are real, #vaccines are safe, and we should get our info from professionals like @gorskon, not disgraced, discredited ex-scientists."* During analysis, such tweets were assigned to the non-conspiracy category as they attempt to debunk the assertions of the documentary and mitigate the spread of conspiracy. Therefore, we created a new topic and manually took out the tweets from Topic 1 that debunked the documentary.

For Topic 2 tweets, the thematic analysis suggested that the tweets corresponded to existential conspiracy motives. The majority of the tweets reflected existential motivational characteristics, such as the presence of power beliefs. Tweets such as *"Fauci's Plandemic Exposed. Video is being censored on YouTube #Plandemic2020 #Plandemicmovie #Plandemic #FreedomOfSpeech #1stAmendment"* signaled how people in power and influence were trying to hide the real truth. Furthermore, the tweets reflected "powerlessness" and a "lack of control," which are characteristic of the existential motives, as the Twitter users displayed anxiety and disempowerment by urging everyone to watch and share the Plandemic documentary before it was removed and censored.

Topic 3 tweets were indicative of epistemic conspiracy motives. The tweets reflected characteristics of epistemic motives of pattern seeking and recognition. Tweets such as *"Fake Virus! Fake Numbers! #Plandemic All you want is your paycheck from Big Pharma for forcing Texans to get vaccines. Evil in a wheelchair. #OpenTexasNow"* expressed beliefs about finding links, patterns, and connections between prominent actors and institutions trying to deliberately create a pandemic to push for the vaccines and other vested agendas. Topic 7 tweets, too, reflected similar epistemic conspiracy motives wherein Twitter users tried to draw connections, patterns, and links between risks of wearing masks and getting vaccines, arguing that such measures enhance the chances of getting COVID.

The tweets in Topic 4 predominantly reflected social conspiracy motives. Consistent with the characteristics of social motives like descriptions of pro and anti-political affiliations, the majority of the tweets in this topic such as *"#AimlessAmy the #DeepState is being exposed. We know this was a #Plandemic and your fellow Democrats were behind it! Probably part of #ObamaGate which means @JoeBiden was part of it!"* focused on talking about how certain political parties like the Democrats had a ploy in planning the health crisis. Furthermore, the tweets like *"The only thing unprecedented about this #PLANdemic is the level of deception and corruption from #Fauci #Gates #Birx Their greed is disgusting. Fauci youâ€™re killing people worldwide for cash you receive from the vaccine patents"* highlighted in-group vs out-group membership wherein powerful elite caused the misfortune of the socially disenfranchised.

Tweets in Topic 5 reflected the existential motives characteristics like projecting beliefs that the pandemic and its consequences like lockdowns are being used by the global elite to destroy businesses and the world economy and push for their own policies. Tweets like *"In the middle of a national emergency and this * is still pushing for socialism The unemployment numbers were planned and unnecessary Plenty of living wage jobs available, you just don't want them to work #Plandemic #BacktoWorkAmerica #BackToWorkNOW"* and *"Those seeking profit orchestrated this #Plandemic in the first place and were successful in making us stay at home whilst destroying the jobs and lives of millions all around"* echoed such beliefs.

Topic 6 tweets continued to call the health crisis of COVID a scam and hoax and attribute its causes and consequences (like masking, lockdown, etc.) to tangible entities and targets like Bill Gates, and the World Health Organization (WHO). Tweets such as *"How can we possibly trust the Government over the #Coronavirus when its members are bribed by the #WHO & #BillGates with lucrative positions? #scamdemic #Plandemic #bbcaq #endthelockdown #Coronabollocks #covidhoax #CoronaHoax"* exemplify epistemic motives wherein people exaggerate the influence and agency of the others in causing the phenomenon. Users harboring epistemic motivations tend to engage in agency detection where they perceive the events to be caused by intentional agents and consider the implicated authorities to be unethical. Additionally, tweets such as *"Tainted tests that are positive for a fruit and goat! #scamdemic #Plandemic #scamdemic2020"* and *"You can take any group and you'll likely get similar results. The tests have shown that they are unreliable and only show you have antibodies for a coronavirus #plandemic #scamdemic"* reflected a sense of uncertainty when conflicting information is made available about the increasing number of cases/death and testing results being manipulated.

Topic 8 tweets reflected the existential conspiracy motives. Some of the sample tweets in this topic were *"It was never about your safety it was about control from day 1 #Plandemic"* and *"US PLAN TO USE BIOTERRORISM ON THE WORLD TO CREATE AUTHORITARIAN CONTROL. MUST WATCH #plandemic #Plandemic2020."* Such tweets indicated power play characteristics of existential motives such that the Twitter users felt that authorities, government, and people in power were trying to exercise control over them by lying to them; tracking them; and taking control of their lives, freedom, liberty, and health.

Topic 9 tweets again corresponded to existential motives. With tweets like *"Dr. Mikovits also alleges that deaths from covid19 are being inflated. The real cause of death could have been from the flu, COPD, or other raspatory issues. Doctors are being pressured by hospitals to say the cause of death was from covid19 for financial reasons. #Plandemic,"* users emphasized that the number of deaths was exaggerated, and all the deaths irrespective of the cause were attributed to COVID. This was indicative of the proportionality bias wherein users attempted to explain the alternative narrative of equal size matching the event (Table 2.2).

2.4 Discussion

The present study employed LDA to understand the observed motives, or stated reasons, for the spread of the conspiracy theory "Plandemic" on the sample of tweets collected during the week the documentary film was released. While we explained the steps involved with conducting an LDA analysis, it is important to note that an important step before analyzing textual data is selecting a topic that is coherent and distinct. From a social science perspective, humans use symbols to communicate for

Table 2.2 Results from the Thematic Analysis

LDA Topic Number	Thematic Analysis Labels	Stated/Observable Motives
1	Expressing distrust in official news of information	Epistemic
2	Powerplay, powerlessness, use of power	Existential
3	Pattern seeking and recognition	Epistemic
4	Political affiliations	Social
5	Causal connections-worsening of economy	Existential
6	Agency detection, uncertainty	Epistemic
7	Links between wearing masks, getting vaccines and COVID-19	Epistemic
8	Exercising social control	Existential
9	Inflated death numbers, proportionality bias	Existential
10	Non-conspiracy tweet (manual topic removal from Topic 1)	

distinctive purposes. Hence, a symbolic- and communication-based dataset needs a rigorous and effective way to ensure the interpretability of the topics generated by the machine learning algorithm. To that end, this chapter demonstrated using the multi-prong approach for determining the LDA topic (k). The results from the tuning run of the LDA indicated that coherence value increased as the number of topics increased. However, after Topic 9, the scores reached a plateau, indicating that the topic interpretability was similar for Topics 9 through 14, followed by an uptick in the coherence value for Topic 15. Based on the coherence value measured alone, one could be tempted to run the LDA model for 15 topics. However, visualizing the topics and the inter-topic distance aids in the optimal number of topics to select. As Figure 2.4 indicates, several topics overlapped in Topic 15, which would make assigning observable motives difficult. Additionally, an advantage of using the pyLDAvis package is that a word can be clustered into different topics, as opposed to traditional clustering techniques (Sivert & Shirely, 2014). Having a more stringent technique allowed for a better model that helps answer the main research question of the study.

While the LDA algorithm (or any other unsupervised topic modeling technique) does not provide labels, or explain their corresponding topics, we recommended a hybrid approach to help fill this void. This hybrid approach of computational and manual tools corroborates findings on the machine-based analysis, and while adding nuance to the findings through manual interpretation and labeling. Finally, we strongly encourage researchers to use a theoretical framework to guide thematic analysis to help understand the nuances of the topics generated by the LDA model.

2.4.1 Observable Conspiracy Theories Motives

Results from the LDA and thematic analysis can be classified as conspiracy theories circulated with existential motives. For such motives, Douglas and colleagues (2017, 2019) suggest that feelings of powerlessness, lack of control, unrest, and the belief that the economy is worsening contribute to conspiracy beliefs. Additionally, "conspiracy theories provide a tangible enemy on which to externalize anger or confusion for problems perceived as too abstract or impersonal" (Hollander, 2018, p. 694). In the context of the current dataset from Twitter, people directed their anger toward certain public figures like Dr. Faucci, Bill Gates, and scientific organizations like the Center of Disease Control (CDC) and the National Institute of Health (NIH). Spreading this type of information may help conspirators feel safer as they have managed to identify, call out, and mitigate threatening individuals (Bost & Prunier, 2013). For example, a tweet belonging to the existential motives read: "I, XXX, from Raleigh, declare I will not be masked, tested, tracked, chipped, or poisoned to support this orchestrated LIE! This will not be my 'new normal'. I DO NOT CONSENT! #IDoNotConsent #MyBodyMyChoice #Plandemic SHARE YOUR #DeclarationOfSovereignty #wwg1wga." Prior research indicates that when people feel powerless in a given situation, they tend to believe in conspiracy theories to feel a sense of empowerment (Difonzo, 2019).

Additionally, some of the tweets indicated the belief that the virus was deliberately created by individuals, and that health agencies and large pharmaceutical companies hide information in order to skirt laws and avoid detection. This explanation assigns blame for negative consequences to others. Another example tweet warned: "Everyone needs to watch Plandemic and the @CDCgov @NIAIDNews @NIH need to be stopped. @realDonaldTrump fire these morons and make it safe for Americans again #FauciFraud #FauciLiedPeopleDied #Plandemic #Plandemicmovie #DrainTheSwamp #covidhoax." Existential motives for conspiracy beliefs may be triggered by threats and a need to find safety, security, and control in response. The COVID-19 pandemic was an event on a global scale, and the magnitude of the threat combined with the uncertainty of the virus may have elicited a type of proportionality bias such that the complexity of explanations behind the Plandemic conspiracy needed to equal the size and scale of the event (Douglas et al., 2019). Thus, the existential motives for using conspiracy theories in this context may also have been compensatory mechanisms to feel more in control resulting in an alternative narrative to explain if not quell the issue.

The data also indicated the presence of epistemic motives that are often understood as means to cognitive closure by seeking information and forming quick judgments by searching for patterns and drawing spurious causal relationships. For example, some tweets pointed to viewing the Plandemic video as a simple way to access the truth, i.e.: "#Plandemic If you want to know the TRUTH: WATCH THIS VIDEO." A smaller percentage of tweets deliberated about the spread of the coronavirus and how the increasing number of COVID-19 infections were fake and a decoy for pharmaceutical companies to profit from vaccines. According to another tweet in this category: "Fake Virus! Fake Numbers! #Plandemic All you want is your paycheck from Big Pharma for forcing Texans to get vaccines. Evil in a wheelchair. #OpenTexasNow." Such tweets reflect the tendency to rely on conspiracy beliefs in order to find patterns and make spurious causal connections where there are none. Another smaller percentage of tweets were grouped within the epistemic category based upon perceived compliance with political beliefs and distrust of information sources.

Results also showed tweets falling within the social motive category. These tweets indicated more limited evidence of users expressing themselves and fellow group members as being harmed by COVID-19, along with powerful elites who appeared to be a threat. One tweet, for example, vilified Democrats as "DemonRats" and labeled their actions as "terrifying," "ridiculous," "tyrannical," and "a scam." Directives that were listed as hashtags at the end of this tweet included: "#GetBackToWork #OpenAmerica #Trump2020Now." Presumably, these users wanted to present a positive image of themselves in relation to fellow Trump followers and Democratic critics (Douglas et al., 2019).

2.4.2 Limitations

Although unsupervised machine learning and LDA topic modeling, in general, have several advantages, there are limitations to this method. First, selecting the number of topics to run the model is a challenging issue as there are no agreed-upon standards for this process. While the present study used the most stringent rules to guide the number of topics run through the model, a different number of topics may be more optimal.

Second, the topics produced by the models are based on numeric output and the interpretability of the model solely rests on human coding and the researchers' perspectives and goals. Like other qualitative analyses, the thematic analysis does not routinely use intercoder reliability (unlike traditional quantitative content analysis).

Third, the data from this study was solely from Twitter; however, several other social media platforms shared the same video with different comments, so the results cannot be generalized. However, this limitation also highlights the need for having machine learning algorithms in place to detect themes and motives on various platforms to be in a position to counter the spread of conspiracy theories and misinformation.

2.4.3 Practical Implications and Conclusions

When conspiracy theories emerge on social media platforms such as Twitter, our analysis suggests that machine learning can help find a vast trail of evidence that includes detectable motives or reasons underlying the conspiratorial beliefs. Detecting these motives subsequently allows the corresponding tweets to be grouped together to identify the prominence of a shared theme or topic. With respect to practical implications, professional communicators can use the dominant themes that emerge as guideposts for subsequent message responses, and design messages that address motives directly.

The efficiency of detection and rate of message responses may also be important factors to "inoculate" individuals from being influenced by weakening the persuasiveness of a conspiracy theory's appeal. As the name implies, inoculation theory of persuasion essentially provides a smaller "dose" of the argument and operates through a combination of forewarning media participants about the ensuing conspiracy theory message, providing evidence of arguments that will likely be made by the message, and examples of refutations or counterarguments to the message (Compton et al., 2021; Pfau et al., 1997). Another consideration for detection and response is that individuals vary in the strength of their conspiracy beliefs, and individuals who hold the strongest conspiracy views may be identifiable but entrenched in their beliefs. Similarly, inoculation benefits may only work if recipients are exposed to the inoculation message first and the conspiracy message second, so detection, message response speed, and widespread dissemination may all play important defensive roles in thwarting the spread. For example, following the detection of a conspiracy motive, a public health communicator could select a corresponding inoculation message and disseminate the message with tweets through an "inoculation corps" of pro-public health bots trained using supervised LDA. Future research could, for example, compare the pre/post effects of inoculation messages and general counterarguments on Twitter users' subsequent tweets and retweets and the resulting spread of information.

Through the preceding chapter, we used "Plandemic" as a novel context that involved the creation and spread of a COVID-19 conspiracy theory containing false misinformation across Twitter. The issue allowed us to illustrate how data science researchers can leverage social science-based theoretical frameworks and Python-based text mining methods to answer inductive observational research questions. Since individuals are drawn to conspiracy theories to fulfill specific epistemic, existential, and social motives, we were able to create corresponding taxonomies defined by unique attributes of the motives. Step-by-step Latent Dirichlet Allocation topic modeling with thematic analysis was detailed to uncover which of these motives were stated in tweets and prevalent within the spread of this misinformation. While the outcome of these analyses is specific to Plandemic and COVID-19, the strategy of coupling theoretical guidance with a rigorous unsupervised learning model and thematic analysis can be broadly applied to detect conspiracy theory motives in other situations.

References

Andrews, T. M. (2020). Facebook and other companies are removing viral 'Plandemic' conspiracy video. *Washington Post*. https://www.washingtonpost.com/technology/2020/05/07/plandemic-youtube-facebook-vimeo-remove/.

Baden, C., Kligler-Vilenchik, N., & Yarchi, M. (2020). Hybrid content analysis: Toward a strategy for the theory-driven, computer-assisted classification of large text corpora. *Communication Methods and Measures, 14*(3), 165–183.

Baines, A., Ittefaq, M., & Abwao, M. (2021). # Scamdemic, # Plandemic, or# Scaredemic: What parler social media platform tells us about COVID-19 vaccine. *Vaccines, 9*(5), 421.

Blei, D. M. (2012). Probabilistic topic models. *Communications of the ACM, 55*(4), 77–84. https://dl.acm.org/doi/fullHtml/10.1145/2133806.2133826?casa_token=AS09DNjvq8EAAAAA:4EjnHFvU-aui9yKs18cL9ndxabOTz76AgztordzSC_Euynbei2QYa2t2FtgwFzQTr8b0icfVTSEpyQ.

Blei, D. M., Ng, A. Y., & Jordan, M. I. (2003). Latent Dirichlet allocation. *Journal of machine Learning research, 3*(Jan), 993–1022.

Bost, P. R., & Prunier, S. G. (2013). Rationality in conspiracy beliefs: The role of perceived motive. *Psychological Reports, 113*(1), 118–128.

Boumans, J. W., & Trilling, D. (2016). Taking stock of the toolkit: An overview of relevant automated content analysis approaches and techniques for digital journalism scholars. *Digital Journalism, 4*(1), 8–23.

Braun, V., & Clarke, V. (2006). Using thematic analysis in psychology. *Qualitative Research in Psychology, 3*(2), 77–101. https://uwe-repository.worktribe.com/preview/1043068/thematic_analysis_revised_-_final.pdf.

Briones, R., Nan, X., Madden, K., & Waks, L. (2012). When vaccines go viral: An analysis of HPV vaccine coverage on YouTube. *Health Communication, 27*(5), 478–485.

Brotherton, R., French, C. C., & Pickering, A. D. (2013). Measuring belief in conspiracy theories: The generic conspiracist beliefs scale. *Frontiers in Psychology, 4*, 279.

Chan, M. P. S., Jones, C. R., Hall Jamieson, K., & Albarracín, D. (2017). Debunking: A meta-analysis of the psychological efficacy of messages countering misinformation. *Psychological Science, 28*(11), 1531–1546.

Choudrie, J., Banerjee, S., Kotecha, K., Walambe, R., Karende, H., & Ameta, J. (2021). Machine learning techniques and older adults processing of online information and misinformation: A covid 19 study. *Computers in Human Behavior, 119*, 106716.

Compton, J., van der Linden, S., Cook, J., & Basol, M. (2021). Inoculation theory in the post-truth era: Extant findings and new frontiers for contested science, misinformation, and conspiracy theories. *Social and Personality Psychology Compass, 15*(6), e12602.

DiFonzo, N. (2019). Conspiracy theory as rumor. In Uscinski, J. E. (Ed.) *Conspiracy Theories and the People Who Believe them* (pp. 257–268). New York: Oxford University Press. DOI: 10.1093/oso/9780190844073.001.0001.

Douglas, K. M., Sutton, R. M., & Cichocka, A. (2017). The psychology of conspiracy theories. *Current Directions in Psychological Science, 26*(6), 538–542.

Douglas, K. M., Sutton, R. M., & Cichocka, A. (2019). Belief in conspiracy theories: Looking beyond gullibility. In Forgas, J. & Baumeister, R. (Eds.). *The Social Psychology of Gullibility*. New York: Routledge. DOI: 10.4324/9780429203787.

El Naqa I., Murphy, M.J. (2015). What is machine learning? In: El Naqa, I., Li, R., and Murphy, M. (Eds.) *Machine Learning in Radiation Oncology*. Cham: Springer. DOI: 10.1007/978-3-319-18305-3_1.

Enders, A. M., Uscinski, J. E., Seelig, M. I., Klofstad, C. A., Wuchty, S., Funchion, J. R., Murthi, M. N., Premaratne, K., & Stoler, J. (2021). The relationship between social media use and beliefs in conspiracy theories and misinformation. *Political Behavior*, 1–24. Advance online publication. DOI: 10.1007/s11109-021-09734-6.

Frenkel, S., Decker, B., & Alba, D. (2020). How the 'plandemic' movie and its falsehoods spread widely online. *The New York Times*. https://www.nytimes.com/2020/05/20/technology/plandemic-movie-youtube-facebook-coronavirus.html.

Hollander, B. A. (2018). Partisanship, individual differences, and news media exposure as predictors of conspiracy beliefs. *Journalism & Mass Communication Quarterly*, *95*(3), 691–713. DOI: 10.1177/1077699017728919.

Islam, M. S., Kamal, A. H. M., Kabir, A., Southern, D. L., Khan, S. H., Hasan, S. M. & Seale, H. (2021). COVID-19 vaccine rumors and conspiracy theories: The need for cognitive inoculation against misinformation to improve vaccine adherence. *PloS One*, *16*(5), e0251605.

Jelodar, H., Wang, Y., Yuan, C., Feng, X., Jiang, X., Li, Y., & Zhao, L. (2019). Latent Dirichlet allocation (LDA) and topic modeling: models, applications, a survey. *Multimedia Tools and Applications*, *78*(11), 15169–15211.

Kata, A. (2010). A postmodern Pandora's box: Anti-vaccination misinformation on the Internet. *Vaccine*, *28*(7), 1709–1716.

Loper, E., & Bird, S. (2002). Nltk: The natural language toolkit. *arXiv preprint cs/0205028*.

Madden, K., Nan, X., Briones, R., & Waks, L. (2012). Sorting through search results: A content analysis of HPV vaccine information online. *Vaccine*, *30*(25), 3741–3746.

Maier, D., Waldherr, A., Miltner, P., Wiedemann, G., Niekler, A., Keinert, A., Pfetsch, B., Heyer, G., Reber, U., Häussler, T., Schmid-Petri, H., & Adam, S. (2018). Applying LDA topic modeling in communication research: Toward a valid and reliable methodology. *Communication Methods and Measures*, *12*(2–3), 93–118. DOI: 10.1080/19312458.2018.1430754.

McClaran, N., & Rhodes, N. (2021). Portrayals of vaccination in entertainment television: A content analysis. *Health Communication*, *36*(10), 1242–1251.

Negara, E. S., & Triadi, D. (2021). Topic modeling using latent dirichlet allocation (LDA) on twitter data with Indonesia keyword. *Bulletin of Social Informatics Theory and Application*, *5*(2), 124–132.

Pfau, M., Tusing, K. J., Koerner, A. F., Lee, W., Godbold, L. C., Penaloza, L. J., & Hong, Y. H. (1997). Enriching the inoculation construct: The role of critical components in the process of resistance. *Human Communication Research*, *24*(2), 187–215.

Řehůřek, R., & Sojka, P. (2011). Gensim—statistical semantics in python. Retrieved from genism. org.

Riffe, D., Lacy, S., & Fico, F. (2014). *Analyzing Media Messages: Using Quantitative Content Analysis in Research* (3rd ed.). Routledge. DOI: https://doi.org/10.4324/9780203551691.

Röder, M., Both, A., & Hinneburg, A. (2015). Exploring the space of topic coherence measures. In *Proceedings of the Eighth ACM International Conference on Web Search and Data Mining*, Shanghai China, pp. 399–408.

Shepherd, K. (2020). Who is Judy Mikovits in 'Plandemic,' the coronavirus conspiracy video just banned from social media? *Washington Post.* https://www.washingtonpost. com/nation/2020/05/08/plandemic-judy-mikovits-coronavirus.

Sievert, C., & Shirley, K. (2014). LDAvis: A method for visualizing and interpreting topics. In *Proceedings of the Workshop on Interactive Language Learning, Visualization, and Interfaces* (pp. 63–70). Retrieved: https://www.aclweb.org/anthology/W14-3110.pdf.

Stefanidis, A., Vraga, E., Lamprianidis, G., Radzikowski, J., Delamater, P. L., Jacobsen, K. H., & Crooks, A. (2017). Zika in Twitter: Temporal variations of locations, actors, and concepts. *JMIR Public Health and Surveillance, 3*(2), e22.

Tangcharoensathien, V., Calleja, N., Nguyen, T., Purnat, T., D'Agostino, M., Garcia-Saiso, S & Briand, S. (2020). Framework for managing the COVID-19 infodemic: Methods and results of an online, crowdsourced WHO technical consultation. *Journal of Medical Internet Research, 22*(6), e19659.

Wang, Y., McKee, M., Torbica, A., & Stuckler, D. (2019). Systematic literature review on the spread of health-related misinformation on social media. *Social Science & Medicine, 240*, 112552.

Warner, B. R., & Neville-Shepard, R. (2014). Echoes of a conspiracy: Birthers, truthers, and the cultivation of extremism. *Communication Quarterly, 62*(1), 1–17. DOI: 10.1080/01463373.2013.822407.

Wasserman, S., & Faust, K. (1994). *Social Network Analysis: Methods and Applications.* New York, NY: Cambridge University Press.

Xue, J., Chen, J., Chen, C., Zheng, C., Li, S., & Zhu, T. (2020). Public discourse and sentiment during the COVID 19 pandemic: Using latent Dirichlet allocation for topic modeling on Twitter. *PloS One, 15*(9), e0239441. DOI: 10.1371/journal.pone.0239441.

Zhou, S., Kan, P., Huang, Q., & Silbernagel, J. (2021). A guided latent Dirichlet allocation approach to investigate real-time latent topics of Twitter data during Hurricane Laura. *Journal of Information Science.* DOI: 10.1177/01655515211007724.

Chapter 3

Near Human-Level Style Transfer

Rahul Pereira, Beryl Coutinho, Jenslee Dsouza,
Cyrus Ferreira, and Vaishali Jadhav

St. Francis Institute of Technology

Contents

3.1 Introduction

Re-drawing images typically mean illustrating some paintings in a different style. This is considered to be a complicated task for computers compared to humans. On the contrary, humans can easily master the method to compose and describe the style between different images. Our brains are masters at determining objects quickly albeit this process is laborious. Creating an art piece for an artist may take a day, weeks, or at times, even months. However, with the help of convolutional neural networks (CNN) and powerful GPUs, this can be transformed into a relatively effortless task that can be achieved within minutes.

Deep learning is empowering people all around the world to experiment with their own creativity, and thus, we can see the importance of style transfer playing out in the commercial art world. Style transfer has various use cases like photo and video editors, virtual reality, gaming, commercial art, etc. from sharing stylized selfies to augmenting user-generated music videos, and beyond, the ability to add famous art styles to images and video clips promises to add unprecedented power to these kind of creativity tools. Style transfer makes high-rated and over-priced artistic work reproducible for office and home decor, or for advertisements. It aims to boost the artistic skills of every person. If you've ever imagined what a photo might look like if it were painted by a famous artist, then style transfer is the computer vision technique that turns this into a reality. Creating an art painting for an artist may take a day or even a week or it can even take a month. But if we train our computer machine to create an art painting, it will be created within an hour or two. It's always fascinating to visualize what we imagine. Style transfer brings your imagination to reality. This system will be built to give an artistic effect to an image. This system will take input content images from the user, and simultaneously, the user will select a style image, and within a moment, the software will process this image and will give a stylized output image. If you've ever imagined what a photo might look like if it were painted by a famous artist, then style transfer is the computer vision technique that turns this into a reality.

The VGG19 CNN model implemented in this project was furthermore trained on the ImageNet dataset specializing in artworks. Specializing in a particular domain assists the model in giving results with increased accuracy. The model can also work on photographs but the best results are obtained when it is provided with artworks. With this, a particular artist's artistic style can effortlessly be applied to another artists' artwork.

CNN is a subset of neural networks that work exclusively on image processing and natural language processing. This system uses the VGG19 CNN, which is 19 layers deep to separate and recombine various aspects of both images, respectively. This yields some great artistic outputs. The results, though, have relatively low resolution due to which a Super-Resolution Generative Adversarial Network (SRGAN) had to be implemented at the end of the system, which upscales the output image to a respectable resolution. SRGANs are specialized Generative Adversarial Networks (GANs) that specialize in converting single images to a super-resolution state.

Evaluation of the research is performed using loss functions as a performance metric. The amount of loss associated with each iteration of the style transfer process helps give an idea about the total number of iterations necessary to output a visually appealing image. Specifically, three types of loss are considered, i.e. style loss, content loss, and variation loss. They measure the difference in content features, style features, and amount of noise between original and output images, respectively. Time is not a major concern here as the time between iterations is constant except for some outliers due to excess loads on the GPU due to external factors.

3.2 Methodology

The style transfer study aims to build a near human-level style transfer model that will combine two images as input: a content image and a style image (Figure 3.1) that will put forth a stylized high-resolution image (Figure 3.2) by combining style and content features of both the input images. In artistic style transfer study, one of the major challenges is creating high-resolution images with meaning preservation, i.e. generating high-resolution images with feature preservation.

3.3 Pre-Processing

We can extract higher representations of image content by using CNNs, which are a type of neural network model. VGG19 convet requires the images to be in an appropriate format that is compatible with VGG19 input. We first need to prepare the images in a format that can be entered into and exited from the VGG19 convet before we can feed them into it. Pre-processing-scale pixel values appropriately for the VGG19 model are also necessary. Therefore, we first have to prepare the images in a format that can be read from and write to the VGG19 convet.

Figure 3.1   Input images.

Figure 3.2   Stylized output image.

3.4 Feature Extraction Using Transfer Learning

The basic idea of style transfer is to transfer the style features of a style image onto a content image. To extract these style and content features, a feature extractor is necessary. CNN is capable of extracting complex features from images. Training all the parameters of the neural network on a large dataset from scratch is not only resource-intensive but also time-consuming. Using this approach, i.e. starting from zero, is like reinventing the wheel; instead, our research proposes using the concept of transfer learning wherein a pre-trained model is reused based on our use case and is fine-tuned as per our requirements. In our model, a pre-trained VGG19 model trained on the ImageNet dataset has been implemented to create a feature extractor.

The features extracted by the feature extractor are produced as features maps, which highlight the important features. Max pooling is a kind of pooling layer that

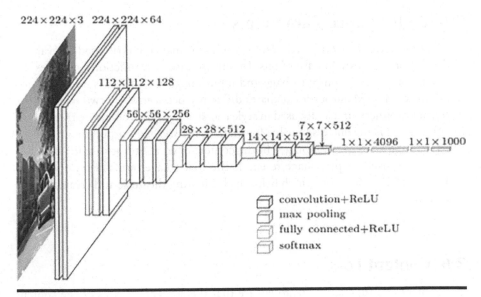

Figure 3.3   VGG19 architecture.

does some spatial invariance for downsampling operations. In max pooling, each pooling operation selects the maximum value of the current view. Max pooling is used in VGG19 to reduce data size and processing time. This allows the identification of features that have the greatest impact and reduces the possibility of over-fitting. VGG19 is a progressive algorithm that first tries to detect edges in the earlier layers, shapes in the middle layer, and some more features in the later layers. It uses multiple layers to extract hierarchical features for images. At each layer, VGG19 keeps learning a few features, which makes it one of the best image classifiers (Figure 3.3). Feature extraction segment takes place from the input layer to the last max-pooling layer in the VGG19 model, and classification segment takes place in the remaining layers. Since our research only requires feature extraction, we have excluded the remaining part of the VGG19 network.

To begin with feature extraction, the VGG19 model is imported from TensorFlow's Keras library. Then, the input images are pre-processed, i.e. scaling pixel values appropriately for the VGG19 model. The feature extraction part of VGG19 is going to be reused, so a new model has to be designed that is a subset of the layers in the full VGG19 model. The new model would have the same input layer as the original model, but the output would be the activation of the layer or the feature map. In the next step, the VGG19 model is loaded with the pre-trained weights for the ImageNet dataset. Python's NumPy library is used to convert pixel data to a NumPy array, which is then fed back into the TensorFlow model that extracts the required features.

3.5 Performance Parameters

To produce optimum and better results, the performance metric used to evaluate model performance are loss functions. In our use case, loss function calculates the difference between the output image and input image since there is no predefined standardized desired output it calculates difference between these two images. The different loss functions usually used in style transfer algorithm comprise three parts: (i) content loss is the one responsible for making the stylized output image and the content image close in resemblance in the context of content features; (ii) style loss makes the stylized output image resemble the style image terms of style features; and (iii) total variation loss, which helps in eliminating the noise and creates a more artistic stylized image.

3.6 Content Loss

The content loss function helps to ensure that the content features of the content image are preserved in the final output image. The higher layers of CNN are more concerned with the content present in the image compared to the lower layers, which deal with individual pixel values. Local features is the technical term used to describe image patches (small group of pixels), while global features describe the entire image. Global image features are features that enable viewers to quickly grasp the gist of a scene. Thus, the content features are extracted by the upper layers in the CNN. The content loss function is used to determine how the generated image differs from the original content image. The content loss is calculated as the root mean-squared error between the activations produced by the output image and the content input image. As stated earlier, activations from earlier layers in a CNN contain local information about the image, whereas activations from higher layers contain increasingly global, abstract information.

3.7 Style Loss

To extract the style features, the model uses the concept of correlation, which is nothing but the co-occurrence of the features. Therefore, if we know the correlation between the channels, we can get to know exactly which features co-occur. This would give us an insight into the style of an image. Style loss is similar to content loss, but the difference lies in that it is used to ensure the style of the style image is preserved in the final generated output image. The style loss function calculates the difference between the style of the input image and the generated output image.

3.8 Total Variation Loss

The total variation loss is the sum of content loss and style loss obtained from the previous states. Total variation loss parameter is used to increase the model accuracy. This metric measures how noisy the images are, hence lesser loss values equate to better the output.

3.9 Optimization

Optimization techniques play an important part in any deep learning model as they are used to increase the accuracy of the model by minimizing the loss function values. Optimizers are heavily dependent on the model's learnable parameters like weights as adjusting weights to reduce the loss is the primary function of the optimizers. A small change in a model's coefficient results in a small and predictable change in the loss value. Therefore, it is important to understand in which direction to move the model's coefficients so as to decrease the loss.

Gatys et al. have used L-BFGS as their primary optimization technique. Since L-BFGS is a very memory-expensive algorithm, our research proposes using gradient descent optimization technique to maximize the model performance. Gradient descent is an optimization technique that tries to change a model's learning parameters iteratively. It is a type of back-propagation method that updates the weights in the neural network by taking into account the actual output and the desired output. First, the loss was computed and then it was back-propagated to get the gradient of the loss with respect to each weight and accordingly update the weights of the network using the gradient.

Gradient descent has the disadvantage that it begins updating parameters only after it has processed the entire training set, but since our research uses a pre-trained model, longer runtimes isn't an issue. Eventually, the optimal weights are obtained by continuously applying gradient descent to them. This minimizes the loss function and makes the neural network better at prediction. Gradient descent is easy to understand as well as easy to implement.

3.10 Super-Resolution

Generating high-resolution images is one of the most challenging parts of the style transfer algorithm. Instead, our research proposes using a GAN to upscale the image after the whole style transfer process. The objective of this research is to generate near human-level artistic style transfer images. Enhanced Super-Resolution Generative Adversarial Network (ESRGAN) was proposed to be used in this part of the model, which is an enhanced version of SRGAN model. The pre-trained model called 'ESRGAN-2' from TensorFlow Hub has been imported to assist in this endeavor.

ESRGAN has Residual in Residual Dense Block (RRDB), which combines multi-level residual network and dense connection without batch normalization. By using a relativistic discriminator, ESRGAN is able to more effectively approximate the probability of an image's genuineness. For fine-tuning this section of the generator, a portion of the complete model is included in this model. The generator uses a linear combination of perceptual difference between real and fake image (using pre-trained VGG19 network), pixel-wise absolute difference between real and fake image, and relativistic average loss between the real and fake image as loss function during adversarial training. The generator is trained in a two-phase training setup. The first phase focuses on reducing the pixel-wise L1 distance of the input and targets high-resolution images to prevent local minimas obtained while starting from complete randomness. The second phase focuses on creating a sharper and better reconstruction of minute artifacts. The final trained model is then interpolated between the L1 loss model and adversarially trained model, to produce a photorealistic reconstruction of the original image with better resolution.

3.11 Results and Implementation

Figure 3.4 shows that our model produces stylized images while keeping most of the content and style features of the input images intact.

To verify the effectiveness of our model, we tested our model on different images (Figures 3.5 and 3.6).

According to Figure 3.7, the difference in loss reduction between iterations 200 and 800 is way more compared to the same between iterations 800 and 1,000. Hence, going for more than 1,000 iterations is not worth it as the point of diminishing returns has already been reached. Figure 3.7 shows that the decline is loss resembling an exponential curve wherein it drops massively at the beginning and then flattens out near but above 0. This further proves that there is no real gain from increasing the iterations beyond a certain point. With this approach, it takes about 8 minutes on average for the whole notebook to complete running on Google Colab's servers using dedicated graphical processing units.

During testing, the results exhibited that around 1,000 iterations of the optimization process are a good enough trade-off where the time taken is manageable while putting forth a visually appealing output image. This can be seen in Figure 3.8.

As seen in Figure 3.8, the most vivid changes to the content image happen during the first 500 iterations but these changes are rough and don't fully incorporate the styles into the content image; therefore, the number of iterations had to be significantly increased to account for refining the output image.

MobileNet model InceptionV3 model

Picsart model NHL Style Transfer

Figure 3.4 Comparison with other models.

The results after the style transfer process showed that the output image was too low in resolution, which led to the ESRGAN-tf2 pre-trained model being implemented at the end of the process, which triples the resolution of the output image (Figure 3.9) while retaining its pre-existing features and styles.

Content Image

Style Image

Style Transfer Output

Upscaled

Figure 3.5 Style transfer on architecture.

Content Image

Style Image

Style Transfer Output

Upscaled

Figure 3.6 Style transfer on human face.

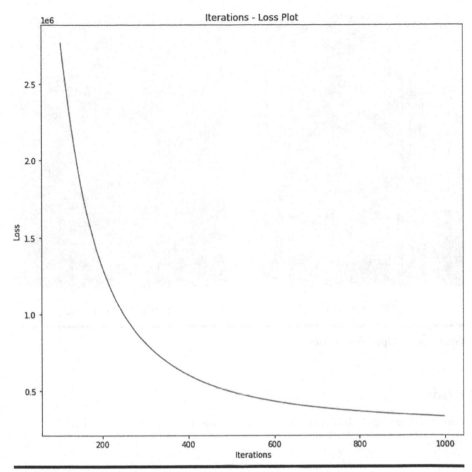

Figure 3.7   Plot of iterations-loss.

Figure 3.8   Changes during the optimization process.

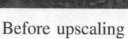

Before upscaling   After upscaling

Figure 3.9   Upscaling process.

Code

Github: https://github.com/LOCKhart07/Near-Human-Level-Style-Transfer

Chapter 4

Semantics-Based Distributed Document Clustering

Neepa Shah
Dwarkadas J. Sanghvi College of Engineering

Sunita Mahajan
M.E.T. Institute of Management

Ketan Shah
MPSTME Mumbai, NMIMS University

Contents

DOI: 10.1201/9781003390220-4

4.1 Introduction

The availability of various powerful and affordable computers, data collection devices, and storage media is tremendous due to the rapid growth in the computer hardware and information technology domains since past few years. This in turn has greatly influenced the database and information industries to produce and store huge amount of information [1]. This change has contributed very large amount (80%–85% [2]) of information in the form of text databases for various sectors like government, industry, business, and other institutions. This tremendous growth in the volume of the text documents leads to the problem of manually organizing and then analyzing this dataset efficiently. Thus, there is a challenge to provide an easy, friendly, effective, and efficient organization of text documents automatically, making smooth navigation and quick subsequent access to the information [1,3].

Document clustering helps to organize documents into different categories known as 'clusters'. The documents in every cluster have some common properties, and these properties are defined as per various similarity and distance measures. The efficient document clustering algorithm plays a very critical role in helping users to organize, browse, and analyze the document dataset.

Semantics for Document Clustering: Most document clustering approaches are based on the Vector Space Model (VSM) [4]. The VSM approach cannot deal with multi-word expressions, synonymous and polysemous terms. Due to this, in VSM, there are generally thousands of features leading to high dimensionality [5]. This problem is mainly because of ignorance of the hidden semantics present in the documents. Thus, there is a need of proper semantic understanding for better-quality clustering.

Distributed Document Clustering: The datasets are increasing at an exponential order. So only the algorithmic and conceptual changes are not enough in current scenario of very large datasets. To solve these problems, many user-friendly and scalable tools for distributed processing are emerging, Hadoop being the most popular one among these. It is an open-source software framework for data-intensive distributed applications. MapReduce is parallel programming for scalable data processing on Hadoop [6].

So, combining these issues and need of efficient clustering solution, we address the below objectives in our research work.

- To device suitable model to represent the dataset
- To reduce high dimensionality
- To support scalability
- To handle semantics
- To increase accuracy of clusters
- To use proper clustering algorithm
- To generate good-quality clusters and assess the same
- To provide efficient pre-processing, and
- To reduce clustering time

4.2 Background and Related Work

We reviewed many research papers of document clustering. We categorized these as basic/traditional algorithms, semantics-driven algorithms, parallel clustering algorithms, and distributed clustering algorithms.

Various basic document clustering methods studied since last few years such as agglomerative, partitional, and their variations are studied. These include document clustering algorithms starting with Croft (only for titles' clustering) followed by K-means (KM) for linear time computation, hierarchical agglomerative clustering (HAC) for better-quality clustering solutions, and variations of KM and HAC algorithms for balancing time and quality parameters. Few other concepts are also studied and explored, which include frequent-itemsets, fuzzy theory, neural network, genetic algorithm, self-organizing map, non-negative matrix factorization, etc. The study of all these methods with respective comparison and analysis is given in Ref. [7]. Various approaches have been proposed to handle semantic relations in document clustering. They differ in document representation, semantic measure used, usage of background semantic information, etc. We studied these methods and made comparison in Ref. [8]. Here, the limitations and drawbacks of various methods are discussed with parameters like the semantic approach, clustering algorithm, experimental datasets, evaluation parameters, suggested future work, etc. We also compared the traditional and semantics-based approaches [9] of document clustering in Table 4.1.

Various parallel and distributed clustering algorithms along with the role of Hadoop and MapReduce in distributed clustering applications are reviewed in detail in Ref. [10]. From the study of various traditional, semantics-driven, parallel, and distributed approaches, we conclude that KM, Bisecting KM, HAS, particle swarm optimization, and self-organized map algorithms are the most widely used ones. So, we summarize these algorithms with respect to advantages, disadvantages, and time complexities in Table 4.2.

Through this rigorous study, we came to the conclusion that the research work focusing on very large dataset is not considering any semantic approach; however, the research work driven by semantics has not applied distributed computing or

Table 4.1 Comparison of Traditional and Semantics-Based Approach of Document Clustering

Criteria	Traditional Approach	Semantic Approach
Data representation method	Bag-of-Words (BOW), Vector Space Model (VSM)	Ontology, Semantic Graph, Latent Semantic Indexing (LSI), Frequent Concept, WordNet
Features	Frequency of words, bags of words, TFxIDF	Concept of words, concepts based on background domain knowledge, sense of a word, frequent concept, concept weight
Background knowledge	No background knowledge is used	Ontology
Function	Focuses on the syntax in a document and ignores the conceptual similarity of terms generating poor-quality clusters	Focuses on computational semantics of the grammar in the document giving more accuracy, quality, and performance of the clustering
Strengths and weaknesses	Weaknesses/Problems: Polysemy, synonymy, ambiguity, and semantic similarities	Strengths: Word Sense Disambiguation resolves ambiguity. Ontology as background knowledge helps in tackling polysemy and synonymy problems

parallel computing for faster calculation. The research work proposed making use of parallel and distributed clustering approaches is difficult from the view point of implementation, cost of extra hardware, and execution to some extent.

From the comparison portrayed in Table 4.2, it is clear that for large datasets, partitional methods like **KM and Bisecting KM are the best candidates as clustering algorithms**. Out of these two, Bisecting KM has no disadvantage and is not yet explored and implemented by any researcher. So, this motivated us to propose **Distributed Bisecting KM** (DBKM) as our clustering algorithm for our approach.

From the survey of semantics-based approaches, we conclude that testing of their proposed method is not done on large datasets. They have proposed enhancement in used current semantic approach as future work. Many researchers have proposed combined usage of syntactic and semantic method for better results. This led us to propose the use of **Part-of-Speech (POS) Tagging** and **WordNet Ontology** as a combined approach for our work. This is needed for background

Table 4.2 Comparison of Most Widely Used Clustering Algorithms

Clustering Algorithm	Advantages	Disadvantages	Time Complexity
K-Means [11,12,16,19,23–26,30]	• Linear time complexity [12] • It produces tighter clusters especially if the clusters are globular [13]	• Thought to produce inferior clusters. [12] • Difficult to predict k-value • Different initial partitions can produce different final clusters • The clusters are non-hierarchical and do not overlap [13]	$O(l*k*n*m)$ l=# of iterations K=# of clusters n=# of vectors m=dimensionality of the vector [31]
Bisecting K-Means [12,15,16,20,24,25,29]	• Better than KM and as good or better than HAC • Linear time complexity • If the number of clusters is large and if refinement is not used, then Bisecting K-Means is even more efficient than the regular k-means algorithm [12] • Low cost and quality of the cluster is satisfactory • More stable as during every split multiple k-Means are used to find better clustering. This reduces the effect of randomness [13] • No need to specify k [31]	No disadvantage as such [13]	$O((k-1)l*n)$ l=# of iterations K=# of clusters n=# of vectors [31]

(Continued)

Table 4.2 (*Continued*) Comparison of Most Widely Used Clustering Algorithms

Clustering Algorithm	Advantages	Disadvantages	Time Complexity
Hierarchical agglomerative clustering [12,14,16,17,24,25,27,28]	• Better-quality clustering approach [12] • No apriori information about the number of clusters required • It can produce an ordering of the objects, which may be informative for display [13]	• Quadratic time complexity [12] • Sometimes it is difficult to identify correct number of clusters using dendrogram • If initial document collection is larger than computation, it could be very time-consuming [13]	O (n^2) n=input vector size [31]
Self-organizing map [18,21,27]	• Data mapping interpretation is easy • It is capable of arranging complex and large datasets [13]	• Determination of input weights is difficult • Requires nearby points to behave similarly [13]	O (nXC) n=# of vectors C=# of documents [31]
Particle swarm optimization [22]	• More stable • Occupies bigger optimization ability [31]	• Too slow • Non-repeatable in terms of computational cost, which makes the comparison hard [13]	O (M*X) M=# of search agents X=# of generations [31]

knowledge and proper Word Sense Disambiguation, leading to more accuracy for our semantics-based clustering.

Majority of the parallel and distributed approaches have not explored semantics at all. Again, testing is not done on standard and large datasets by them. There are few methods wherein specialized server setup is needed. So, for distributed document clustering, we propose to make use of **Hadoop-MapReduce**. Hadoop supports complete transparency and does not need any specialized server or hardware; it supports the commodity platform.

4.3 Proposed Approach: Semantics-Based Distributed Document Clustering

In this section, we will discuss our approach of distributed document clustering with a detailed description of each module. The architecture of our system is given in Figure 4.1.

Figure 4.1 demonstrates different stages of our proposed approach. It involves dataset pre-processing (addressing syntactic and semantic analysis), dataset representation model (using Ontology-based VSM), distributed clustering algorithms (KM and Bisecting KM), followed by finally the evaluation of output solution (clusters).

The objective of the text data pre-processing is to enhance the quality of data and at the same time to reduce the difficulty of mining process [32]. We have done extensive pre-processing of datasets. In our approach, we have used Ontology-based VSM [33], a hybrid approach to represent our dataset. This is possible due to extensive pre-processing in the first stage of the document clustering. Third module is distributed document clustering where we used distributed KM (DKM) and DBKM algorithms. For these algorithms, the generated vector and centroids are copied to

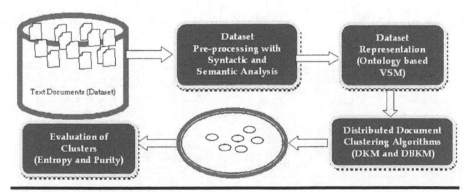

Figure 4.1   Proposed approach.

Hadoop Distributed File System (HDFS) and the algorithm is run over Hadoop framework. For evaluation of the clusters, we have used entropy and purity.

4.3.1 Dataset Pre-Processing

Dataset pre-processing is based on Natural Language Processing. It is divided into two stages: syntactic and semantic analysis. We have used Stanford Parser [34] for syntactic analysis and WordNet [35] for semantic analysis. The proposed approach of enhanced pre-processing has reduced the size of the original dataset by a factor of 2. Due to this, the major issue of dimensionality curse of traditional document clustering is resolved. The details of pre-processing with its experiments and results are in Ref. [36]. We give the diagrammatic representation in Figure 4.2.

4.3.2 Document Representation: Ontology-Based VSM

After dataset pre-processing, we apply term weighting and pruning and then generate Ontology-based VSM in this phase. For this, we first took the pre-processed dataset as input. It then calculates the number of unique words and asks the user to provide the pruning level. It then creates Dictionary instance to calculate and store these frequency values for these top unique words and generates TFxIDF vector. Further, it normalizes the same as per TFxIDF. This process is shown in Figure 4.3.

4.3.3 Distributed K-Means and Bisecting K-Means Algorithm for Document Clustering

As the time complexity of hierarchical clustering algorithms is quadratic, for clustering large datasets, we prefer partitional algorithms like KM and Bisecting BM due to their linear time complexity. We have developed distributed version of both

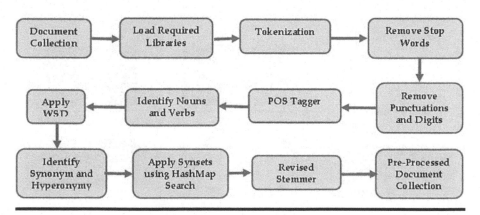

Figure 4.2   Dataset pre-processing steps.

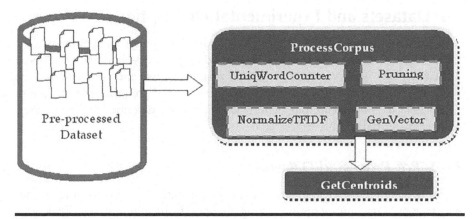

Figure 4.3   Dataset representation.

these algorithms. Distributed document clustering using KM is stated in Ref. [37]. The Bisecting KM is hybrid approach of clustering, which combines partitional and hierarchical clustering approaches. For DBKM, the dataset is first pre-processed and then Ontology-based VSM is generated similar to DKM approach. After that, generating centroids, copying vector and centroids to HDFS is also the same. The algorithm and working of MapRed (Distributed) Bisecting KM are different. It interacts with the user to ask inputs as 'data file to select the cluster and number of clusters to form'. The first input is '/data' in the HDFS directory where we moved our vector file and the second input is the count of clusters, as per our requirement.

The algorithm for the DBKM is given below:

1. Choose 'k' random initial reference points, centroids, which lead to a provisional partition.
2. Consider all Document Vectors and assign each of them to the cluster identified by the centroid from which it has less distance.
3. Calculate the centroid of each of the k groups thus obtained.
4. Choose the cluster that has more documents.
   a. From the selected cluster, you select two documents as initial centroids.
   b. Calculate the distance of each Document Vector from each centroid obtained in the previous step.
   c. Assign it to the cluster identified by the centroid from which it has less distance.
   d. Calculate the new centroid of each of the groups thus obtained. These centroids become the reference points for the new cluster.
   e. If the minimum distance is not obtained in the group centroid membership, then you return to step 4-b.
5. Return to step 4, as long as they are not counted K clusters.

4.4 Datasets and Experimental Description

Two real-world text corpuses are used for conducting extensive experiments. The first corpus is Reuters-21578 [38], and the second corpus is 20-NewsGroups (20NG) [39] Collection. We have experimented on partial datasets and complete datasets (with 70% pruning) for both the corpuses. We also used pre-processed versions of the datasets for inferencing our hypotheses. Below, we describe baseline datasets followed by partial and pre-processed datasets.

4.4.1 Pre-Processed Datasets

As mentioned in proposed approach, we applied syntactic and semantic understanding (stage-by-stage) during pre-processing phase to the baseline datasets. These gave us various pre-processed datasets. With this pre-processing, we also could see reduction in the number of words and size in bytes for whole datasets. We give table to indicate this reduction in the size of datasets with calculation of percentage reduction in Table 4.3. It clarifies that pre-processing reduces the size of dataset almost by a factor of 2.

4.4.2 Experimental Setup

For our experiments, we used Hadoop version 1.2.1. Each machine (node) has two single-core processors (running at 2.33 GHz), 1GB memory, and 130 GB disk, and the network bandwidth is 100 Mbps. The node configuration is given below:

- Distributed, Multi-node Apache Hadoop cluster: with Ubuntu Linux 14.04 Operating System (as dual boot with Windows 8) and Hadoop version 1.2.1
- The processor is Intel i5 Quad Core Processor

There are two setups: single-node and multi-node. In multi-node cluster, master node acts as slave too.

4.5 Results and Discussion

In this section, we first lay the background of the experiments using various test cases and hypotheses. Then, we discuss experiments, followed by the results. The outcomes are explained and discussed.

We categorize the test cases as per our problem statement and objectives. These are

1. Test cases for stability of algorithms (count of clusters and stability)
2. Test cases for accuracy/quality of syntactic and semantic analysis

Table 4.3 Reduction in Size (Bytes) of Datasets after Pre-Processing

Dataset	Reuters			20-NewsGroup		
	Bytes	**MBs**	**% Reduction**	**Bytes**	**MBs**	**% Reduction**
Baseline	1,861,4879	18.6	-	46,655,479	46.5	-
Stop words removed	1,203,7532	12.0	35.48	27,526,368	27.5	40.86
Stop and Modified stem	1,084,2925	10.8	41.93	25,290,864	25.3	45.59
Stop, POS, and Modified stem	1,586,3092	15.9	14.52	38,307,507	38.3	17.63
Stop, POS, WordNet	1,146,2937	11.5	38.17	26,304,766	26.3	43.44
Stop, POS, WordNet, Mod stem	**1,046,1830**	**10.5**	**43.55**	**24,299,238**	**24.3**	**47.74**

Bold values signify the best reduction

3. Test cases for scalability (of cluster and both the algorithms)
4. Test cases for clustering time

4.5.1 Test Cases for Stability of Algorithms (Count of Clusters and Stability)

This test case is designed to decide the best-performing clusters' count as per the classes of the datasets. For this, we first experiment DKM and DBKM algorithms on 5 nodes setup to generate 5, 10, 15, and 20 clusters. We then calculate entropy and purity of these clusters. The entropy and purity for both DKM and DBKM are found the best for 5 clusters, so we ran the job to generate clusters near to count 5, i.e. 5, 6, 7, and 8 clusters. The analysis of these experiments shows that the best-performing cluster count is 6 compared to 5, 7, and 8 for both DKM and DBKM algorithms. So, for further experiments, we have generated 5 or 6 clusters.

4.5.2 Test Cases for Accuracy/Quality of Syntactic and Semantic Analysis

This test case is to prove one of our contributions. Here, we are trying to prove the usage and benefits of syntactic and semantic understanding to the datasets.

We performed experiments to cluster the documents over different pre-processed datasets for DKM and DBKM algorithms and calculated entropy and purity values for the variations of both the datasets. Then, we compared the clustering results of these datasets to justify our hypothesis. For this, we further calculated improvement in percentage for various cases like:

■ Usage of Part-of-Speech Tagger and WordNet over original datasets
■ Usage of Modified Stemmer over Part-of-Speech Tagger and WordNet
■ Usage of Modified Stemmer, Part-of-Speech Tagger, and WordNet over original datasets

These improvement values for entropy and purity using DKM algorithm are given in Table 4.4.

It can be clearly seen that applying syntactic and semantic understanding to the original dataset has given considerable improvement ranging from 19% to 24% and on top of that application of modified stemmer gave further improvement of 25%– 38% for DKM algorithm.

We executed similar experiments for DBKM also to prove our test case. These improvements for entropy and purity values are given in Table 4.5.

As we can see, compared to DKM, DBKM gave better performance. By adding syntactic and semantic understanding over baseline dataset gave considerable

Table 4.4 % Improvement in Entropy and Purity Values for Different Levels of Pre-Processing: DKM

Test Cases	% Improvement in Entropy		% Improvement in Purity	
	Reuters	*20NG*	*Reuters*	*20NG*
POS and WordNet over Baseline Dataset	22.404	19.870	23.711	20.884
Modified Stemmer over POS and WordNet	7.075	6.098	11.667	6.645
Modified Stemmer with POS, WordNet over Baseline Dataset	27.893	24.756	38.144	28.916

Table 4.5 % Improvement in Entropy and Purity Values for Different Levels of Pre-Processing: DBKM

Test Cases	% Improvement in Entropy		% Improvement in Purity	
	Reuters	*20NG*	*Reuters*	*20NG*
POS and WordNet over Baseline Dataset	21.495	25.914	27.700	30.479
Modified Stemmer over POS and WordNet	17.063	15.022	20.956	12.861
Modified Stemmer with POS, WordNet over Baseline Dataset	34.891	37.043	54.460	47.260

improvement of 21%– 30% and applying modified stemmer over syntactic and semantic understanding (which will be discussed in next test case) gave higher improvement of 35–54%. The performance improvement for both DKM and DBKM is due to the use of Ontology WordNet.

Test cases for scalability of clusters and of both the distributed algorithms are given in Ref. [40].

Table 4.6   Comparing Time for BL and PP Datasets and Corresponding Improvements: DKM

| Dataset | Partial DS | | Full DS | | | |
	Baseline Dataset (BL DS)	Pre-Processed Dataset (PP DS)	Baseline Dataset (BL DS)	Pre-Processed Dataset (PP DS)	% Improvement for Partial DS	% Improvement for Full DS
Reuters	170	128	318	219	24.71	31.13
20NG	240	151	639	347	37.08	45.70

Table 4.7   Comparing Time for BL and PP Datasets and Corresponding Improvements: DBKM

| Dataset | Partial DS | | Full DS | | | |
	Baseline Dataset (BL DS)	Pre-Processed Dataset (PP DS)	Baseline Dataset (BL DS)	Pre-Processed Dataset (PP DS)	% Improvement for Partial DS	% Improvement for Full DS
Reuters	397	281	567	348	29.22	38.62
20NG	736	396	1007	489	46.20	51.44

4.5.3 Test Cases for Clustering Time

For this test case, we compared time taken by partial and full datasets along with their improvements for both baseline and pre-processed collection of Reuters and 20-NewsGroups using DKM and DBKM algorithms. These outcomes are narrated in Table 4.6 for DKM, where we can see that there is considerable improvement ranging from 25% to 46% and in Table 4.7 for DBKM with improvement of 29%– 51%.

We represent the results of comparison of running time results for partial dataset and full dataset in Figures 4.4 and 4.5 for DKM and DBKM, respectively. It depicts the evident improvement using pre-processed dataset over baseline dataset.

4.6 Conclusion and Future Scope

Due to ever-increasing rate of the information, there is need of finding, filtering, and managing this information. Document clustering, a domain under data mining, helps in document organization and management. In this chapter, the approach of

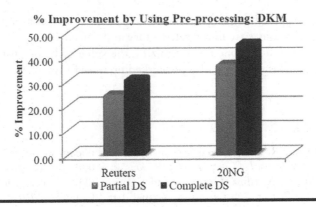

Figure 4.4   % improvement using pre-processed datasets: DKM.

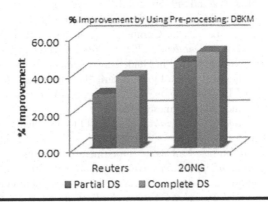

Figure 4.5   % improvement using pre-processed datasets: DBKM.

semantics-based distributed document clustering is discussed. This method mainly addresses two requirements of text data mining, which are semantics and scalability. This chapter also focuses on other requirements like quality and accuracy.

For scalability, DKM with semantics is proposed and it is proved to be better with respect to quality, time, and accuracy when compared with DKM without semantics. In addition to this, a new algorithm, DBKM with semantics, is proposed and implemented. The results are evaluated using entropy and purity. DBKM with semantics performs better in terms of quality, accuracy, time, and scalability compared to DKM with semantics.

For better quality and accuracy, syntactic and semantic understanding is added to the baseline datasets using POS tagging and WordNet Ontology. This approach improved the performance of generated clusters. Also, the dataset size is reduced to almost half using this effective pre-processing. Various test cases are designed to justify stability, scalability, quality, and time. For all the test cases, improvement is calculated and outcomes are found satisfactory and considerable.

Further work can be done for optimizing the value of K for Distributed KM. Soft/overlapping clustering can also be worked upon as future scope.

References

[1] R. Baghel and R. Dhir, "A frequent concepts based document clustering algorithm," *International Journal of Computer Applications*, 4, 5, 0975–8887, 2010.

[2] Volkan Tunalı, A. Yılmaz Çamurcu, and T. Tugay Bilgin, "An empirical comparison of fast and efficient tools for mining textual data," In *ISCSE 2010, 1st International Symposium on Computing in Science and Engineering*, Izmir, Kusadasi, Turkey, 2010.

[3] A. Huang, "Similarity measures for text document clustering," In *Proceedings of the Sixth New Zealand Computer Science Research Student Conference NZCSRSC*, Christchurch, New Zealand, 49–56, 2008.

[4] A. Hotho, S. Staab, and G. Stumme. Explaining text clustering results using semantic structures. In: N. Lavrač, D. Gamberger, L. Todorovski, and H. Blockeel (eds) *Knowledge Discovery in Databases: PKDD 2003. PKDD 2003. Lecture Notes in Computer Science*, vol 2838. Berlin, Heidelberg: Springer, 2003.

[5] Loulwah AlSumait and Carlotta Domeniconi, "Local semantic kernels for text document clustering," In *Workshop on Text Mining, SIAM International Conference on Data Mining*, Minneapolis, Minnesota, 2007.

[6] Tom White, "*Hadoop: The Definitive Guide*," O'Reilly Media, Inc., 2009. ISBN: 9780596521974.

[7] Neepa Shah and Sunita Mahajan, "Document clustering: A detailed review," *International Journal of Applied Information Systems*, 4, 5, 30–38, 2012.

[8] Neepa Shah and Sunita Mahajan. "Semantic based document clustering: A detailed review," *International Journal of Computer Applications*, 52, 5, 42–52, 2012.

[9] M. P. Naik, H. B. Prajapati, and V. K. Dabhi, "A survey on semantic document clustering," In *2015 IEEE International Conference on Electrical, Computer and Communication Technologies (ICECCT)*, Coimbatore, 1–10, 2015. doi: 10.1109/ICECCT.2015.7226036.

[10] Neepa Shah and Sunita Mahajan, "Semantics based distributed document clustering: Proposal," *International Journal of Computer Science Engineering and Information Technology Research*, 3, 2, 379–388, 2013.

[11] S. C. Punitha and M. Punithavalli, "Performance evaluation of semantic based and ontology based text document clustering techniques," *Procedia Engineering*, 30, 100–106, 2012.

[12] Michael Steinbach, George Karypis, and Vipin Kumar, "A comparison of document clustering techniques," In *KDD Workshop on Text Mining*, Boston, MA, USA, 2000.

[13] M. P. Naik, H. B. Prajapati, and V. K. Dabhi, "A survey on semantic document clustering," In *2015 IEEE International Conference on Electrical, Computer and Communication Technologies (ICECCT)*, Coimbatore, 1–10, 2015. doi: 10.1109/ICECCT.2015.7226036.

[14] Peter Willett, "Recent trends in hierarchic document clustering: A critical review," *Information Processing & Management*, 24, 5, 517–597, 1988.

[15] Ying Zhao and George Karypis, "Evaluation of hierarchical clustering algorithms for document datasets", Technical Report, 2002.

[16] R. Kashef and M.S. Kamel, "Enhanced bisecting k-means clustering using intermediate cooperation," *Journal of Pattern Recognition,* 42, 11, 2557–2569, 2009.

[17] M. Muhammad Rafi, Shahid Shaikh, and Amir Farooq, "Document clustering based on topic maps," *International Journal of Computer Applications,* 12, 1, 0975–8887, 2010.

[18] B. Choudhary and P. Bhattacharyya, "Text clustering using semantics," In *Proceedings of the 11th International World Wide Web Conference,* Geneva at CERN, 2002.

[19] Andreas Hotho, Alexander Maedche, and Steffen Staab, "Ontology-based text document clustering," *K¨unstliche Intelligenz,* 16, 4, 48–54, 2002.

[20] Andreas Hotho, Steffen Staab, and Gerd Stumme, "Wordnet improves text document clustering," In *Proceedings of the SIGIR 2003 Semantic Web Workshop,* 2003.

[21] Chihli Hung, Stefan Wermter, and Peter Smith, "Hybrid neural document clustering using guided self-organization and WordNet," *Journal IEEE Intelligent Systems Archive,* 19, 2, 68–77, 2004.

[22] Liang Feng, Ming-Hui Qiu, Yu-Xuan Wang, Qiao-Liang Xiang, Yin-Fei Yang, and Kai Liu, "A fast divisive clustering algorithm using an improved discrete particle swarm optimizer," *Journal of Pattern Recognition Letters,* 31, 11, 1216–1225, 2010.

[23] Deng Cai, Xiaofei He, and Jiawei Han, "Document clustering using locality preserving indexing," *IEEE Transactions on Knowledge and Data Engineering,* 17, 12, 2005.

[24] Yong Wang and Julia Hodges, "Document clustering with semantic analysis," In *Proceedings of the 39th Annual Hawaii International Conference on System Sciences, HICSS 2006,* vol. 3, 54c–54c, 2006.

[25] Hai-Tao Zheng, Bo-Yeong Kang, and Hong-Gee Kim, "Exploiting noun phrases and semantic relationships for text document clustering," *Journal of Information Sciences,* 179, 13, 2249–2262, 2009.

[26] S.Vijayalakshmi and D. Manimegalai, "Query based text document clustering using its hypernymy relation," *International Journal of Computer Applications* 23, 1, 13–16, 2011.

[27] Mari-Sanna Paukkeri, Alberto Pérez García-Plaza, Víctor Fresno, Raquel Martínez Unanue, and Timo Honkela, "Learning a taxonomy from a set of text documents," *Applied Soft Computing,* 12, 3, 1138–1148, 2012.

[28] Aboutabl Amal Elsayed and Elsayed Mohamed Nour, "A novel parallel algorithm for clustering documents based on the hierarchical agglomerative approach," *International Journal of Computer Science & Information Technology,* 3, 2, 152, 2011.

[29] Yanjun Li, "High performance text document clustering," PhD Thesis, Wright State University, USA, 2007.

[30] Zakaria Elberrichi, Abdelattif Rahmoun, and Mohamed Amine Bentaalah, "Using WordNet for text categorization," *The International Arab Journal of Information Technology,* 5, 1, 2008

[31] N. Y. Saiyad, H. B. Prajapati, and V. K. Dabhi, "A survey of document clustering using semantic approach," In *2016 International Conference on Electrical, Electronics, and Optimization Techniques (ICEEOT),* Chennai, 2555–2562, 2016. doi: 10.1109/ICEEOT.2016.7755154.

[32] Anil Kumar, "Text data pre-processing and dimensionality reduction techniques for document clustering," *International Journal of Engineering Research & Technology (IJERT),* 1 5, 2012, ISSN: 2278-0181.

[33] S.C. Punitha, K. Mugunthadevi, and M. Punithavalli, "Impact of ontology based approach on document clustering," *International Journal of Computer Applications*, 22, 2, 0975–8887, 2011.

[34] Stanford Lexicalized Parser v3.7.0, 2016-10-31, available at https://github.com/stanfordnlp/CoreNLP/tree/master/doc/lexparser.

[35] WordNet, A lexical database for English, available at http://WordNet.princeton.edu/.

[36] S. Mahajan and N. Shah, "Efficient pre-processing for enhanced semantics based distributed document clustering," In *3rd International Conference on Computing for Sustainable Global Development (INDIACom)*, New Delhi, 338–343, 2016.

[37] Neepa Shah and Sunita Mahajan, "Distributed document clustering using K-means", *International Journal of Advanced Research in Computer Science and Software Engineering*, 4, 11, 24–29, 2014.

[38] Reuters-21578, Text categorization collection data set, UCI machine learning laboratory, available at https://archive.ics.uci.edu/ml/datasets/Reuters-21578+Text+Categorization+Collection, 2013.

[39] Tom Mitchell, 20 newsgroups dataset, available at http://kdd.ics.uci.edu/databases/20newsgroups/20newsgroups.html, 1999.

[40] Neepa Shah and Sunita Mahajan, "Scalability analysis of semantics based distributed document clustering algorithms," In *International Conference on Intelligent Computing, Instrumentation and Control Technologies (ICICICT)*, Kerala, India, 2017, 763–768, doi: 10.1109/ICICICT1.2017.8342660.

Chapter 5

Application of Machine Learning in Disease Prediction

Sannidhi Rao, Shreya Kulkarni,
Shikha Mehta, and Neha Katre

Dwarkadas J. Sanghvi College of Engineering

Contents

5.1 Introduction

In the healthcare system, people try to opt for the best possible treatment available while keeping in mind the costs that will be incurred depending on the quality of treatment [1]. Nowadays, diseases like heart attacks and diabetes are common, especially among patients between the ages of 30 and 50 [2], wherein most patients are clueless about the nature of the disease and are unsure about what

DOI: 10.1201/9781003390220-5

treatment they should undergo. Surveys suggest that patients have a challenging time differentiating heart attacks from acidity and eventually succumb to fatality [3]. Similarly, in the case of diabetes, patients are reluctant to accept they have diabetes and end up delaying their treatments, which further deteriorates their health and exacerbates the already worse situation [4]. On the other hand, breast cancer is a rare disease observed in women in or above the age of 50 in the past but is now observed in even younger people [5]. Furthermore, breast cancer patients are unaware of the risks posed by this disease and unwilling to take any action until it is too late [6]. Therefore, an early and effective diagnosis is the key solution to all problems as it ensures a patient's well-being and simultaneously educates them about that medical condition. Machine learning (ML) has manifested a vast and impressive potential in medical diagnosis. One such application is effective digital diagnosis since ML can detect patterns of anomalies recorded in patient health records. Thus, this powerful subset of Artificial Intelligence (AI) assists in evaluating the medical condition of the patient with the help of data extrapolated from large medical datasets [7]. ML is the study of how computers act without being programmed explicitly. In addition to medical diagnosis, it even has variegated applications in automatic language translation, image recognition, traffic prediction, online fraud detection, self-driving cars, practical speech recognition, product recommendations, effective web search, stock market trading, understanding of the human genome, and email and malware filtering. It is the best way to make progress toward advanced-level AI [8]. Most effective ML techniques have been studied and implemented for more than a decade now. In addition, the practical knowledge needed to apply these techniques intends to manage large and complex data effectively. There is a broad spectrum of ML types, which include (i) supervised learning (task-driven), concerned with classification and regression; and (ii) unsupervised learning (data-driven), concerned with clustering, dimensionality reduction, and association. Due to the extensive number of supervised and unsupervised algorithms in ML, choosing the correct algorithm for a large dataset to obtain the maximum accuracy may seem complicated and time-consuming since each algorithm takes a different approach to learning [9]. An algorithm works on a trial-and-error basis since there is no way to tell whether an algorithm will work without trying it out. An appropriate algorithm is selected based on the size and the type of data the user is currently working on. Not only does this help in getting insights from the data but also helps in creating a clear picture of how those insights can be useful [10]. An automated classifier for disease prediction aims to build an efficient process for patients to predict disease accurately and give proper justification behind that prediction. By doing so, the system prioritizes urgent patients and keeps satisfaction levels high [11]. For this purpose, an investigation into the patient's behavior is significant for the administrators to make necessary adjustments to the system by analyzing the insights derived from past patient records, detecting areas of improvement, and keeping the target audience (patients) as the core focus around which the entire system revolves.

Disease prediction by ML has become a pivotal interest of research and development for many professionals working in the medical field [12]. Although notable results have been procured, there is still scope for improvement. A patient should be familiar with the disease and the corresponding treatment he is receiving for that disease. Early detection of a disease is necessary to avoid complications in health. Therefore, the focus should be on tasks that provide more value while improving the whole patient experience. Ensuring that the patient is in the right hands helps achieve time and cost-effectiveness. In the proposed model, patients enter specific data from their medical reports and expect an accurate disease prediction (heart disease, diabetes, or breast cancer) with a detailed elucidation after analysis is performed using a pre-trained ML model [13].

5.2 Literature Review

There is an ample amount of work done in the field of health care using ML and AI. Understanding the significance of the amount of data available today and using various data mining techniques to derive meaningful insights predicting the outcome of giving a diagnosis based on patient input [14]. The paper has implemented the K-Nearest Neighbor (KNN) and Convolutional Neural network (CNN) ML algorithms to give a general disease prediction to the patients based on their symptoms. In this process of diagnosis, different parameters such as the living habits of a person and previous health records were the information considered for accurate predictions. The results showed that the accuracy of the CNN algorithm was 84.5% compared to that of the KNN algorithm, which showed lower accuracy and an increased amount of time and memory requirements.

In Ref. [15], the developed model helps in the early prediction of diabetes; this study has used the real data collected by the Security Force Primary Health Care. The current model uses the combination of two ML algorithms, namely, Support Vector Machine (SVM) and Random Forest (RF) to predict diabetes. The model achieved an accuracy of 98%, and RF was found to give better results compared to the SVM algorithm. Diabetes is rapidly increasing among people in different age groups; if not detected, early diabetes can further grow toward type 2 diabetes, which is more fatal and gives rise to more complications; a study in Ref. [16] has found the use of different ML algorithms and different data mining techniques could help in the early detection and treatment of even type 2 diabetes mellitus. On the PIMA dataset, RF was found to give the highest accuracy as compared to the other ML algorithms. The study [17] was motivated to develop a model with precision to prognosticate the likelihood of diabetes using three ML classification algorithms, namely, SVM, Naïve Bayes (NB), and Decision Tree. The model here gives the highest accuracy (76.30%) with the NB algorithm.

The study in Ref. [18] aims at the identification of different ML algorithms for the effective diagnosis along with achieving the highest accuracy for the prediction of heart disease. The comparison of different supervised learning algorithms on the dataset obtained by Kaggle RF was found to give the highest accuracy for heart disease prediction. In Ref. [19], the proposed system considering the dangers of heart disease helps in the prediction of getting any kind of heart disease in advance by implementing KNN along with a Decision Tree as the ML algorithms to predict the risk level for an individual related to heart disease. The study in Ref. [20] compares the performance of different ML algorithms, namely, Artificial Neural Network (ANN), RF, and SVM, for the prediction of heart disease. Here, SVM provides the highest accuracy of 84.0%, while ANN and RF classifier achieved the accuracy of 83.5% and 80.0%, respectively.

Breast cancer is affecting women worldwide; hence, early detection becomes more necessary to prevent loss of life. The paper [21] observed that the discrimination of malignant breast lesions from benign ones and the accurate prediction is critical in successful clinical decision making. Hence, the paper discussed has trained a large dataset of consecutive mammographic values on the ANN so that it could discriminate between benign and malignant diseases and give the predictions accurately. The study [22] compared the performance of C4.5, NB, SVM, and K-NN to find the best classifier in WBC. SVM proves to be the most accurate classifier with an accuracy of 96.99%. An accuracy of 69.23% was achieved using a decision tree classifier (CART) in breast cancer datasets. Another study [23] compared the performance of decision trees (C4.5), SVM, and ANN. The dataset used was obtained from the Iranian Center for Breast Cancer. Simulation results showed that SVM was the best classifier followed by ANN and DT.

Some of the other supervised ML algorithms used for predictions are Logistic Regression, DT, KNN, RF, and SVM. LR can be explained as an extension of the ordinary regression algorithm; it helps in finding the probability of a new instance belonging to a particular class. Since the outcome lies between 0 and 1, a threshold needs to be assigned to differentiate the two classes [24]. SVM algorithm can classify both linear and nonlinear data; in SVM, each data point is plotted as a point in an n-dimensional space (n is the number of features), to find the classification of the hyperplane which classifies or partitions the plane with the maximum margin. In the DT algorithm, the data is split continuously considering certain parameters that correspond outcome to be a tree-like structure. DT has multiple levels where the topmost level is the root node and the internal nodes represent the different attributes; at last, the leaf node will represent the test outcomes. A RF could be called the collection of various decision trees, as decision trees that grow too deep tend to have overfitting [24], which further results in a large variation in the outcome over an insignificant change in the data; hence, RF trains various decision trees with distinct parts of the training data. KNN can be thought of as a simpler version of the NB classifier [24], which unlike the NB does not consider probability values; the K in KNN stands for several nearest neighbors where different values of K would generate various classification outcomes for the same sample. Table 5.1 depicts the comparison between various ML algorithms.

Table 5.1   Comparison of Different Supervised Learning Algorithms

Algorithm	Advantages	Disadvantages
K-Nearest Neighbors (KNN)	It stores the training dataset and learns from it only at the time of making real-time predictions. This makes the KNN algorithm much faster than other algorithms that require training [25] in case of prediction.	KNN is called 'Lazy Learner' (instance-based learning). It does not learn anything in the training period. It does not derive any discriminative function from the training data. In other words, there is no training period for it [25].
Logistic Regression (LR)	The predicted parameters (trained weights) give inference about the importance of each feature. The direction of association, i.e., positive or negative, is also given. So, we can use LR to find out the relationship between the features [26].	LR is a statistical analysis model that attempts to predict precise probabilistic outcomes based on independent features. On high-dimensional datasets, this may lead to the model being overfit on the training set, which means overstating the accuracy of predictions on the training set, and thus, the model may not be able to predict accurate results on the test set [26].
Decision Tree (DT)	DT takes less training time compared to other machine learning algorithms [27].	Overfitting is the main drawback of decision trees, which leads to wrong predictions [27].
Support Vector Machine (SVM)	SVM gives satisfactory results even if there is no sufficient information [28].	SVM gives reliable results even if there is no sufficient information [28].
Random Forest (RF)	The chances of overfitting are reduced as compared to DT; as compared to DT, the RF fares well for disease predictions with higher accuracy [23].	Overfitting can occur easily as the data from medical reports vary from patient to patient. RF is computationally expensive and complex for a disease prediction model. As RF favors those attributes that take a higher number of values, it is not suitable for disease prediction [23].

(Continued)

Table 5.1 (*Continued*) Comparison of Different Supervised Learning Algorithms

Algorithm	Advantages	Disadvantages
Naïve Bayes (NB)	As the amount of training data required to make predictions is less, NB outperforms some of the other algorithms. NB is appropriate for both discrete and continuous data types, which may be the case for different diseases [23]. NB makes faster predictions that can be used for large medical datasets.	NB considers the attributes to be normally distributed, and the presence of any dependency between attributes negatively impacts the prediction 23].

From Table 5.1, it is evident that NB [29] is an eagerly learning classifier that is fast compared to other methods and hence could be used to give real-time predictions.

Different medical reports that are required for using the prediction model depend on the disease for which you need the predictions. The report needed for undergoing a diabetes prediction would be the 2-hour glucose tolerance test with insulin, also known as the 'oral glucose tolerance test' (OGTT) [30], which would consist of all the details needed by the model. In the case of heart disease, an electrocardiogram (ECG) is a test that is used to determine patients' heart rhythm and electrical activity. Sensors are attached to the skin to help detect the electrical signals produced by your heart each time it beats [31]. For breast cancer, a mammogram report shows an assessment of the breast density, which is a description of how much fibrous and glandular tissue is in the breasts, as compared to fatty tissue. The denser the breasts, the harder it can be to see abnormal areas on mammograms. BI-RADS (Breast Imaging-Reporting and Data System) provides a widely accepted lexicon and reporting schema for imaging of the breast. It applies to mammography, ultrasound, and MRI [32].

5.3 System Architecture

The system architecture is shown in Figure 5.1. The datasets for the respective diseases need to be imported from their respective data sources, which are in the form of numeric data. Before pre-processing the data, there is a need to standardize the

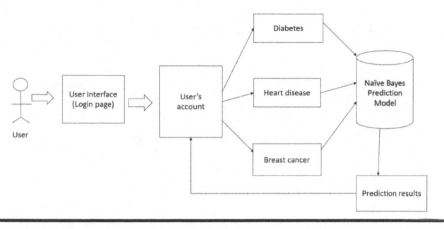

Figure 5.1   System architecture for prediction model.

data. After the pre-processing step next, the data is split into training and testing datasets. Then, classification algorithm is applied to the training dataset using the NB classifier.

When an individual would like to use the system, they may log in to the system or sign up if new to the system. While signing in, the user needs to enter his/her personal details like name, date of birth, contact number, email id, any previous medical history, and address; then, the user can set his password. Once an id is created, the user may log in to the system using the registered email id as a username and by entering the correct password. Once the user has logged in, the user may need to select any one of the diseases which he may like to have the prediction made. When a particular disease is selected, the patient/user needs to fill in the information asked or needed by the system referring to the medical reports of the particular disease.

Figures 5.2–5.4 depict the testing of the developed model on values given to determine the chances of having diabetes, heart disease, and breast cancer, respectively.

For diabetes, the user needs to enter the number of pregnancies, age (years), glucose level (from the OGTT report), insulin level (from the OGTT report), skin thickness (in mm), blood pressure (in mm Hg), BMI, and diabetes pedigree function. For predicting heart disease, age, gender (1: male and 0: female), chest pain type (0: typical angina, 1: atypical angina, 2: non-anginal pain, 3: asymptomatic), resting blood pressure (in mm Hg), serum cholesterol (in mg/dL), fasting blood sugar and gt [(120 mg/dL) (1 = true; 0 = false)], resting electrocardiographic results, maximum heart rate achieved, exercise-induced angina (1 = yes; 0 = no), the slope of the peak exercise ST segment (Value 1: upsloping, Value 2: flat, Value 3: downsloping), ST depression induced by exercise relative to rest ('ST' relates to positions on the ECG plot), number of major vessels (0–3) colored by fluoroscopy, a blood

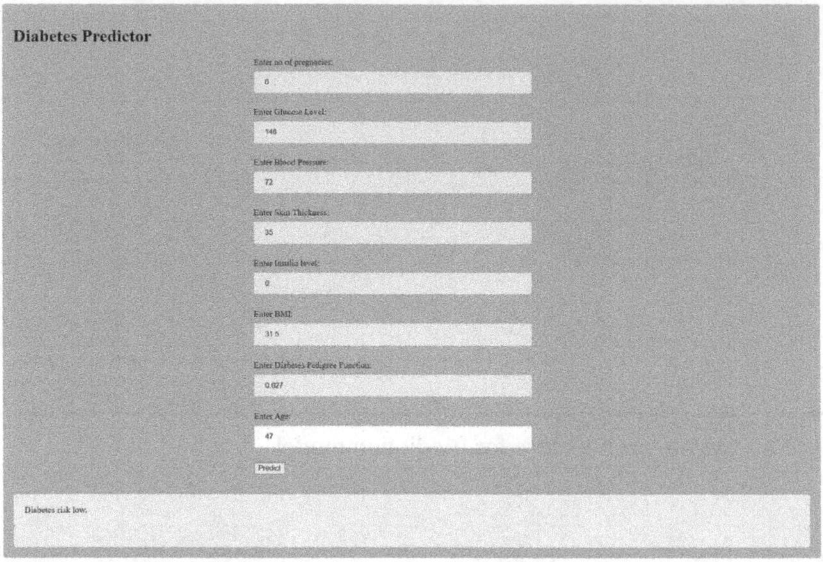

Figure 5.2   Testing of the diabetes prediction model.

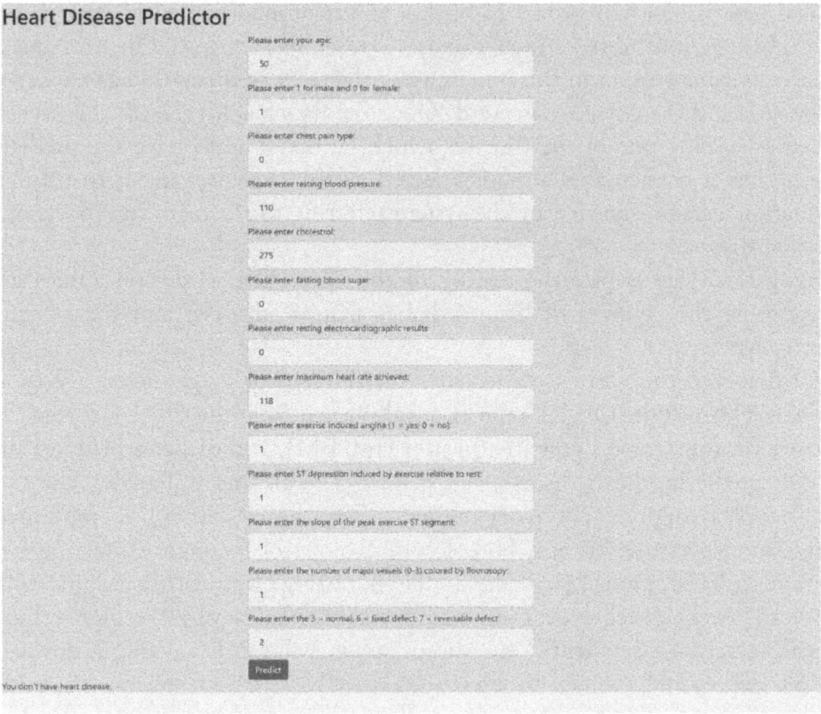

Figure 5.3   Testing of heart disease prediction model.

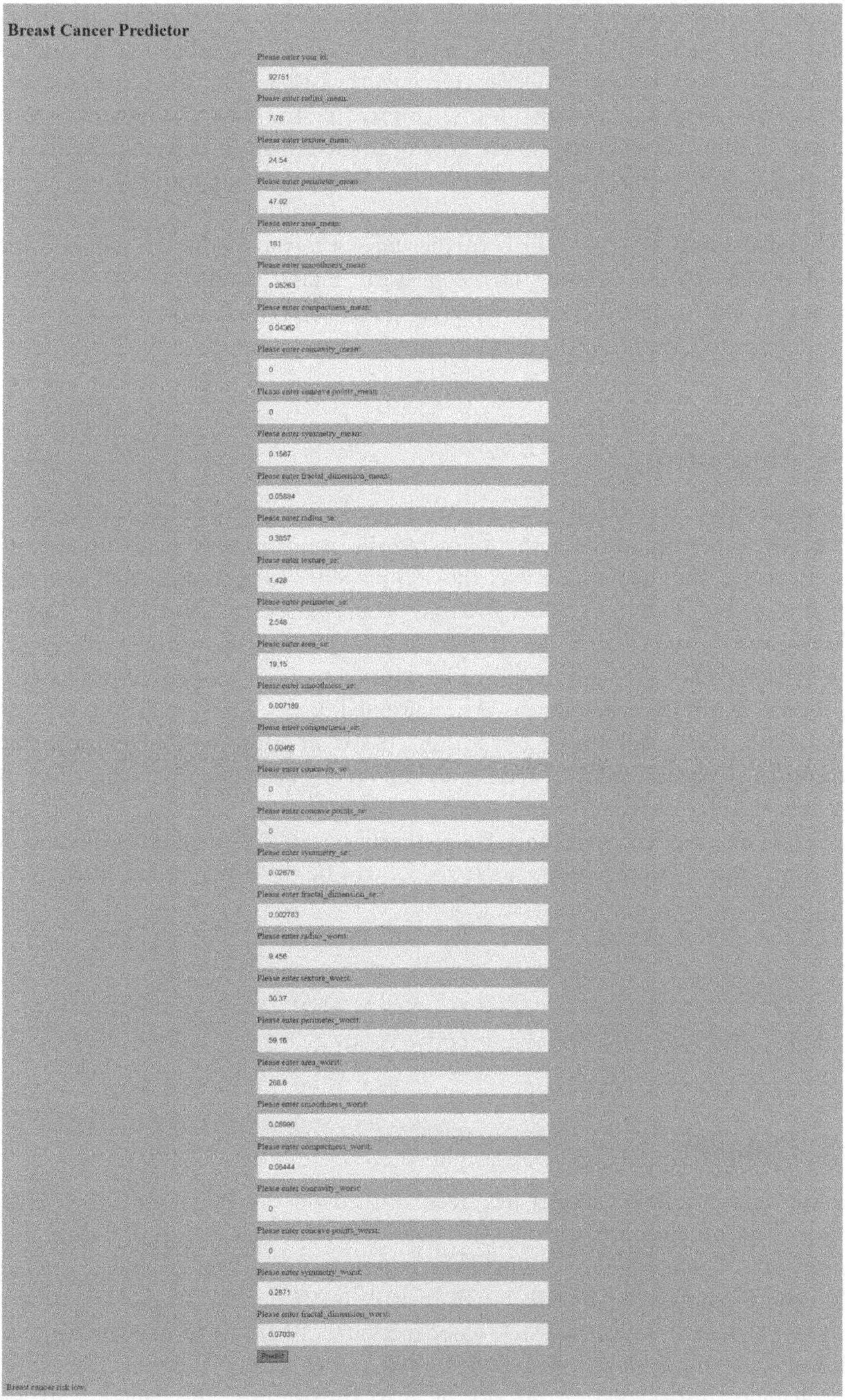

Figure 5.4   Testing of breast cancer prediction model.

disorder called 'thalassemia' (1 = normal; 2 = fixed defect; 3 = reversible defect). For breast cancer prediction, a patient is required to enter the following parameters: radius mean, texture means, perimeter means, area mean, smoothness means, compactness means, concavity means, concave points mean, symmetry means, and fractal dimension means. These parameters will help in determining the correct diagnosis, i.e., whether the cell mass is malignant (diagnosis = M) or benign (diagnosis = B).

The data entered by the user is further passed to the prediction model, which was developed by the training of the medical dataset using the NB algorithm, which gives the final prediction of whether the person is positive or negative for the disease that is displayed on the user's page.

5.4 Algorithm

This section describes the algorithm used to make the predictions. The developed model gives the diagnosis for the following diseases: diabetes, heart disease, and breast cancer. The model here uses the NB classifier to accurately diagnose individual diseases. The NB classifier is based on the Bayes Theorem and is the most effective classification algorithm. Also in the NB classifier, the features are independent of a given class. It is a probabilistic classifier since it makes predictions based on the probability of the other objects. As mentioned, Bayes Theorem is used as it used to determine the probability of a hypothesis based on prior knowledge. It considers each of the symptoms to contribute individually or independently to the diagnosis of a person suffering from the disease.

Let A1 and A2 represent the person suffering from a particular disease and not suffering, respectively. Let x = [x1, x2, x3, …, xn] be the different test attributes of the disease.

As per the NB classifier, P(A|X) = P(x1|a) * P(x2|a) * … * P(xn|a) * P(a)

As per the Bayes Theorem, $P(A|B) = \dfrac{\left(P(B|A)P(A)\right)}{P(B)}$

5.5 Dataset

The diabetes prediction model has been trained on the Pima Indians Diabetes Dataset [33], which consists of data from different patients who are all female above the age of 21 belonging to the Pima Indian heritage. The database consists of various medical parameters and one target variable outcome. The medical parameters include pregnancies, glucose level, blood pressure, BMI (body mass index), skin thickness, insulin level, age, and diabetes pedigree function. The heart disease prediction model for predicting the risk of heart disease used the dataset [34] with the following attributes: age, sex, type of chest pain, resting blood pressure, serum cholesterol in mg/dL, fasting blood sugar level, resting electrocardiographic results (values 0, 1, 2), maximum heart rate achieved, exercise-induced angina, and few more attributes. As breast cancer is the most common type of cancer in women and the second highest in terms of mortality rates, the diagnosis becomes more crucial at an early stage. Hence, the prediction model has been trained on the dataset [35], which contains real-valued features that have been computed for each cell nucleus. The database contains various attributes computed for each cell nucleus and one target variable: diagnosis, which can have any one of the two outcomes that are benign (not cancerous) or malignant (considered cancerous).

5.6 Results and Discussion

NB model was chosen for disease prediction where the datasets were split into training and testing sets in the ratio of 80:20 to get the most accurate answer for prediction. NB performs well in multi-class prediction and performs better compared to other models especially when an assumption of independence holds, and less training data is required. The use of the NB algorithm is an effective method for the diseased sequence classification with better accuracy since most of the disease datasets contain sequential information. NB has a higher bias and lower variance when compared to the LR model. Hence, the former is preferred over the latter. It even performs better than the DT since pruning may neglect some key values in training data, which can lead to the accuracy of a loss. NB is much faster than KNN because of the large real-time computation needed by the latter. Similarly, the NB performs better than RF in cases where the model size is quite low and constant concerning the data. The NB model cannot represent complex behavior, so it will not get into overfitting. RF, on the other hand, works with large-size models and is more likely to result in overfitting. When the data is dynamic and keeps changing, NB can adapt quickly to the changes and new data while using an RF model you would have to rebuild the forest every time something changes.

A classification report is a performance metric that is used to define the quality of prediction for a classification algorithm. Figures 5.5–5.7 depict the classification report for each of the three diseases, respectively. It depicts the models' precision, which is the model's ability to label an instance positive when it is negative; recall is the ability of the classifier to find all positive instances; f1-score is the weighted harmonic mean of precision and recall where the best score is 1.0 and the worst being 0.0 on a per-class basis [36]. All these metrics are calculated using the true-positive (TP), true-negative (TN), false-positive (FP), and false-negative (FN) values. TP is when a case is positive and is even predicted as positive, TN stands when a case was negative and predicted negative, the case becomes FP when the outcome was negative but predicted positive, and the case becomes FN when the outcome was

	precision	recall	f1-score	support
0	0.81	0.88	0.85	100
1	0.73	0.62	0.67	53
accuracy			0.79	153
macro avg	0.77	0.75	0.76	153
weighted avg	0.79	0.79	0.79	153

Figure 5.5 Classification_report for diabetes.

	precision	recall	f1-score	support
0	0.78	0.73	0.76	100
1	0.76	0.81	0.78	105
accuracy			0.77	205
macro avg	0.77	0.77	0.77	205
weighted avg	0.77	0.77	0.77	205

Figure 5.6 Classification_report for heart disease.

	precision	recall	f1-score	support
B	0.99	0.79	0.88	102
M	0.34	0.92	0.50	12
accuracy			0.81	114
macro avg	0.67	0.86	0.69	114
weighted avg	0.92	0.81	0.84	114

Figure 5.7 Classification_report for breast cancer.

positive but predicted negative. The formulae for the calculation of precision, recall, and f1-score is as follows:

$$\text{precision} = \frac{TP}{TP+FP} \qquad \text{recall} = \frac{TP}{TP+FN} \qquad \text{f1-score} = \frac{2*\text{precision} * \text{recall}}{\text{precision} + \text{recall}}$$

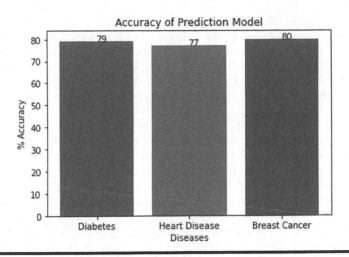

Figure 5.8   **Accuracy of prediction model.**

Figure 5.8 represents the accuracies obtained by using NB classifier for diabetes, heart disease, and breast cancer.

5.7 Conclusion

The chapter presented the technique of predicting diseases based on the health reports of an individual patient. Subsequently, NB was found to give the following accuracies for the given datasets with an accuracy of 77% for heart disease prediction, 79% for diabetes prediction, and 80% for breast cancer prediction. This model would help in lowering the cost required in dealing with the disease and would also help the patient understand the nature of these diseases. ML is an effective tool for doctors to detect these aforementioned diseases at an early stage and can be used for the diagnosis, detection, and prediction of the same. This, in turn, helps to provide prompt and timely treatment to patients and avoid severe consequences.

References

[1] Price Setting and Price Regulation in Healthcare. (Online) Available at: https://www.oecd.org/health/health-systems/OECD-WHO-Price-Setting-Summary-Report.pdf [Accessed on 14 September 2021].

[2] Diabetes, Heart Disease & Stroke. (Online) Available at: https://www.niddk.nih.gov/health-information/diabetes/overview/preventing-problems/heart-disease-stroke [Accessed on 12 October 2021].

[3] Treatment of Heart Attack. (Online) Available at: https://www.medicalnewstoday.com/articles/312964#treatment_for_heart_attack [Accessed on 17 November 2021].

[4] Rushforth, B., McCrorie, C., Glidewell, L., Midgley, E., & Foy, R. (2016). Barriers to effective management of type 2 diabetes in primary care: A qualitative systematic review. *The British Journal of General Practice: The Journal of the Royal College of General Practitioners, 66*(643), e114–e127. https://doi.org/10.3399/bjgp16X683509.

[5] Key Statistics for Breast Cancer. (Online) Available at: https://www.cancer.org/cancer/breast-cancer/about/how-common-is-breast-cancer.html [Accessed on 23 September 2021].

[6] Safizadeh, H, Hafezpour, S, & Mangolian Shahrbabaki, P. (2018). Health damaged context: barriers to breast cancer screening from viewpoint of Iranian health volunteers. *Asian Pacific Journal of Cancer Prevention, 19*(7), 1941–1949. Published 2018 Jul 27. https://doi.org/10.22034/APJCP.2018.19.7.1941.

[7] A Practical Application of Machine Learning in Medicine. (Online) Available at: https://www.macadamian.com/learn/a-practical-application-of-machine-learning-in-medicine/ [Accessed on 29 August 2021].

[8] Machine Learning. (Online) Available at: https://www.coursera.org/learn/machine-learning [Accessed on 4 December 2021].

[9] Machine Learning. (Online) Available at: https://searchenterpriseai.techtarget.com/definition/machine-learning-ML [Accessed on 4 December 2021].

[10] Machine Learning Explained. (Online) Available at: https://mitsloan.mit.edu/ideas-made-to-matter/machine-learning-explained [Accessed on 5 December 2021].

[11] Sutton, R.T., Pincock, D., Baumgart, D.C. et al. (2020) An overview of clinical decision support systems: Benefits, risks, and strategies for success. *npj Digital Medicine, 3*, 17. https://www.nature.com/articles/s41746-020-0221-y.

[12] Tohka, J. & van Gils, M. (2021). Evaluation of machine learning algorithms for health and wellness applications: A tutorial. *Computers in Biology and Medicine, 132*, 104324, ISSN 0010-4825, https://doi.org/10.1016/j.compbiomed.2021.104324.

[13] Caballé, N., Castillo-Sequera, J., Gomez-Pulido, J. A., Gómez, J., & Polo-Luque, M. (2020). Machine learning applied to diagnosis of human diseases: A systematic review. *Applied Sciences, 10*, 5135. https://doi.org/10.3390/app10155135.

[14] Dahiwade, D., Patle, G., & Meshram, E. (2019). Designing disease prediction model using machine learning approach. *2019 3rd International Conference on Computing Methodologies and Communication (ICCMC)*, pp. 1211–1215. https://doi.org/10.1109/ICCMC.2019.8819782.

[15] Alanazi, A. S. & Mezher, M. A. (2020). Using machine learning algorithms for prediction of diabetes mellitus. *2020 International Conference on Computing and Information Technology (ICCIT-1441)*, pp. 1–3. https://doi.org/10.1109/ICCIT-144147971.2020.9213708.

[16] Mounika, V., Neeli, D. S., Sree, G. S., Mourya, P., & Babu, M. A. (2021). Prediction of Type-2 Diabetes using Machine Learning Algorithms. *2021 International Conference on Artificial Intelligence and Smart Systems (ICAIS)*, pp. 127–131. https://doi.org/10.1109/ICAIS50930.2021.9395985.

[17] Sisodia, D. & Sisodia, D. P. (2018). Prediction of diabetes using classification algorithms, *Procedia Computer Science, 132*, 1578–1585, ISSN 1877-0509. https://doi.org/10.1016/j.procs.2018.05.122.

[18] Ali, Md M., Paul, B. K., Ahmed, K., Bui, F. M., Quinn, J. M.W., & Moni, M. A. (2021). Heart disease prediction using supervised machine learning algorithms: Performance analysis and comparison. *Computers in Biology and Medicine, 136*, 104672, ISSN 0010-4825. https://www.sciencedirect.com/science/article/pii/S0010482521004662.

[19] Arul Jothi, K., Subburam, S., Umadevi, V., & Hemavathy, K. (2021). Heart disease prediction system using machine learning. *Materials Today: Proceedings*, ISSN 2214-7853. https://doi.org/10.1016/j.matpr.2020.12.901.

[20] Rindhe, Baban, Ahire, Nikita, Patil, Rupali, Gagare, Shweta, & Darade, Manisha. (2021). Heart disease prediction using machine learning. *International Journal of Advanced Research in Science, Communication, and Technology*. 267–276. https://doi.org/10.48175/IJARSCT–1131.

[21] Ayer, T., Alagoz, O., Chhatwal, J., Shavlik, J. W., Kahn, C. E., Jr, & Burnside, E. S. (2010). Breast cancer risk estimation with artificial neural networks revisited: Discrimination and calibration. *Cancer, 116*(14), 3310–3321. https://doi.org/10.1002/cncr.25081.

[22] Asri, H., Mousannif, H., Moatassime, H. A., & Noel, T. (2016). Using machine learning algorithms for breast cancer risk prediction and diagnosis. *Procedia Computer Science*, 83, 1064–1069, ISSN 1877-0509. https://doi.org/10.1016/j.procs.2016.04.224.

[23] Omondiagbe, David, Veeramani, Shanmugam, & Sidhu, Amandeep. (2019). Machine learning classification techniques for breast cancer diagnosis. https://doi.org/10.1088/1757–899X/495/1/012033.

[24] Uddin, S., Khan, A., Hossain, M. et al. Comparing different supervised machine learning algorithms for disease prediction. *BMC Medical Informatics and Decision Making*, 19(281). https://doi.org/10.1186/s12911-019-1004-8.

[25] Advantages and Disadvantages of KNN Algorithm in Machine Learning. (Online) Available at: http://theprofessionalspoint.blogspot.com/2019/02/advantages-and-disadvantages-of-knn.html#:~:text=It%20stores%20the%20training%20dataset,e.g.%20SVM%2C%20Linear%20Regression%20etc [Accessed on 27 February 2022].

[26] Advantages and Disadvantages of Logistic Regression. (Online) Available at: https://iq.opengenus.org/advantages-and-disadvantages-of-logistic-regression/ [Accessed on 27 February 2022].

[27] Advantages and Disadvantages of Decision Trees in Machine Learning. (Online) Available at: http://theprofessionalspoint.blogspot.com/2019/02/advantages-and-disadvantages-of.html [Accessed on 27 February 2022].

[28] Support Vector Machine. Available at: https://www.researchgate.net/figure/Support-Vector-Machines-Advantages-and-Disadvantages_tbl2_338950098 [Accessed on 28 February 2022].

[29] 6 Easy Steps to Learn Naive Bayes Algorithm. (Online) Available at: https://www.analyticsvidhya.com/blog/2017/09/naive-bayes-explained/ [Accessed on: 14 January 2022].

[30] Stumvoll, M., Mitrakou, A., Pimenta, W., Jenssen, T., Yki-Järvinen, H., Van Haeften, T., Renn, W., & Gerich, J. (2000). Use of the oral glucose tolerance test to assess insulin release and insulin sensitivity. *Diabetes Care*, 23(3), 295–301. https://doi.org/10.2337/diacare.23.3.295.

[31] Electrocardiogram (ECG). (Online) Available at: https://www.nhs.uk/conditions/electrocardiogram/#:~:text=An%20electrocardiogram%20(ECG)%20is%20a,heart%20each%20time%20it%20beats [Accessed on 27 February 2022].

[32] Weerakkody, Y. & Ashraf, A. (2022). Breast imaging-reporting and data system (BI-RADS). Reference article. Radiopaedia.org [Accessed on 28 Feb 2022] https://doi.org/10.53347/rID–10003.

[33] Pima Indians Diabetes Database. Available at: https://www.kaggle.com/uciml/pima-indians-diabetes-database.

[34] Heart Disease UCI. Available at: https://www.kaggle.com/ronitf/heart-disease-uci.

[35] Breast Cancer Wisconsin (Diagnostic) Data Set. Available at: https://www.kaggle.com/uciml/breast-cancer-wisconsin-data.

[36] Understanding the Classification report through sklearn. (Online) Available at: https://muthu.co/understanding-the-classification-report-in-sklearn/ [Accessed on: 28 February 2022].

Chapter 6

Federated Machine Learning-Based Bank Customer Churn Prediction

Chirag Jagad, Chirag Jain, Dhrumil Thakore, Om Naik, and Vinaya Sawant

Dwarkadas J. Sanghvi College of Engineering

Contents

DOI: 10.1201/9781003390220-6

6.1 Introduction

Because of artificial intelligence, or AI, which seems to be on everyone's lips these days, the world is progressing to new heights. While science fiction depicts AI as robots that intimate humans, AI is much more than that and has impacted many industries by assisting them in making data-driven strategic decisions. Machine learning, a subset of AI, focuses on using data and algorithms to mimic how humans learn, gradually improving its accuracy. Machine learning has helped a variety of industries, including the financial sector. It includes financial institutions that are vulnerable to potential intrusions such as distributed denial-of-service (DDoS) attacks, data breaches, and TCP/IP spoofing attacks. A bank's day-to-day operations include numerous monetary transactions such as ATM (automated teller machine) transactions, credit card, and debit card transactions. Banks must carry out these transactions efficiently, without jeopardizing the customer's personal data or, more importantly, their money, in order to maintain their trust and meet their expectations. Simultaneously, banks require some access to their customers' personal data in order to modernize and improve their services, making their resources faster, easier to use, more reliable, and secure. While consumer privacy is a legitimate concern for consumers, banks can use this information to gain a better understanding of their business, a better understanding of their customers, and the ability to establish more personal communication with them.

In general, we generate a continuous stream of data in the centralized cloud model, where we perform analysis and feature extraction. As a result, existing models are trained on more powerful servers. When there is a lot of interaction with the cloud services, more training data is collected, and highly intelligent ML-based applications are produced as a result. However, the confidentiality of available data used for training and the enormous success of deep learning are raising concerns among users. Such information can be highly confidential and of any type, including personally identifiable information, payment data, and protected health information. When this data is shared with centralized models, the likelihood of a user's data being compromised by an eavesdropping attack increases dramatically. Apart from eavesdropping attacks, the centralized model architecture has some disadvantages such as high latency, long learning time, greater server load, expensive transmission time, and resources.

Cross-device FedML [1] can be described as a decentralized approach to centralized machine learning. In federated learning (FL), all the edge devices have their own local machine learning model, whereas the global machine learning model resides in a central server. Each edge device uses its private data to train its local model and then sends all its calculated model parameters to the central server. The central server then aggregates all the model parameters received from the edge devices to develop the global model. Thus, with this federated approach, the central server can build a joint global ML model without collecting any personal data.

FL can be classified into three main types. Horizontal FL is used in scenarios in which datasets share the same feature space but different spaces in samples. Vertical FL is applicable to the cases in which two datasets share the same sample ID space but differ in feature space. Federated transfer learning applies to the scenarios in which two datasets differ not only in samples but also in feature space [2,3].

Advantages of FedML are as follows:

a. **Privacy:** In FL, only parameter weights and gradient updates are sent from the edge devices to the central server. Thus, the data never leaves the device, and the need for a data pool is eliminated.

b. **Less load on central server:** Because most of the model training computation is performed on the client, the computational load on the central server is reduced dramatically. As a result of FL, the central server can run on low-cost hardware.

c. **Ability to collaborate without sharing data:** Cross-silo FL [4] is an implementation of FedML, which allows for sharing of results of machine learning between companies, thus allowing them to collaborate without sharing actual data with each other.

6.2 Related Works

Customer churn and engagement have become one of the top issues for most businesses, including banks. There are numerous algorithms that are used to predict customer churn. In references [5,6], the authors have compared various algorithms for customer churn prediction, and the research conducted showed that the random forest algorithm gave the highest accuracy against any other algorithm. In both papers, the authors have noted that, while the centralized models have great accuracy, one of the main problems associated with these models is privacy-related attacks.

FL was first proposed by Google in 2016 in reference [1] for GBoard word prediction to reduce uplink communication costs and increase accuracy. Since then, many FL algorithms have been developed. In reference [7], authors had compared different FL algorithms using multilayer perceptron models, namely federated averaging (FedAvg) and federated stochastic variance reduced gradient (FSVRG). The experimental results proved that the FedAvg algorithm showed better accuracy than FSVRG and had comparable accuracy with centralized models.

Following significant advancements in the FL approach since its initial demonstration, it has found application in a variety of sectors. Reference [8] shows one such application, in which the authors used an FL-based model to identify high-value airline passengers. To classify a passenger based on their data, the model used logistic regression. When compared to the centralized model approach, the model also achieved higher accuracy and privacy.

FL has been a significant method in the fields related to security. One such example can be seen in reference [9], where misbehavior on the Internet of Vehicles is detected using FL. The model created to detect questionable vehicle behavior ensures the safety of both the driver and the passenger in addition to protecting the user's data. The results proved that a federated strategy with a centralized one yielded the best results.

FL has also been used in the medical domain, with one example being [10], where the authors used FL to implement a breast cancer detection model. The model demonstrates a method for protecting patients' confidential data by providing a safe and secure way to train models using FL without sending their data to a central server. The results also demonstrated that the FL model could achieve accuracy comparable to conventional models while requiring less training time.

FL has also made inroads into the banking industry. The authors of reference [11] used FL to build a credit card fraud detection system. Experiment results revealed that FL for credit card fraud detection systems improved significantly in terms of both privacy and accuracy, allowing banks to train central fraud detection systems without sending their private data to data centers.

Taking inspiration from all of the preceding works, we designed our system to provide banks with a secure system for predicting customer churn. Banks can use the proposed system without jeopardizing the user's confidential data by sending it to a central system for learning. In subsequent sections, we will go over the proposed system and its results.

6.3 Dataset

We used the Bank Churn Data Exploration and Churn Prediction Dataset [12], which contains critical information about the bank's customers as well as an attrition flag column that indicates whether or not they have left the bank. The dataset contains 20 distinct features. There are 10,127 rows, 1,627 of which are customers who have been churned out and the remaining 8,500 are customers who are still with the bank.

To avoid biased prediction of our classifier, we used the synthetic minority oversampling technique (SMOTE) [13], which generates synthetic samples for the minority class and assists in overcoming the overfitting problem caused by random oversampling. After balancing our dataset, we have 17,000 rows with 8,500 rows under each category. The dataset is shuffled and split into a training set having 13,600 rows and a testing set having 3,400 rows, where the training set is distributed among the clients.

6.4 Experimental Setup

Our setup consists of a simulation of ten clients with equal power and one central server. We divided the training data between the clients in two ways: equal distribution and random distribution. Each client trains their model using only the data that has been assigned to them. The test data is then evaluated on the global model, and the model's efficiency is assessed using various performance metrics.

6.5 Proposed Approach

To avoid any confidentiality, availability, and integrity issues as well as to solve any privacy and scalability issues, we have proposed an algorithm based on a federated approach over a centralized one to predict whether an existing customer of a bank gets churned out, i.e., decides to terminate their bank account at that bank, using data from multiple branches of a bank. The global model is shared across the clients, i.e., the local branches and they perform collaborative learning. Since data is not shared from the local branch to the central server, we can reduce the risk of any digital attack and guarantee the security of personal data.

Figure 6.1 shows our proposed customer churn model. Initially, we perform data preprocessing on our dataset, which involves removal of noisy data, extraction of important features, and balancing the dataset to avoid any bias and get accurate predictions. After the preprocessing, we end up with about 13,600 rows in our training dataset. As mentioned before, we distribute the training data among the

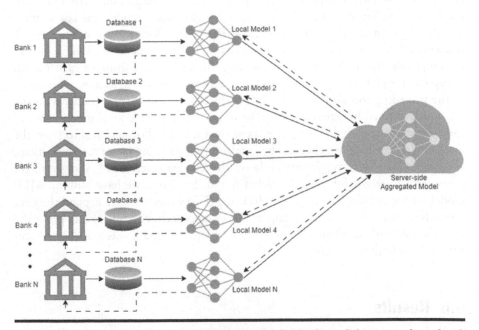

Figure 6.1   Illustration of our proposed FL method. The solid arrows show bank to server communication for local updates. The dashed arrows show server to bank communication for global updates.

clients in two ways. In our first approach, we divide this dataset equally among ten clients so that each client is assigned 1,360 rows for training. However, as equally allocated data is possible only in an ideal setting, we also chose to include random allocation of training data.

Then, we build a four-layer multilayer perceptron (MLP) model. An MLP model is a type of feed-forward artificial neural network with one input layer, one or more than one hidden layer, and one output layer. In our four MLP layers, we have used non-linear activation functions in the order Leaky ReLU ($\alpha = 0.01$), ReLU, ReLU, and Sigmoid, respectively. Sigmoid is an activation function that maps the perceptron's potential to a value between 0 and 1, whereas Rectified Linear Unit (ReLU) is an activation function that returns 0 if the input is negative and returns the value if positive. Leaky ReLU is an improvement over the ReLU function in that it returns a value dependent on a parameter α, which is the slope of the graph on the negative side of the x-axis. To prevent overfitting, we have added Dropout layers after each Dense layer that randomly set the input units to 0 with a frequency rate of 0.2 at each step during training. We have used binary cross-entropy, which is the negative average of the log of corrected predicted probabilities, in order to calculate the losses and to update the weights. To optimize these losses, we have used the Adam optimizer, which is an adaptive optimizer and requires less memory. It is a combination of the Gradient Descent with Momentum and the Root Mean Square Propagation algorithms. We have also performed hyperparameter tuning to optimize our MLP model further. We then run all our ten individual MLP models for ten rounds. For the aggregation of the results back to the central server, we use FedAvg [7]. It allows all our clients to perform more than one batch update on local data and exchanges the updated weights. In this method, at the beginning of each round, we update the global weights in accordance with the changes in local weights made in the preceding round. Following this, each client creates a local model with the previously defined hyperparameters. The initial weight of the local model is set to the weight of the global model. The client then uses its allocated data to train the local model. The local weights are then scaled using a scaling factor for every client, and after all the local weights are updated, they are aggregated and averaged to get a new global weight for the next global round. Similarly, we have built an MLP model for a simulation of centralized learning (CL) where we have kept all the data accessible to a single server. To compare our FL approach with CL, and to prove the efficaciousness of our approach, we have the same hyperparameters and activation function for both approaches.

6.6 Results

We trained our centralized MLP model with the entire dataset and got an accuracy of 95.18% on the validation dataset in the first round, which increased to 96.76% in the last round. To prove the robustness of our MLP model, we foremost compare

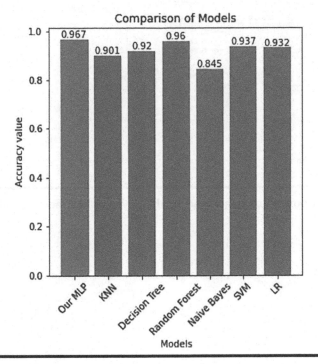

Figure 6.2   Comparison of models.

it with other classification algorithms like Random Forest, Decision Tree, Naïve Bayes, K-Nearest Neighbors, Logistic Regression, and Support Vector Machines. Figure 6.2 displays the accuracy scores of our MLP model and other classification algorithms on the validation dataset. Our MLP model overpowered other classification algorithms with an accuracy of 96.76%. Following, we tested the efficiency of our proposed FedML approach based on various parameters by comparing it with the centralized machine learning approach.

Figure 6.3 displays the accuracy and loss values of CL, FL with equal distribution, and FL with random distribution. We obtained an accuracy of 93.12% and 93.71% in the first round for equal distribution and random distribution, respectively. The accuracy advanced to 95.97% and 96.38%, respectively, in the last round. The accuracies of our proposed FL method are comparable to the accuracy of CL, which was 96.76%. Additionally, our proposed method gives an edge to CL with the advantages of FL.

Figure 6.4 demonstrates the training accuracy of the client or local models against the number of epochs when experimenting with our proposed method with an equal distribution of data among clients. Each graph depicts the training process in the corresponding communication round, and each client is represented by a unique color. In the first training round itself, all the client models attained

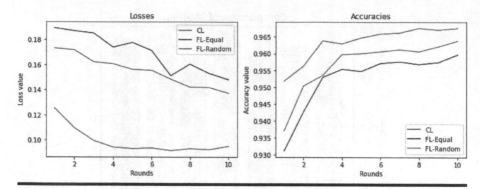

Figure 6.3 **Comparison of accuracy and loss values between centralized and FL models.**

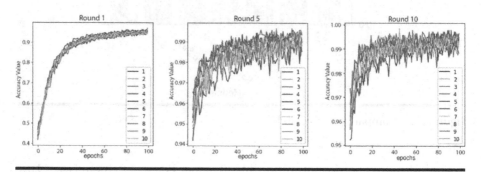

Figure 6.4 **Accuracy values of ten clients over ten training rounds.**

accuracy in the range of 94%–96%. These results are understandable as the dataset is split among the client models, and each client has a trivial amount of data to train. Talking about the final round, we can notice that all the clients achieved an accuracy above 99%, and they are performing sufficiently on their local data. We can assume similar kinds of graphs for our proposed method with a random distribution of data among clients. We get a new global aggregated model after each communication round, and this model is tested on a validation dataset.

Figure 6.5 shows the average time taken in each round to train the global model in CL and local models in the FL approaches. From the graph, it is clearly perceptible that local models can be trained faster due to the little amount of data. The average time taken by CL to train a model was 4.65s, whereas FL approaches took 1.7s. Therefore, FL took 63.44% less time to train a model. In FL, the load is divided between the clients, hence reducing the load of the central server, unlike CL, where the entire dataset is sent to the server for training. When training FL and

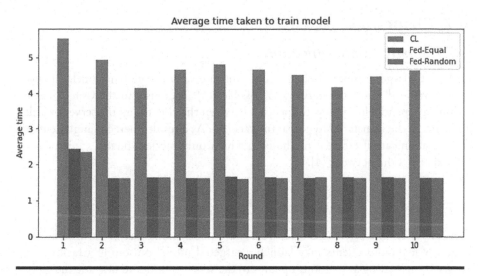

Figure 6.5   Average time taken to train model.

CL models on our machine, we uncovered that the time taken by FL (63.14 with equal distribution and 69.96 with random distribution) was more than CL (46.86) because all the clients were run successively. But in real-life scenarios, all the clients would be running simultaneously, hence boosting the FL process. This scenario can be established with our proposed FL approach by taking into consideration the average time taken per client to submit gradient updates instead of the time taken for the successive implementation. For FL with equal distribution, the total time taken was 63.14s when local models were run sequentially while all the clients took 17.12s to train local models. The average time of 10 clients can be estimated as 1.71s. If all the clients were run simultaneously, the estimated time would be 47.72s (63.14 − 17.12 + 1.71). Likewise, for FL with random distribution, 54.71s (69.96 − 16.94 + 1.69) is the estimated time if all the clients were run simultaneously. These times are comparable to the time taken by CL for convergence which was 46.86s. However, these numbers do not account for the time taken in transmission. In CL, the entire dataset must be uploaded, so transmission time can be expensive. On the other hand, in FL, only the model weights are to be uploaded and downloaded. These weights are not dependent on the size of the dataset, so the transmission time would remain constant even if the data size increases. Thus, FL can achieve high accuracy in less time.

In CL, the datasets must be transmitted, merged, and then a model is trained on the central server. This model is utilized by devices by sending queries on the Internet, which retards the process. Far from it, in FL, local updates are computed on the device, and the latest model is already present on the device itself. Hence, real-time predictions can be achieved with low latency.

6.7 Challenges

6.7.1 Costly Communication

In FL, if a large number of clients communicate with the global model, an enormous overhead across the network is possible [14]. There is also the issue of establishing a dependable wireless connection between the clients and the server in order to facilitate the transfer of hyperparameters [15]. As a result, there is a high demand for communication-efficient methods in which only model updates are iteratively shared across the network [4].

6.7.2 Detection of Malicious Clients

Because all of the clients involved in FL are anonymous due to secured averaging, any malicious clients may launch a targeted model poisoning attack on the server by uploading ambiguous updates to the server in order to degrade the global model's performance [16]. It is critical to probe and detect these malicious model updates, as well as the associated attackers. Few defense mechanisms against suspicious clients include Byzantine-robust FL methods, but these mechanisms cannot empirically guarantee whether the predicting labels used for testing are affected or not [17].

6.7.3 Privacy Concern

Though FL is preferred in domains where security, reliability, and privacy are paramount, there are a few impediments to a flawless FL system. In the case of mobile clients, for example, they require a central service provider in order to create data channels for other mobile clients. That is, mobile clients cannot communicate directly with one another. The authors of reference [18] propose a Secured Aggregation Protocol to address this issue.

6.7.4 System Heterogeneity

Since FL involves multiple clients, there is a good chance that the core architecture of these devices will differ significantly. Because of the flexibility of hardware, network connectivity, and power, different storage, computational, and communication capabilities can exacerbate challenges such as straggler mitigation and fault tolerance. It is fairly normal for an active device to drop out during the iterative process of FL due to connectivity or energy constraints [14]. To overcome such challenges, the FL method system should support heterogeneous hardware, run the loop body on a small subset of all devices, and tolerate a certain failure rate among those devices [4].

6.8 Conclusion

In this chapter, we have proposed a FedML-based approach for bank customer churn prediction. We have compared our MLP model with other classification models and verified its effectiveness. Further, we use that MLP model to compare our proposed FL method with CL. We were successively able to prove the robustness of our FL method concerning accuracy and computation expenses. We uncovered that the accuracies of our FL method and CL method are comparable. FL can have a relatively lesser transmission time when real-life scenarios are considered, even with larger datasets. Moreover, with our proposed FL method, the privacy of the bank customers is protected as the data is never transmitted to the central server.

References

[1] McMahan, Brendan, Eider Moore, Daniel Ramage, Seth Hampson, and Blaise Aguera y Arcas. "Communication-efficient learning of deep networks from decentralized data." In *Proceedings of the 20th International Conference on Artificial Intelligence and Statistics*, Ft. Lauderdale, FL, USA, pp. 1273–1282. PMLR, 2017.

[2] Shome, Debaditya, Omer Waqar, and Wali Ullah Khan. "Federated learning and next-generation wireless communications: A survey on bidirectional relationship." *arXiv e-prints. arXiv–2110*, 2021.

[3] Yang, Qiang, Yang Liu, Tianjian Chen, and Yongxin Tong. "Federated machine learning: Concept and applications." *ACM Transactions on Intelligent Systems and Technology (TIST)*, 10(2): 1–19, 2019.

[4] Kairouz, Peter, Brendan McMahan, Brendan Avent, Aurélien Bellet, Mehdi Bennis, Arjun Nitin Bhagoji, Keith Bonawitz et al. "Advances and open problems in federated learning." *Foundations and Trends® in Machine Learning*, 14(1–2): 1–210, 2021.

[5] Bhuse, Pushkar, Aayushi Gandhi, Parth Meswani, Riya Muni, and Neha Katre. "Machine learning based telecom-customer churn prediction." In *2020 3rd International Conference on Intelligent Sustainable Systems (ICISS)*, SCAD Institute of Technology, Palladam, India, pp. 1297–1301. IEEE, 2020.

[6] Rahman, Manas, and V. Kumar. "Machine learning based customer churn prediction in banking." In *2020 4th International Conference on Electronics, Communication and Aerospace Technology (ICECA)*, Coimbatore, India, pp. 1196–1201. IEEE, 2020.

[7] Nilsson, Adrian, Simon Smith, Gregor Ulm, Emil Gustavsson, and Mats Jirstrand. "A performance evaluation of federated learning algorithms." In *Proceedings of the Second Workshop on Distributed Infrastructures for Deep Learning*, Rennes, France, pp. 1–8. 2018.

[8] Chen, Sien, Dong-Ling Xu, and Wei Jiang. "High value passenger identification research based on Federated Learning." In *2020 12th International Conference on Intelligent Human-Machine Systems and Cybernetics (IHMSC)*, Zhejiang University, Hangzhou, China, vol. 1, pp. 107–110. IEEE, 2020.

[9] Uprety, Aashma, Danda B. Rawat, and Jiang Li. "Privacy preserving misbehavior detection in IoV using federated machine learning." In *2021 IEEE 18th Annual Consumer Communications & Networking Conference (CCNC)*, Las Vegas, USA, pp. 1–6. IEEE, 2021.

[10] Dagli, Saloni, Kashvi Dedhia, and Vinaya Sawant. "A proposed solution to build a breast cancer detection model on confidential patient data using federated learning." In *2021 IEEE Bombay Section Signature Conference (IBSSC)*, ABV-IIITM, Gwalior, India, pp. 1–6. IEEE, 2021.

[11] Yang, Wensi, Yuhang Zhang, Kejiang Ye, Li Li, and Cheng-Zhong Xu. "Ffd: A federated learning-based method for credit card fraud detection." In *International Conference on Big Data*, pp. 18–32. Springer, Cham, 2019.

[12] Bank Churn Data Exploration and Churn Prediction Dataset. https://www.kaggle.com/thomaskonstantin/bank-churn-data-exploration-and-churn-prediction (accessed December 9, 2021).

[13] Chawla, Nitesh V., Kevin W. Bowyer, Lawrence O. Hall, and W. Philip Kegelmeyer. "SMOTE: Synthetic minority over-sampling technique." *Journal of Artificial Intelligence Research*, 16: 321–357, 2002.

[14] Li, Tian, Anit Kumar Sahu, Ameet Talwalkar, and Virginia Smith. "Federated learning: Challenges, methods, and future directions." *IEEE Signal Processing Magazine*, 37(3): 50–60, 2020.

[15] Niknam, Solmaz, Harpreet S. Dhillon, and Jeffrey H. Reed. "Federated learning for wireless communications: Motivation, opportunities, and challenges." *IEEE Communications Magazine*, 58(6): 46–51, 2020.

[16] Li, Suyi, Yong Cheng, Wei Wang, Yang Liu, and Tianjian Chen. "Learning to detect malicious clients for robust federated learning." *arXiv preprint arXiv:2002.00211*, 2020.

[17] Cao, Xiaoyu, Jinyuan Jia, and Neil Zhenqiang Gong. "Provably secure federated learning against malicious clients." *Proceedings of the AAAI Conference on Artificial Intelligence*, 35(8): 6885–6893, 2021.

[18] Bonawitz, Keith, Vladimir Ivanov, Ben Kreuter, Antonio Marcedone, H. Brendan McMahan, Sarvar Patel, Daniel Ramage, Aaron Segal, and Karn Seth. "Practical secure aggregation for federated learning on user-held data." *arXiv preprint arXiv: 1611.04482*, 2016.

Chapter 7

Challenges and Avenues in the Sophisticated Health-Care System

Rajesh Shardanand Prasad and Jayashree Rajesh Prasad
MIT Art, Design and Technology University, Pune

Nihar M Ranjan
Rajarshi Shahu College of Engineering

Contents

DOI: 10.1201/9781003390220-7

7.1 Introduction

Since the pandemic across the globe, the health-care sector was going through the stress of fighting the coronavirus and its variants as well as the challenges in the medical field that can be a direct threat to human life. As the world anticipates curbing the spread of pandemics and other unanticipated challenges, online data that refers to healthcare will in general pull the attention of researchers from analytics and security perspectives. Thus, data mining techniques are getting more attention along with the model to stop cybercriminals to infect the systems to hack the information and interrupt in digital operations of the health-care management systems.

The health-care sector has immediately become an objective for the society, business, and research community. Health-care data is particularly delicate and sensitive to such assaults as any interruption or manipulation or even disclosure of patient data can have extensive consequences. Europol stated that the health-care services were found to be a lucrative target in the form of ransom. This chapter narrates the challenges and avenues in sophisticated health-care systems from the data mining and cybersecurity perspective.

The first part of the chapter focuses on analytics (predictive and descriptive) using data mining in the health-care sector to predict the market for drug discovery, therapy patterns, medicinal effects, patient response, etc.; the second part of the chapter will intend to the recommendations for "cyber hygiene" to mitigate outbreaking coronavirus-related online scams.

7.2 Organization of the Chapters

The challenges associated with health-care systems are explained in the first part of the chapter (Section 7.3). The algorithms used for the application of data mining in healthcare have a lot of positive impacts and also have life-saving outcomes, which are explained in the second part of the chapter (Section 7.4). In essence, data mining refers to the vast quantities of information created by the digitization of everything, which gets consolidated and analyzed by specific technologies. Applied to healthcare, it will use specific health data of a population (or of a particular individual) and to potentially help prevent epidemics, cure disease, cut-down costs, etc. [1,5].

The related literature review has been conducted by studying various research papers and online publications. The study shows that technology alone cannot protect us from challenges in healthcare, but proper sanitization of the population is also needed. Health-care organizations should encourage the use of technologies and methodologies culture by implementing data mining awareness programs [3].

The research on the security of healthcare is sparse. With the advent of technology in healthcare, there is a need to identify the intelligent measures using advanced techniques like artificial intelligence (AI) to give researchers and medical practitioners a better insight into it. We aim to highlight the related issues and suggest solutions and opportunities through this work.

7.3 The Challenges Faced By Health-Care Systems

7.3.1 Patients Predictions

It is one of the classic problems that any hospital administrator faces: how many staff do I put on duty at any given period? Too many workers may add up labor costs, and too few workers can lead to poor customer service – which can be fatal for patients in the hospital. Data mining (DM) techniques can help hospitals to solve this problem. The system can take data from a variety of sources to come up with daily and hourly predictions of how many patients are expected to be at each hospital in a particular duration [2,4].

7.3.2 Electronic Health Records (EHRs)

It's the most important application of data mining in health-care industries. Every patient has his/her digital record, which includes demographics, medical history, allergies, pathological test results, etc. Records are shared through secure information systems and are accessible to both public and private sector suppliers. Every record is made up of a single editable file, which means doctors may make changes over time without having to deal with paperwork or the risk of data replication. EHRs can also send out alerts and reminders when a patient needs a fresh laboratory test, as well as track prescriptions to see if they've been followed. "The integrated system has improved outcomes in cardiovascular disease and delivered an estimated $1 billion in savings from reduced office visits and laboratory testing," according to McKinsey's research on healthcare [2,7].

7.3.3 Real-Time Alerting

Clinical decision support (CDS) software analyses medical data on the spot in hospitals, assisting doctors while they make prescriptive decisions. Doctors, on the other hand, prefer that people avoid hospitals to avoid costly in-house therapies. Analytics, which is already one of the hottest business intelligence buzzwords for 2019, has the potential to become a new strategy. Wearables will continuously collect patient health data and send it to the cloud. Furthermore, this information will be linked to a database on the general public's health, allowing clinicians to examine the data in a socio-economic context and adjust delivery techniques accordingly. Institutions and care managers can monitor and react to this vast data stream using sophisticated techniques. They will utilize sophisticated tools to monitor this large data stream and respond immediately if the results are alarming. For example, if a patient's blood pressure rises dangerously, the system will transmit a warning to the doctor in real-time prompting the doctor to contact the patient and give pressure-lowering measures [4,7].

7.3.4 Patient Engagement

Many potential patients are already interested in smart devices that track their every step, heart rate, sleeping habits, and other data continuously. All this essential data can be combined with other trackable data to uncover hidden health hazards. For example, chronic sleeplessness and an increased heart rate can indicate a future risk of heart disease. Patients are directly involved in their health monitoring, and health insurance incentives can encourage them to live a healthy lifestyle [4].

7.3.5 Less Use of Health Data for Informed Strategic Planning

Because of deeper insights into people's motives, the use of big data in healthcare enables strategic planning. Care managers can look at the results of checkups among persons from various demographic categories to see what factors deter people from seeking treatment. The University of Florida created heat maps for a variety of topics, including population growth and chronic diseases, using Google Maps and open public health data. Academics then linked this information to the availability of medical care in the hottest places. They were able to reassess their delivery plan and add more care units to the most problematic locations as a result of the information they gained [7, 9].

7.3.6 Lack of Predictive Analytics in Healthcare

We have already diagnosed predictive analytics as one of all the largest commercial enterprise intelligence tendencies years in a row; however, the ability packages attain a way past commercial enterprise and plenty in addition with inside the future. Optum Labs, a US studies collaborative, has accumulated EHRs of over 30 million sufferers to create a database for predictive analytics gear to enhance the transport of care. The purpose of health-care online commercial enterprise intelligence is to assist medical doctors to make data-pushed selections in seconds and enhance sufferers' treatment. This is especially beneficial with inside the case of sufferers with complicated clinical histories, tormented by more than one condition. New BI answers and gear could additionally be capable of predicting, for example, who's prone to diabetes and thereby be advised to utilize extra screenings or weight management.

7.3.7 Fraud and Lack of Security

Several studies have shown that 93 health-care institutions suffer from data breaches [2]. The reason for this is simple. Certain dates are very valuable and informative with black demands. The violation will have dramatic consequences. With this in mind, many associations are beginning to address security pitfalls by using analytics to correlate network operations or other gesture changes that reflect cyberattacks. Of course, these data have serious security issues, and many believe that using these data will make their connections more vulnerable than before. However, security advances such as encryption technology, firewalls, and antivirus software meet this need for further security, and the associated benefits largely offset the pitfalls.

7.3.8 Less Integration of Enormous Data with Medical Imaging

Medical images are very important, and about 600 million image processes are performed each year in the United States [2]. Manually analyzing and storing these images is both times consuming and costly as the radiologist needs to inspect each image individually, while the hospital needs to keep them for several years. Carestream, a medical imaging provider, explains how big data analytics in healthcare can change the way images are read. Algorithms that analyze hundreds of thousands of images identify specific patterns within a pixel and convert them into numbers to identify doctors who are useful in making a diagnosis. Going further, the Carestream says that radiologists may no longer need to see the image but instead analyze the results of the algorithm. This will undoubtedly affect the role of radiologists, their training, and the skills required [11, 15].

7.3.9 Risk & Disease Management

Data mining techniques in healthcare are essential for managing hospital risk for specific patients with chronic illnesses. It also helps prevent deterioration. By analyzing insights such as drug type, symptoms, and frequency of doctor visits, health-care facilities can perform accurate screening and ultimately reduce hospitalizations. This level of risk calculation not only reduces spending on home patient care but also makes space and resources available to those who need them most. This is a clear example of how health-care analysis can improve and save people's lives. As a result, big data in healthcare can improve the quality of patient care while streamlining organizations in all key areas more economically [21].

7.3.10 Increase in Suicide & Self-Harm

Nearly 800,000 people die from suicide every year around the world [2]. In addition, 17% of the world's population self-harm at some point in their lives. These numbers are alarming. However, while this is a very difficult area to tackle, the use of big data in healthcare has helped make positive changes around suicide and self-harm. As a company that sees large numbers of patients daily, health-care facilities can use data analysis to identify individuals who may harm themselves.

7.4 The Technology/Methodology behind Data Mining

Data mining is the process of pattern recognition and extraction involving large amounts of data. Both the data mining and health-care industries are creating reliable early detection systems and separate systems, which are health-related systems from clinical and diagnostic data. Data is being collected and accumulated at an alarming rate in all areas. There is an urgent need for a new generation of computing theory and tools that help humans extract useful information (Knowledge) from rapidly increasing digital data. The focus of the process is applying specific data mining techniques for pattern recognition and extraction. Recently developed mining technologies include the generalization of data mining techniques, characterization, classification, clustering, association, evolution, pattern matching, and data visualization [23].

In general, there are two types of data mining models: predictive models and descriptive models. Predictive models often apply supervised learning functions to predict unknown or future values or other variables of interest. Descriptive models, on the other hand, often apply unsupervised models, learning the ability to find patterns that explain human-interpretable data. The predictive model is more commonly used in health-care systems.

After defining the data mining model and tasks, the next step is the data mining method for creating the data mining model. An approach based on the discipline involved. The methods used to detect anomalies are standard support vector data description, density induction support vector data description, Gaussian mixture, and vector quantization methods, which are often used for clustering. The most widely used classification methods are statistical, discriminant analysis, decision tree, Markov base, swarm intelligence, closest neighbor, genetic classifiers, artificial neural networks, support vectors, and association rules.

Healthcare includes illness, injury, and other physical and mental disorders in humans. The health-care industry can be seen as a place where a wealth of data is generated. A huge amount of data including electronic medical records, management reports, etc., is generated, stored, maintained, and used. However, this health data is not fully utilized. Data mining can search for new and valuable information from these large amounts of data. Health-care mines are primarily used to predict and support a variety of illnesses, and diagnoses for physicians in their clinical decisions [24].

An explanation of various methods/algorithms of data mining in the health-care industry is presented below:

Anomaly detection: Anomaly detection is used to detect the most important changes in a dataset. B. Lie et al. used three different anomaly detection methods, a standard support vector data description, a density induction support vector data description, and a Gaussian mixture to assess the accuracy of the anomaly. Detection of liver disease datasets obtained from UCI with uncertain datasets. The method has been evaluated using AUC accuracy. Results obtained with a balanced dataset averaged 93.59%. The mean standard deviation obtained from the same dataset is 2.63. Unsafe records anomaly detection is a good way to solve this problem, as it is likely to be available on all datasets [12].

Clustering: Clustering is a common descriptive task that seeks to identify or group a finite set of categories. Rui Veloso used vector quantization in clustering [20,26]. The algorithm used in vector quantization methods is K-means, K-mediods, and X-means. The dataset used in this study was collected from the patient's clinical process and test results. The evaluation of each algorithm is as follows. K-means achieved the best results, and X-means scored fair results while K-mediods gave the worst results. From the results of these tasks, researchers provide useful results by helping to characterize different types of patients with higher scores and probability of recovery [6,13].

Classification: Classification is the discovery of a predictive learning function that classifies data items into one of the following predefined classes. The tasks related to classification are described below [16,17].

Statistical analysis: The MTS algorithm is widely applied in multivariable statistical analysis. Mahalanobis distance (MD) is used to make statistical decisions to distinguish one group from another. Mahalanobis space (MS) is used to represent the extent of observational anomalies from known observations. For statistical classifiers, the author Su et al. [14] used Mahalanobis-Taguchi System (MTS) to develop a predictive model for pressure ulcers. Class imbalance problem is prevalent in health records. The use of data mining algorithms is often affected if a biased or unbalanced dataset is used, the distribution will be biased. This problem is often the tendency to generate highly predictable classification accuracy for the majority class and poor accuracy with minority classes.

Discriminant analysis: Linear discriminant analysis (LDA) is commonly used in the discriminant analysis for class-based prediction. A specific set of measurements for new unlabeled observations. Authors Armañanzas et al. [25] and Jen et al. use linear discriminant analysis in each study. Jen et al. had the algorithm for predicting the severity of Parkinson's disease patients using non-exercise values symptoms. Their research aims to quantitatively analyze the internal behavior of both engine and non-motor symptoms. Linear discriminant analysis is a conditional probability density function. The number of predictors follows a normal distribution based on the specified class value. It is suitable for investigating the linear constraints of this study to discover synergies between motor and non-motor symptoms. The proposed model achieved a 69% accuracy estimate compared with other models. If the dependencies are linear, the performance of the algorithm will be significantly improved, and so will the algorithm's shape. Based on the same type of algorithm, the author Armañanzas et al. used an algorithm to evaluate the accuracy of the classification to find the most important risk factors and determine the initial set of risk factors. A significant risk factor for early warning in chronic illness. The algorithm gives good results and says it is suitable to use to identify significant accuracy when the relationship between health data is linear.

Decision tree: Several studies have explored decision tree methods to analyze clinical data. Authors Sharma [10] & Om, Wang et al., and Zolbanin et al. [25] used the decision tree algorithm. In essence, their work is to examine data, generate a tree, and use the tree's rules to make predictions. All three works have used dataset decision trees to improve predictive performance, in exact terms. Rather, the nature of the dataset used in this study is a set of balanced datasets.

Comparing the works, we conclude that decision trees cannot be used to suggest predictions. Decisions solve unbalanced problems because decision trees recursively split observations into branches to form a tree.

Swarm intelligence: The particle swarm optimization (PSO) algorithm can efficiently find optimal or near-optimal solutions in large search spaces. Authors tried optimization problem-solving, which often involves features in classification problems. The classification process will be faster and more accurate if fewer features are used. The PSO-based approach demonstrates improving the results of the global classification because PSO is being used to select the appropriate parameters in the relevant classifiers [19,20].

Nearest neighbor: The authors García Laencina et al. [22], Armañanzas et al. [25], Jen et al., Bagui et al., and a Şahan et al. used the nearest neighbor in their respective prediction models. The smartest person, neighbors are an instance-based classification method. Parameter units include samples used in this method and the algorithm then assumes all cases involving points in Space RN. The algorithm is very fast because the information contained in the training data is never lost.

However, this algorithm will be suitable if the training dataset is large because this algorithm is very time-consuming when each sample in the training set is processed in the new data classification and this process requires classification time to be longer. According to the works of the mentioned authors, what is the accuracy of the classification? They want an approach instead of classification time because classification accuracy is more important in medical diagnosis.

Logistic regression: Logistic regression (LR) is a method that will use a given set of characteristics, either continuous, discrete, or a mixture of the two types and a binary objective. LR will then compute a linear combination of the inputs and go through the logistic function [8]. This method is often used because it is easy to perform and delivers competitive results. The authors García Laencina et al. [22], Mamiya et al. [25], Su et al. [14], Wang et al. [17], Zolbanin et al. [18], and Thompson et al. [14] applied LR in their respective study. Results obtained from all authors are not very important since the size of the input dataset has significantly reduced. Results that will be available make more sense if the dataset is large since the precision limit will be larger. LR works well for large datasets.

7.5 Conclusion

From the articles reviewed and discussed, the accuracy of data mining methods varies depending on the characteristics of the dataset and the size of the dataset between the training and test sets. Shared characteristics among health-care datasets are very unbalanced datasets, where the majority and the minority classifier are unbalanced, leading to false predictions when run by the classifier. Missing values are another characteristic of the health-care dataset. The data sample size is usually considered another characteristic since the available data are often on a small scale.

Data mining plays a critical role in the health-care industry, especially in predicting various types of diseases and drug discovery. The diagnosis is widely being used in predicting diseases, and they are extensively used in medical diagnosing and imaging. To obtain the highest accuracy among classifiers, which is important in medical diagnosis, with the characteristics of data being taken care of; we need to design a hybrid model which could resolve the mentioned issues. The health-care industry is also struggling with its management and strategic planning to resolve the related issues as discussed in Section 7.3. Data mining methods and analytics are now gaining popularity due to their intelligent predictive nature.

References

[1] S. H. Liao, P. H. Chu, and P. Y. Hsiao, "Data mining techniques and applications - A decade review from 2000 to 2011," *Expert Syst. Appl.*, vol. 39, no. 12, pp. 11303–11311, 2012.

[2] I. H. Witten, E. Frank, and M. Hall, *Data Mining: Practical Machine Learning Tools and Techniques (Google eBook)*, Morgan Kaufmann, Elsevier, USA, 2011.

[3] D. K. Bhattacharyya and S. M. Hazarika, *Networks, Data Mining and Artificial Intelligence: Trends and Future Directions*, 1st ed. Narosa Pub House, New Delhi, 2006.

[4] M. Kantardzic, *Data Mining: Concepts, Models, Methods, and Algorithms*, 2nd ed. Wiley-IEEE Press, New Jersey, 2011.

[5] D. R. Hardoon, S. Szedmak and J. Shawe-Taylor, "Canonical correlation analysis: An overview with application to learning methods," *J. Neural Comput.*, vol. 16, no. 12, pp. 2639–2664, 2004.

[6] M. Chau, R. Cheng, B. Kao, and J. Ng, "Uncertain data mining: An example in clustering location data," *Lect. Notes Comput. Sci. (including Subser. Lect. Notes Artif. Intell. Lect. Note Bioinformatics)*, vol. 3918, pp. 199–204, 2006.

[7] Z. Wu and C. Li, "L0-constrained regression for data mining," In Zhou, Z. H., Li, H., and Yang, Q. (eds), *Advances in Knowledge Discovery and Data Mining. PAKDD*

2007. Lecture Notes in Computer Science (vol. 4426, pp. 981–988). Springer, Berlin, Heidelberg. https://doi.org/10.1007/978-3-540-71701-0_110, 2007.

[8] A. Genkin, D. D. Lewis, and D. Madigan, "Large-scale bayesian logistic regression for text categorization," *American Statistical Association and the American Society for Quality Technometrics*, vol. 49, no. 3, pp. 291–304, 2007. https://doi.org/10.1198/004017007000000245

[9] J.-J. Yang, J. Li, J. Mulder, Y. Wang, S. Chen, H. Wu, Q. Wang, and H. Pan, "Emerging information technologies for enhanced healthcare," *Comput. Ind.*, vol. 72, pp. 306–313, 2015. ISSN 1877-0509, https://doi.org/10.1016/j.procs.2015.12.145.

[10] Dwivedi, A. N., R. K. Bali, R. N. G. Naguib (2007), Building New Healthcare Management Paradigms: A Case for Healthcare Knowledge Management. In Bali, R. K., Dwivedi, A. N. (eds), *Healthcare Knowledge Management. Health Informatics*. Springer, New York, NY. https://doi.org/10.1007/978-0-387-49009-0_1.

[11] U. Fayyad, G. Piatetsky-Shapiro, and P. Smyth, "From data mining to knowledge discovery in databases," *AI Mag.*, vol. 17, pp. 37–54, 1996.

[12] B. Liu, Y. Xiao, L. Cao, Z. Hao, and F. Deng, "SVDD-based outlier detection on uncertain data," *Knowl. Inf. Syst.*, vol. 34, no. 3, pp. 597–618, 2013.

[13] R. Veloso, F. Portela, M. F. Santos, Á. Silva, F. Rua, A. Abelha, and J. Machado, "A clustering approach for predicting readmissions in intensive medicine," *Procedia Technol.*, vol. 16, pp. 1307–1316, 2014.

[14] C. T. Su, P. C. Wang, Y. C. Chen, and L. F. Chen, "Data mining techniques for assisting the diagnosis of pressure ulcer development in surgical patients," *J. Med. Syst.*, vol. 36, no. 4, pp. 2387–2399, 2012.

[15] R. Armañanzas, C. Bielza, K. R. Chaudhuri, P. Martinez-Martin, and P. Larrañaga, "Unveiling relevant non-motor Parkinson's disease severity symptoms using a machine learning approach," *Artif. Intell. Med.*, vol. 58, no. 3, pp. 195–202, 2013.

[16] C.-H. Jen, C.-C. Wang, B. C. Jiang, Y.-H. Chu, and M.-S. Chen, "Application of classification techniques on development an early-warning system for chronic illnesses," *Expert Syst. Appl.*, vol. 39, no. 10, pp. 8852–8858, 2012.

[17] K.-J. Wang, B. Makond, and K.-M. Wang, "An improved survivability prognosis of breast cancer by using sampling and feature selection technique to solve imbalanced patient classification data," *BMC Med. Inform. Decis. Mak.*, vol. 13, p. 124, 2013.

[18] H. M. Zolbanin, D. Delen, and A. Hassan Zadeh, "Predicting overall survivability in the comorbidity of cancers: A data mining approach," *Decis. Support Syst.*, vol. 74, pp. 150–161, 2015.

[19] W.-C. Yeh, W.-W. Chang, and Y. Y. Chung, "A new hybrid approach for mining breast cancer pattern using discrete particle swarm optimization and statistical method," *Expert Syst. Appl.*, vol. 36, no. 4, pp. 8204–8211, 2009.

[20] S. W. Fei, "Diagnostic study on arrhythmia cordis based on particle swarm optimization- based support vector machine," *Expert Syst. Appl.*, vol. 37, no. 10, pp. 6748–6752, 2010.

[21] M. J. Abdi and D. Giveki, "Automatic detection of erythematous-squamous diseases using PSO-SVM based on association rules," *Eng. Appl. Artif. Intell.*, vol. 26, no. 1, pp. 603–608, 2013.

[22] P. J. García-Laencina, P. H. Abreu, M. H. Abreu, and N. Afonoso, "Missing data imputation on the 5-year survival prediction of breast cancer patients with unknown discrete values," *Comput. Biol. Med.*, vol. 59, pp. 125–133, 2015.

[23] S. C. Bagui, S. Bagui, K. Pal, and N. R. Pal, "Breast cancer detection using rank nearest neighbor classiÿcation rules," *Pattern Recognit.*, vol. 36, pp. 25–34, 2003.

[24] S. Şahan, K. Polat, H. Kodaz, and S. Güneş, "A new hybrid method based on fuzzy-artificial immune system and k-nn algorithm for breast cancer diagnosis," *Comput. Biol. Med.*, vol. 37, no. 3, pp. 415–423, 2007.

[25] H. Mamiya, K. Schwartzman, A. Verma, C. Jauvin, M. Behr, and D. Buckeridge, "Towards probabilistic decision support in public health practice: Predicting recent transmission of tuberculosis from patient attributes," *J. Biomed. Inform.*, vol. 53, pp. 237–242, 2015.

[26] B. Zheng, S. W. Yoon, and S. S. Lam, "Breast cancer diagnosis based on feature extraction using a hybrid of K-means and support vector machine algorithms," *Expert Syst. Appl.*, vol. 41, no. 4, pp. 1476–1482, 2014.

Chapter 8

Unusual Social Media Behavior Detection Using Distributed Data Stream Mining

Aakash Sangani, Princy Doshi, and Vinaya Sawant

Dwarkadas J. Sanghvi College of Engineering

Contents

8.1 Introduction

With the advent of social media, our day-to-day lives are heavily influenced by its presence. This is appropriately evident through its different uses apart from socializing, such as discourse and job-hunting. Hence, one can say that a person's social media profile is to be an accurate representation of their interests, personality, and present life. This online image of a person can be hampered by several means, of which one of the most notorious means to do so remains hacking and misinformation. If an attacker were to take control of our social media profiles, they could make any decisions on that platform using our identity. It could be something as innocent as interacting with posts that we wouldn't normally interact with, or something as sinister as leaking or stealing personal information for their own gain. It has been noted that even with all of our advancements in cyber security, hacking of social media accounts has increased by 13% in the last 2 years. These hacked accounts are further reportedly used to spread propaganda and misrepresent discourse online. Such misrepresentation of one's person on social media has grave consequences in today's day and age.

This misrepresentation of one's person can be referred to as "Unusual behavior," which is contrary to a user's usual behavior, which refers to their interests, common topics talked about, active hours on the site, etc. Of course, there is a chance that the unusual behavior is just that user's new online behavior, but that does not disqualify "usual behavior" as a valid indicator of a user's authenticity. To better handle this, such false-positive detections of unusual behavior can be corrected by keeping concept shift in mind for our solution. Hence, the solution works on clickstream data based on the user's activity on that social media platform. Use a classification algorithm for every user to keep track of their usual behavior by using data labeled as usual behavior mixed in with a bot's data labeled as unusual behavior. Of course, applying a separate model for every user on a large scale wouldn't be feasible. Hence, clustering can be used to group together users with similar online activities, helping them make use of the same model.

8.2 Related Works

As the usage of social tools for business communications is becoming widespread, social media security is more vital and in demand than ever. It is a platform for many artists, small enterprises, etc. Online social networks (OSN) have attracted significant attention, arising from the main concern with their security. Detecting malicious users in an OSN is a crucial issue for the proper operation of such networks. According to the latest EY Global Information Security Survey [1], 59% of organizations had a "material or significant incident" in the past 12 months. Currently, research is being conducted on developing different mechanisms to detect malicious activities in an OSN [2].

So many techniques have arisen in the case of detecting unusual behavior. Few significant user behavior analyses have been surveyed in references [2,3]. A hacked account will exhibit different patterns than the regular user to fulfill their objectives. It could be posting malicious content or advertising things against the user's ideology. We get an in-depth understanding of user intent and the importance of detecting hostile social bot accounts in OSN through user behavior analysis. User behavior will likely change under different situations [2].

8.2.1 User Behavior Analysis

Through user behavior, one observes the pattern's change by watching it. A few of the essential behavioral attributes identified are usage frequency, information control, social association, egomaniacal, cooperation, social boldness, and social investigation. The context under which user behavior is looked upon includes trust, privacy, age, culture, gender, information sharing, and distance.

Almost 4.5 billion people use social media in one way or another, thereby citing the issues of security and user behavior analysis as significant issues. It is a rapidly growing industry in a business platform and an employment source. So, in reference [4], we can see that a social media model is created to classify the users. It is based on the frequency of social media content sharing and classified into individual users (light users), heavy users, and automated users.

User behavior depends upon one's schedule, environment, essential changes in life, workload, and a few more factors. User behavior will likely change under different situations. By analyzing the user behavior and typical characteristics, we get a load of information to gain insightful understanding of user intent and play a crucial role in detecting malicious social bots' accounts in OSN.

In reference [2], a four-layer system is created. It acquires data from a social media sensor and manipulates it, thereby detecting patterns in behavioral changes. The layers are: social sensing layer, data acquisition and preparation layer, data storage management layer, and analysis representation layer. The first layer is an interface that lists the users and their queries or searches, and then, a connection is established with APIs of OSNs where the data is observed. Then, it is classified and sorted according to the parameters. The second layer cleans the data, and then in the third layer, information is extracted from the data extractor between the second and third layers. Hadoop framework comes into the picture and forms the data into specific trends. Analyzing these trends requires the process of extracting explicit features and implicit features. A detailed element can be removed in real-time, and implicit features, in contrast, require offline calculations. Then, an algorithm is implemented.

Few papers have stated that users include connections with the features as they interact in the network, e.g., through communication with other users. An answer is formed by keeping a check on the users. Researchers use data and machine-learning methods to find users that do not conform to specific rules; such techniques usually compare the user activities to a predefined set of actions [5,6].

A paper presented a framework for discovering user behavior patterns in multimedia video recommendation services on online social networks. Their framework is based on social context and analyses the changes in user need for different social situations. Such user behavior data can be obtained by accessing the user's logs [7] or user's clickstreams (e.g., recorded by social network platforms). The difference in user behavior can be obtained, for example, by analyzing the image search logs of users to study the search intention of different users [3], and this approach can facilitate the optimization of search engines.

8.2.2 Social Media Bots

Social media bots as programs come in numerous sizes. The size varies depending on their function, capacity, and design, and they are very functional on social media platforms to do various valuable and hostile tasks while imitating human behavior. Social media bots can be trained for multiple processes, not just restricting themselves to detecting unusual behavior.

At times, few social media bots very evidently exhibit non-human behavior or mechanical behavior; there is no 100% accurate method for identifying sophisticated bot accounts. A study conducted by the University of Reading School of Systems Engineering found that 30% of people could be deceived into believing a natural person ran a social media bot account.

In some cases, it can be tough to spot a bot. For example, some bots use real users' accounts previously hijacked by an attacker. These hijacked bot accounts have even persuasive pictures, post histories, and social networks. In fact, even a non-hijacked account can create an entire social network: A study found that one in five social media users always accept friend requests from strangers.

So, when we look for a technique to identify social media bots, the advanced ones can be hard to spot even for experts; there are a few plans of action to detect some less sophisticated bot accounts. They are: (i) We try to run a reverse image search on their profile photograph if another account has taken it and been using it. (ii) We will see the timing and how a post is being posted. Suppose an account that frequently posts at a time does not match, has been posting randomly, or is making posts every few minutes every day. In that case, these are indications that the account is automated or even persuasive; (iii) Using a bot detection service that uses machine learning to detect bot behavior [8].

In reference [9], social media bots had behaviors more than the malicious ones, for example, posting tweets, commenting, etc. They focused on behaviors not necessarily threatening but likely to be performed by malicious ones. Here, they used a semi-supervised clustering method to detect malicious bots. It was real-time detection. The user and social bots' behavior was analyzed based on temporal and spatial dimensions features. Based on the constrained seed K-means algorithm, a sample mean square error threshold determines the number of iterations and then obtains the social bots detection algorithm. Also, a hybrid feature of transition probability features and time feature was used to increase the robustness of the features, thus improving the accuracy of detection.

8.2.3 Existing Mechanisms/Methods/Algorithms

Classification is a data mining function that assigns items in a collection to target categories or classes. The classification objective is to foresee the target class accurately and precisely for every case in the data. Classification algorithms could be classified as follows: (i) linear classifiers (logistic regression, naive Bayes classifier, Fisher's linear discriminant), (ii) support vector machines (least squares support vector machines), (iii) quadratic classifiers, (iv) kernel estimation (k-nearest neighbor), (v) decision trees (Random forests), (vi) neural networks, and (vii) learning vector quantization.

A decision tree divides the training set acting like a class discriminator recurrently until each partition consists of vital examples from one class. Here when a node is considered, if it is a non-leaf node of the tree, it consists of a split point that tests one or more characteristics and determines how the data is partitioned.

Decision trees are very constructive and appealing classification tools, majorly as they give us quickly interpretable and well-organized outcomes and are computationally efficient and capable of dealing with noisy data. Decision tree techniques build the classification or prediction models based on recursive partitioning of data, which begins with the entire body of data, then splits the data into two or more subsets based on the values of one or more attributes, and then repeatedly breaks each subset in more exemplary subsets until the stopping criteria are met [1].

In reference [5], a very fast decision tree (VFDT) is implemented to detect credit card fraudulent use. VFDT is a method based on Hoeffding inequality to establish a classification decision tree for a data stream mining environment. It is generated by continuously replacing leaf nodes with branch nodes, and the sample attributes studied are discrete attributes [10]. For data stream, an ID3 is inefficient, and an online decision tree brings VFDT learner into play and the concept drift method [11]. The examples collected in leaf nodes are only a part of all the available examples. Therefore, they can include errors. However, the set of measures that arrive at each leaf node can be regarded as perfect data sets in an offline-type decision tree, which can consider infinitely long data streams produced stochastically based on stationary distribution [5].

A way of dividing the population or the data points into many groups so that data points in the same group are similar to the data point of the same group than of the other is called clustering [12]. In simpler words, the aim is to set apart groups with similar traits and combine them into clusters. We use feature pruning based Clickstream Clustering [13] specifically. At a high level, this system uses similarity metrics between clickstreams to build similarity graphs that capture behavioral patterns between users. Edges catch similar distances between users' clickstreams, and clusters represent user groups with similar behavior. It uses a hierarchical clustering approach to detect the most prevalent behavior patterns and uses an iterative feature pruning technique to remove the influence of dominating features from each subsequent layer of clusters. The result is a hierarchy of behavioral clusters where higher-level clusters represent more general user behavior patterns. Lower-level clusters further identify smaller groups that differ in critical behavioral ways.

8.3 Proposed System

The system can be bifurcated into two parts. One part is used to train or retrain models (like in Figure 8.1), while the other part contains the trained models to detect unusual behavior in real-time-on-real-time data streams (Figure 8.2). We further elaborate on the two sections below:

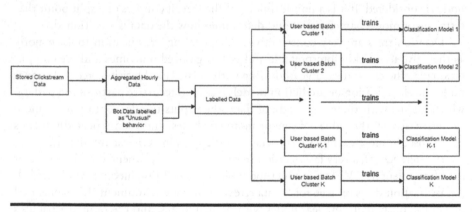

Figure 8.1 Training models.

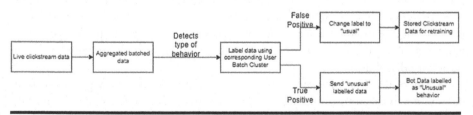

Figure 8.2 Unusual behavior detection.

8.3.1 Training Models

The two primary data sources that are used to train the model (in Figure 8.1) to be able to classify usual and unusual user behavior for a specific cluster were the past clickstream data of Users and the Hourly Aggregated data of users when they were genuinely detected as behaving unusually, hence, like a bot. These two data sources are used to source data with two labels, "usual" and "unusual," in the "behavior" attribute. The percentage of "usual behavior" is 80%, while that of unusual behavior is 20% to keep the data's distribution consistent with the actual world rates at which bot accounts operate.

A method in unsupervised learning is clustering, which is used to find a definite structure, deep-sited explanatory procedures, numerous features, and groupings of different inherent in a set of examples. Here, we draw references from datasets lacking labeled responses. Clustering is used to cluster the aggregated labeled data into K clusters. Each collection contains users who exhibit similar behavior and their dummy bot behavior. Each cluster represents N number of users that exhibit identical online behavior to simplify the task at hand. These K clusters are used to label the data with their cluster number. We use clustering here to decrease the number of classifiers to be used, had we not used clustering, we'd have to train and use N number of classifiers, one for each user's behavior. By clustering users in K clusters, we eliminate the need to train N models instead of having to train only the K number of models (where $K < N$).

A decision tree is a flowchart-like tree structure, where each internal node denotes a test on an attribute, each branch represents an outcome of the trial, and each leaf node (terminal node) holds a class label. A VFDT is implemented to achieve better accuracy. Based on the Hoeffding tree algorithm, VFDT makes improvements in-memory optimization. When the current data fills the memory space, the VFDT system will temporarily remove the space used by the child nodes that have the most negligible impact on the classification decision. The data is then used to train cluster-specific very fast decision tree classifiers.

At a time, many algorithms combined are used by decision trees to split a node into two or more sub-nodes. The creation of sub-nodes increases the homogeneity of sub-nodes, thereby increasing clarity. The working of the decision tree is that it first splits the nodes on all present chargeable and then selects the split, thereby forming the most homogeneous sub-nodes.

This means that each classifier will be able to tell when a user behaves unusually for that specific cluster. These classifiers can be trained parallelly using distributed data mining, using Apache Spark. Then by clustering, a similar set is clustered together, and a behavioral pattern is observed. One of the significant characteristics of a clustered solution is the option of automatic recovery in case of failure with no user intervention.

8.3.2 Unusual Behavior Detection

In this section of the system (Figure 8.2), we detect the unusual behavior exhibited in a live data stream by aggregating user behavior data hourly. This data has no labels in the "behavior" attribute. Now, according to the cluster the user belongs to, we let the corresponding model detect if a day (24 consecutive entries) presented unusual behavior or not. The corresponding model that sees this unusual behavior is trained for that specific cluster. If this "unusual behavior" labeling is continued for four straight days (four rounds of detection), then the system can positively say that the user is exhibiting suspiciously continuous unusual behavior.

Now, upon positively detecting unusual behavior, there are two possible scenarios. In case of a false positive, the label assigned as uncommon for the user's behavior is changed to usual, and the user's data is put through the first section again. It would probably be assigned a new cluster, or if it is not, it will help retrain the model to accommodate this natural change in user behavior better. This step is taken to handle concept change, which could be a user's behavior changing with time, using relabeling and rapid retraining of the models accordingly.

Suppose the unusual behavior is, in fact, a bot or somebody taking a user's accounts control without their approval. In that case, the system will send these "bot-like" unusual behavior data to the bot data repository. This data can later be reused to train our models on what real-world unusual (or bot-like) behavior looks like and behaves.

In this system, detecting a user account getting hacked would be much more efficient with fewer false positives. It must be implemented in real-time. The information/data available for detection is a bit tedious. Also, after implementing the model, the security of the data is a significant crisis. There could be an information breach as to raising privacy concerns.

8.4 Data Format to Be Used

Data suitable for this system to work should be clickstream, i.e., the data tracks the user's every click and action since logging onto their account. This typical use by them is indicative of their behavior when aggregated over some time. In our system, we aggregate the user's actions over an hour. For example, if a user were to like 70 posts in 1 hour between 12 noon and 1 pm on Saturday, 29th of January, it will be considered the aggregated number of likes over that 1 hour. Hence, every user will have 24 rows for each day of their activity, even when they are not logged in. For example, if not logged in, the user's hourly activity would be 0 newly liked posts. This is done to signify their inactivity through the data and create similarly shaped data for all the users.

Apart from this, to optimize the system, distributed systems can be used with an increasing number of clusters. Parallel computing would become much more practical to implement as the only feasible solution to not having enough computing power. Similarly, for detection, every cluster's corresponding model would need to detect unusual behavior to keep up with the real-time streaming data and to be able to scale up to more users if necessary.

8.5 Conclusion

In this text, we saw concepts such as classification, clustering, and distributed systems can be used as building blocks to build a much more complex, use-intensive, ensemble system. This ensemble system's primary application is to classify usual behavior from unusual behavior in a user through their past data. But that would require a lot of computational costs, especially at a larger scale. This computational cost is lowered by using clusters to use one similar classification model for all users exhibiting similar behavior. Leveraging VFDTs could help us retrain the model multiple times to combat concept change, i.e., a user might see a difference in their behavior over the course of time.

We conclude that upon the availability of necessary data in the specified format, the proposed system theoretically offers a good application for distributed data stream mining, which can be further explored upon such data being made available.

References

[1] Jia, Shuangying. (2020). "A VFDT algorithm optimization and application thereof in data stream classification." *J. Phys. Conf. Ser.*, 1629, 012027.

[2] Al-Qurishi, M., Hossain, M. S., Alrubaian, M., Rahman, S. M. M., and Alamri, A. (2018). "Leveraging analysis of user behavior to identify malicious activities in large-scale social networks." *IEEE Trans. Industr. Infor.*, 14(2), 799–813.

[3] Shi, Peining, Zhiyong, Z. & Kim-Kwang Raymond, C. (2019). "Detecting malicious social bots based on clickstream sequences." *IEEE Access*, 7, 28855–28862.

[4] Park, J. Y., O'Hare, N., Schifanella, Jaimes, A., and Chung, C. W. (2015). "A large-scale study of user image search behavior on the web." *Proc. 33rd Annual ACM Conf. Hum. Fact. Comput. Syst. Proc.*, Seoul, Korea.

[5] Fedoryszak, Mateusz, Frederick, Brent, Rajaram, Vijay & Zhong, Changtao. (2019). "Real-time event detection on social data streams." *The 25th ACM SIGKDD International Conference*, Anchorage, AK, USA.

[6] Minegishi, Tatsuya & Niimi, Ayahiko. (2013). "Proposal of credit card fraudulent use detection by online-type decision tree construction and verification of generality." *Int. J. Inf. Secur. Res.*, 3(1), 229–235.

[7] Campos, G. F., Tavares, G. M., Igawa, R. A. & Guido, R. C. (2018). "Detection of human, legitimate bot, and malicious bot in online social networks based on wavelets." *ACM Trans. Multimedia Comput. Commun. Appl.*, 14(1s), 1–27.

[8] Cloudflare. "What is a social media bot? | Social media bot definition." https://www.cloudflare.com/en-in/learning/bots/what-is-a-social-media-bot/ [accessed January 2022].

[9] Global Information Security Survey Ernst & Young Global Limited. https://www.ey.com/en_gl/giss [accessed January 2022].

[10] Hu, H., Chen, Y. & Tang, K. (2009). "A dynamic discretization approach for constructing decision trees with a continuous Label." *IEEE Trans. Knowl. Data Eng.*, 21(11), 1505–1514.

[11] Agrahari, Supriya & Singh, Anil. (2021). "Concept drift detection in data stream mining: A literature review." *J. King Saud Univ. – Comput. Inf. Sci.*, 34(10), Part B, 9523–9540.

[12] Sayed, Doaa, Rady, Sherine & Aref, Mostafa. (2020). "Enhancing clustream algorithm for clustering big data streaming over sliding window." *12th International Conference on Electrical Engineering (ICEENG)*, Cairo, Egypt.

[13] Wang, Gang, Zhang, Xinyi, Tang, Shiliang, Zheng, Haitao & Zhao, Ben. (2016). "Unsupervised clickstream clustering for user behavior analysis." 225–236. doi: 10.1145/2858036.2858107.

Chapter 9

Market Basket Analysis Using Distributed Algorithm

Vinaya Sawant

Dwarkadas J. Sanghvi College of Engineering

Ketan Shah

MPSTME Mumbai, NMIMS University

Neeraj Parolia

Townson University

Contents

DOI: 10.1201/9781003390220-9

9.1 Introduction

The association rule mining (ARM) aims at identifying patterns among the different items bought in a given set of transactions [1]. The patterns are constructed based on the relationship between the data items. An association rule exists in a transaction if buying of one product results in buying another product as well. These association rules play a major role in an application of market basket analysis for shop owners to identify the common buying patterns of the customers so that group of products can be displayed together to earn a profit. The various applications of association rules exist in pattern matching, marketing, inventory management, and shopping malls. The relationship between data items and occurrence of common patterns in the given transaction set represents the association rule. The data nowadays is not centrally located and dispersed across various geographical locations. The idea of ARM can be combined with the concept of distributed systems where the ARM algorithms work on distributed data in a distributed environment. This technique is known as distributed ARM or DARM. Since the data is available at huge amount, data mining algorithms need to be evolved from centralized systems to support increasing levels of data distribution. The rate of data growth is fast, and applying data mining algorithms in a distributed environment is very challenging. Most of the data in organizations are inherently distributed. The organizations perform data mining tasks on homogeneous or heterogeneous distributed databases. The common way is to perform the task locally, and then, the integration of the data is done globally. The distributed environment can be considered as geographically separated data sources. The distributed nature of data available at different locations enforces a challenging issue of effective communication between the nodes using message passing. The communication cost also increases with an increase in the number of nodes due to large amount of data transfer in a distributed environment. It is difficult to rely on the traditional data mining algorithms in a distributed environment to deal with the problems of the distributed environment. The work is to be carried out in the direction where an improvement in the existing algorithms to be done where the data mining aspects can be efficiently handled in a distributed environment.

The data stored at either single or multiple data nodes is given as input to the algorithm. The fragments achieved from data fragmentation are assigned to each node in a distributed environment.

The chapter includes the challenges encountered for DARM. Further, it includes the literature work related to concerned topic. The outcome of literature work is used to formulate the proposed algorithm - transaction reduction using enhanced distributed DARM (TR-EDARM), its working, and experimental results.

9.2 Challenges of DARM

The very commonly used approach for data mining when data is located at different nodes is that data can be moved to a single central location and then data mining task is executed. But here, a huge amount of data is exchanged across all the sites and execution time increases as data mining operation is executed at one single point on a large amount of dataset. A different approach that can be followed is to build the local models at each node by performing data mining task and then moved to a shared location where they are combined. The current research work focuses on second approach that involves local models created at local nodes and global models created after knowledge integration. While considering knowledge integration, an efficient technique to reduce communication costs needs to be focused. The data transfer cost, which is in the estimate of time and number of messages that are transferred from the local sites to a global server, is enormous. The goal is that the volume of the data shipped between the various sites need to be reduced. The data distribution across the nodes is another significant problem in distributed data mining. The major task is to distribute large dataset efficiently across the nodes. There are different ways of fragmentation, but the commonly used technique where data in each dataset is divided into various partitions row-wise is called horizontal fragmentation.

The continuous streamed data, where new incoming data is received at regular intervals, poses a major challenge. Applications such as e-commerce and network traffic analysis are classical example of continuous streamed data. It is difficult for data mining algorithms to consider the new incoming transactions. In conventional approach, algorithm is re-executed on the combined set of transactions. This led to previous results as invalid and overwritten by the new set of rules [2].

Distributed frequent itemsets mining need to be actively researched on the following features:

- Reduction in execution time by reducing the number of database scans to generate frequent k-itemsets
- Reduction in communication cost by exchanging a fewer number of messages in a distributed environment

■ Handling of increasing data in a distributed environment so that the new set of transactions can be combined and processed along with the rules generated from the previous transaction set.

The literature and research work proposes many algorithms for DARM but algorithms can still be improved to increase the performance concerning execution time and communication cost [3,4].

Since the main aim of ARM is to generate both frequent itemsets and association rules, the primary focus of the proposed algorithm presented in this chapter is on generation of frequent itemsets.

When new records are included, the results of original association rules become invalid, and the chances of new implicit valid rules might be identified in updated database. The time taken to execute the algorithm with original database and new database is approximate equal, and hence, if the size of the original database is very large, then most of the execution time is wasted in maintaining the association rules when new set of transactions are added.

The data in various organizations that is dispersed at various geographical locations can be of high frequency or density; data can be static or dynamic. The knowledge and data integration at one common location are challenging to operate. The weakness of existing distributed data mining systems results in a need for more flexible, intelligent, and scalable distributed algorithms. The field of data mining needs to be developed with new approaches and technologies to identify the patterns for the distributed data [5].

The main aim of distributed data mining applications to design in such a way that will reduce the execution time and communication cost. A relationship between the set of products bought together by a customer in a supermarket is one the significant functionality of data mining. They are called as association rules that are generated from a set of frequent itemsets that are found in the transactional database. The insertion of new transactions in original database may result in old association rules may no longer be valid or new association rules may appear because of new transactions. The process of producing new association rules by considering and comparing the previously generated association rules and the new transaction set is called as incremental ARM. Here, the results of the association rules of previous transactions are exploited to generate association rules when new transactions are inserted. In few cases, few of the large itemsets in the previous transaction set may remain large when new transaction set is inserted. That will further lead to duplication of the recomputing the support count of same itemsets again and again as the support count is previously stored in the database. The computation time can be saved in this case [6].

9.3 Literature Work

The literature work includes the work done by the researchers in DARM. An improvement in communication cost in DARM need to be done using agent based

DARM architecture is suggested by Ogunde et al. [7,8]. An overview of all the algorithms in ARM was given by Kotsiantis et al. [9], and due to the generation of a considerable number of frequent itemsets and association rules, the suggestion of parallelization and reduction in the number of database scans were given. An improvement in the Apriori algorithm was suggested by reducing the generation of candidate itemsets in the paper [10]. Though the paper [11] has suggested a data representation similar to FP-tree called as N-list, but most of the researchers had considered Apriori as a base algorithm for DARM.

Hongjun Lu [12] had extended the scope of mining association rules from traditional single-dimensional intra-transaction associations to multidimensional inter-transaction associations. In paper [13], author has suggested that local algorithms are one of the most efficient families of algorithms developed for distributed systems. The paper [14] presented a new DARM algorithm that uses the communication efficiency of the DDM algorithm to parallelize the single-scan sampling algorithm. In paper [14], authors had proposed a novel algorithm that to raise the throughput of resulted data over distributed databases. In their research work, they had proposed a novel algorithm to process a large quantity of data at a variety of servers and collect the processed data on customer machine as much as necessary. The authors in paper [10,15,16] had suggested making use of only join step for candidate itemsets generation instead of join and pruning steps in the traditional approach. The researchers had suggested the use of XML data in DARM algorithms for improving the response time through paper [17]. In paper [11], author had done the comparison between the two most used DARM algorithms, i.e., CDA and FDM. Here, the researchers concluded that the performance of FDM is better than CDA with respect to execution time and communication cost. A suggestion was given in paper [6] that instead of transmitting all itemsets and their counts, they propose to transmit a binary vector and count of only frequently large itemsets. Parallel processing technique is exploited to avoid broadcasting among data sites. The paper [10] had suggested an improvement in CDA algorithm to reduce the generation of candidate itemsets for faster execution time.

In paper [14], researchers make use of L-matrix for improving the efficiency of the Apriori algorithm when implemented on the partitioned dataset, where L-matrix represents an object-by-variable compressed structure to represent the transaction set. The various algorithms used for parallel and distributed data mining are discussed in paper [18] and had suggested the areas of research work in the field of DARM. The incremental mining using closed itemset is described in [19]. The paper [20,21] suggests a parallel version of the incremental mining algorithm. The paper [19] suggests various algorithms that can be used for incremental mining of association rules, their significance, and working of all the algorithms. A novel parallel algorithm for frequent itemset mining for incremental dataset using MPI is suggested in [22].

Most of the literature work concentrated on three DARM algorithms, i.e., count distribution algorithm (CDA), fast data mining (FDM), and optimized distributed mining (ODAM). Though FP-tree is used for ARM in a few research works, the significant concentration was on Apriori algorithm that works efficiently in a distributed environment.

9.4 Proposed Algorithm: Transaction Reduction Using Enhanced Distributed ARM (TR-EDARM)

The aim of this proposed algorithm is lower the required space and increase the execution time of the algorithm using the concept of transaction reduction in a distributed environment. A level-wise search option is used in iterative manner, where (k + 1)-itemsets are explored from k-itemsets. The first pass calculates the support count of 1-itemset and verifies against the support threshold, and then, the frequent 1-itemset is determined if the itemset satisfies the minimum support. The support of an item (or items) is defined as the percentage of transactions in which that item (or items) occurs. L1 is used to represent the resulting set. L2 is determined using frequent 2-itemset. Using L2, L3 is generated until no more frequent k-itemsets can be determined. For determining each Lk, the algorithm requires one full scan of the database. The time complexity increases as the database increases for a greater number of database scans.

The problems faced by the existing algorithms will be addressed in the proposed algorithm. They are as follows:

1. The original transaction set need to be scanned after generation of frequent itemsets at each pass. At each pass, there are also few infrequent itemsets, which will not become frequent in later passes. These are not eliminated in the next passes of the algorithm.
2. A large number of candidate's itemsets could be generated in a significant transaction database if infrequent itemsets are not deleted and the transaction set is not updated for each pass.

The abovementioned problems result in increased transaction scanning time that results in higher processing cost.

The proposed technique is explained with the help of an example. An existing DARM algorithm that uses the principle of Apriori requires k number of database scans to generate a frequent k-itemset. The proposed algorithm had suggested an improvement by eliminating all infrequent 1-itemset after the first pass and generates candidate support counts for later pass efficiently. In TR-EDARM, the remaining passes till the final set of candidate itemsets are generated used this technique by eliminating the infrequent itemsets. Using this technique, the average transaction length as well as database size is reduced significantly. This technique of eliminating the infrequent itemsets from each pass increases the chances of finding similar

Table 9.1 Sample Transactions

Tr. No.	Tr. Count	Items
1	1	Bread, butter, milk
2	1	Butter, milk, maggi
3	1	Bread, butter, jam
4	1	Bread, butter, milk, biscuit
5	1	Bread, milk, jam
6	1	Bread, butter, maggi
7	1	Milk, Jam, biscuit
8	1	Bread, jam
9	1	Butter, milk, biscuit
10	1	Bread, butter, milk, jam

transactions, and these similar transactions are considered a single transaction for database scans of next passes. This will considerably reduce the transaction size. The below example describes TR-EDARM passes.

For a specified minimum support of 0.5, consider the sample dataset in Table 9.1. The candidate itemsets in the first pass = {Bread, Butter, Milk, Jam, Biscuit, Maggi}. The infrequent 1-itemset based on minimum support is Biscuit and Maggi. After eliminating these items, more identical transactions are found, and the results are shown in Table 9.2.

In the second pass, candidate itemsets are {(BREAD, BUTTER), (BREAD, MILK), (BREAD, JAM), (BUTTER, MILK), (BUTTER, JAM), (MILK, JAM)}. Based on the minimum support, the non-frequent itemset is {JAM}. Table 9.3 represents the similar transactions by eliminating JAM.

The candidate itemset is now {(BREAD, BUTTER, MILK)}, which becomes the last iteration of the algorithm. In the above example, the number of transaction scans in the first pass is 10, in the second pass is 8, and in the third pass is 6, making a total of 24 scans. As compared to Apriori, the number of transaction scans get reduced from 30 to 24. Applying the above technique to the real dataset, the significant amount of variation is achieved in transaction size, thus reducing the execution time.

Due to large amount of data available, performing ARM is the challenging assignment. Apriori algorithm is the commonly used approach to find out the frequent itemsets from the large dataset. The generation of large number of candidate itemsets while finding the frequent itemsets from transactions leads to failing of the algorithm in certain situations. The repeated scanning of dataset while

Table 9.2 Transaction Set for Pass 2

Tr. No.	Tr. Count	Items
1,4	2	Bread, butter, milk
2,9	2	Butter, milk
3	1	Bread, butter, jam
5	1	Bread, milk, jam
6	1	Bread, butter
7	1	Milk, jam
8	1	Bread, jam
10	1	Bread, butter, milk, jam

Table 9.3 Transaction Set for Pass 3

Tr. No.	Tr. Count	Items
1,4,10	3	Bread, butter, milk
2,9	2	Butter, milk
3,6	2	Bread, butter
5	1	Bread, milk
7	1	Milk
8	1	Bread

finding frequent itemsets makes the algorithm more inefficient. The inefficiency will increase if it requires more I/O load when the database is accessed frequently.

The above steps can be summarized as proposed algorithm **TR-EDARM** as follows:

INPUT

Horizontal Partitioned Transactional Database located at each site
Min_Support is the threshold value to find Frequent Itemsets
Min_Confidence is the threshold value to find association rules

OUTPUT

Frequent k-Itemsets and Association Rules

STEPS

Step 1: Read the fragmented transaction set generated from the input dataset at each node in a distributed environment.

Step 2: Scan the local transaction set to determine the value of TRANSACTION COUNT (TR_COUNT) in parallel at each node.

Step 3: Determine the candidate 1-itemsets from the local transaction set at each node.

Step 4: Determine the frequent 1-itemsets based on the support count given as an input parameter.

Step 5: Eliminate the non-frequent itemset identified in step 4.

Step 6: The above steps result in similar transactions (transactions containing same itemsets) that can be considered a single transaction while scanning during the next pass.

Step 7: Scan the local transaction set again to determine the new value of TR_COUNT in parallel at each node.

Step 8: Increment the TR_COUNT for those transactions that are similar and can be considered as a single transaction.

Step 9: Load the local data set at each node with a new set of transactions based on the similar transactions identified in the previous step. This set of transactions is called a reduced set of transactions, and it eliminates the scanning of the original transaction at every pass, thereby reducing the transaction set size and thus reducing the execution time.

Step 10: Determine the candidate k-itemsets from the new local transaction set at each node.

Step 11: The local candidate k-itemsets along with the count from all the clients are sent to the server for finding the frequent global k-itemsets

Step 12: Determine the frequent global k-itemsets based on the support count given as input parameter and send it to all the clients to generate candidate k-itemsets for the next pass.

Step 13: Repeat steps 5–12 for k-itemsets and finally generate the frequent k-itemsets after iterating through all the passes at each node in the distributed environment.

Step 14: Generate association rules from frequent k-itemsets and save the result.

It is difficult to apply the algorithm in the single set of the dataset. It is desirable to partition the entire database into smaller partitions that can be tested and mined in a single scan. The horizontal fragmentation technique is used to form the smaller partitions to reduce the number of transaction lengths. During each scan, a set of all potentially large frequent itemsets are generated by scanning the local dataset. These frequent itemset is also a superset of all frequent itemsets in the local partition and might not be frequent when the whole DB was finally considered. The infrequent itemsets are eliminated in the remaining passes, and new transaction set is loaded in the main memory for next database scans.

9.5 Reduction in Communication Cost Using Efficient Communication in TR-EDARM Algorithm

The distributed system aims at reducing the number of messages exchanged between the nodes in a distributed environment that will significantly reduce the communication cost in a distributed environment. The communication overhead arises due to dense datasets or small minimum supports.

The existing distributed ARM algorithms are characterized by many messages that are exchanged during the data mining tasks. One of the significant contributions in this proposed approach is to reduce the number and sizes of messages exchanged in a distributed algorithm. In previous works, the algorithms exchange the messages among all the processes in the distributed network. In the proposed algorithm, the message passing involves optimized many-to-one technique for data exchange in a distributed environment. At each node, the data mining algorithm executes locally on local datasets and then waits for the global server to assemble the global results. Figure 9.1 illustrates the total number of messages exchanged for n number of sites. If there are 10 client nodes in a distributed environment, the total number of messages exchanged will be from (10–1) senders to one receiver. The knowledge integration and global processing are performed at receiver end to generate frequent global itemsets. These frequent global itemsets are then sent to all the senders for generating candidate itemsets for the next pass. The main advantage of this method is that it uses less exchanges of messages between the receiver and senders. Here, receiver is global server, and the senders are the client nodes. Due to this technique, the performance improved with an increasing number of data sites.

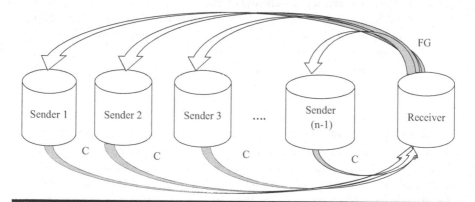

Figure 9.1   Number of data sites involved in message communication.

The aggregation of senders and receiver's messages constitute the total message. Here, n is taken as the number of sites, local frequent itemset is FL, and the global frequent itemsets is FG. |FL| represents the size of local frequent itemsets, and |FG| represents the size of globally frequent itemsets. The knowledge integration involves adding of all message sizes at n-1 data site that gives the total message size.

The message communication cost calculated based on the number of messages that are passed among the local nodes and the global node at each iteration while generating the frequent itemsets. At each local node, the support counts of each itemset generated and all of them are broadcasted to all the remaining sites in the network. The global frequent itemsets for that pass are generated using the support count. Each node has a capacity to broadcast $(n-1 * |C|)$ number of messages. The globally frequent itemsets are sent to all other nodes in the network. Here, the number of messages exchanged will be more as each node sends and receives support counts from all the remaining nodes in the network. Since the global support counts are sent to all connecting nodes in the network, due to large number of candidate itemsets there will be increase in the communication cost. The total number of messages broadcast from the global node to all other nodes is $(n-1)*FG$.

The total message size is defined as below:

$$T = \sum_{i=1}^{n} (n-1)*C + (n-1)*FG$$

where n is the total number of sites, C is number of candidate itemsets, and FG is globally large frequent itemsets.

In TR-EDARM, the use of the locally large frequent itemsets that are sent to the server is considered as communication cost. The calculation of communication cost also involves the concept of local pruning and global pruning in a distributed environment. The reduction in message size can be implemented if each sender sends only frequent local itemsets instead of candidate itemsets to the receiver site. Since using only frequent local itemsets from each sender will not determine the frequent global itemsets, the receiver then communicates with only other senders for the counts of those itemsets that are not locally frequent at their node. The total message size can be calculated using

$$T = \sum_{i=1}^{n} |FL| + (n-1)*|FG|$$

where FL = Locally Large Frequent Itemsets.

At each pass, the globally large frequent itemsets are considered as candidate itemsets for the next pass. From these candidate itemsets, the local frequent itemsets are determined at each node using the support threshold value. At the receiver end in global server, these local frequent itemsets are used to generate global frequent itemsets using knowledge integration. To generate global frequent itemsets, the receiver needs the support count of all the itemsets from all the nodes. The itemsets may be frequent in one node and may not be frequent in another node. The receiver then communicates with only those senders for the support counts of those itemsets that are not locally frequent at their respective nodes.

9.6 Datasets

The datasets from UCI Machine Learning Repository [23] were used for testing the performance of proposed algorithm in a distributed environment. The UCI Repository is the collection of different datasets used for various types of data mining algorithms. The following datasets that are used for testing the results are selected based on the nature of their implementation for ARM algorithms. Full descriptions of the characteristics of these datasets are shown in Tables 9.4–9.7.

9.7 Results and Discussion

9.7.1 Experiment 1: Improvement in Execution Time (Comparative Analysis of TR-EDARM with Three Benchmark Algorithms)

In TR-EDARM algorithm, there is reduction in the number of transaction scan that in turn reduces the execution time. The execution time of existing algorithms, CDA, FDM, and ODAM, is compared with the execution time of the TR-EDARM algorithm. Here, the improvement in the execution time takes place due to the reduction in the number of transaction scans, thus avoiding the rescanning of the original transaction set at every pass of the algorithm.

Result: The experimental setup consists of three different client nodes and a global server connected in a distributed environment. The input of support threshold is varied from 4% to 20% to visualize the result for varying values of the execution time. Figure 9.2 represents the improvement with respect to time taken to execute CDA, FDM, ODAM, and TR-EDARM for four different datasets by varying the support threshold.

9.7.2 Experiment No. 2: Improvement in Communication Cost (Comparative Analysis of CDA, FDM, ODAM, and TR-EDARM Based on Communication Cost)

All the algorithms were executed in a distributed environment to analyze the communication cost involved in passing the messages between the nodes. For various

Table 9.4   Zoo Dataset

Characteristics of Zoo Dataset
1. Number of items: 17
2. Number of records: 101
3. Date donated: 1990-05-15
4. Number of web hits as at when downloaded: 223321
5. Filename: zoo.data
6. Area: Life
7. Relevant Information: A simple database containing 17 Boolean-valued attributes. The "type" attribute appears to be the class attribute. Here is a breakdown of which animals are in which type
8. Attribute Information: (name of attribute and type of value domain) • animal name: Unique for each instance • hair   Boolean • feathers   Boolean • eggs   Boolean • milk   Boolean • airborne   Boolean • aquatic   Boolean • predator   Boolean • toothed   Boolean • backbone   Boolean • breathes   Boolean • venomous   Boolean • fins   Boolean • legs   Numeric (set of values: {0,2,4,5,6,8}) • tail   Boolean • domestic   Boolean • catsize   Boolean • type   Numeric (integer values in range [1,7])

levels of support threshold, the number of bytes transferred were examined. As expected, when there is decrease in the minimum support threshold, the number of candidate itemsets that is generated will increase. This will further increase the total number of bytes that need to be transferred across the nodes, since the algorithms exchanges the support count of candidate itemsets and also of frequent itemsets. From this, it is also concluded that the number of messages exchanged and in turn the communication cost is increased if the greater number of nodes are connected in a distributed environment. In this case, the increasing factor is not linear. The

Table 9.5   Tic-Tac-Toe Dataset

Characteristics of Tic-Tac-Toe Dataset
1. Number of items:9
2. Number of records:958
3. Date donated:1991-08-19
4. Number of web hits as at when downloaded:173995
5. Filename: tic-tac-toe.data
6. Area: Game
7. Relevant Information: This database encodes the complete set of possible board configurations at the end of tic-tac-toe games, where "x" is assumed to have played first. The target concept is "win for x" (i.e., true when "x" has one of eight possible ways to create a "three-in-a-row").
8. Attribute Information: (name of attribute and type of value domain) • top-left-square: {x,o,b} • top-middle-square: {x,o,b} • top-right-square: {x,o,b} • middle-left-square: {x,o,b} • middle-middle-square: {x,o,b} • middle-right-square: {x,o,b} • bottom-left-square: {x,o,b} • bottom-middle-square: {x,o,b} • bottom-right-square: {x,o,b} • Class: {positive, negative}

data skewness increases if a greater number of nodes are involved and the number of candidates itemset generation is also increased.

Result: The following graphs (Figures 9.3 and 9.4) represent the comparison of two different algorithms with respect to communication cost for TTT and Zoo dataset. The results were compared with all the three benchmark algorithms and TR-EDARM. Figure 9.5 shows the result of DS dataset where the communication cost was measured with support threshold varying from 40% to 80% and minimum confidence of 70%. Figure 9.6 shows the result of Grocery dataset where the communication cost was measured with support threshold varying from 40% to 80% and minimum confidence of 70%. Since the size of all the datasets is different, the value of support threshold and confidence is different. Also, for each dataset, varying values of support threshold is considered to visualize the communication cost effectively.

The resulting analysis shows that there is a reduction of 10%– 40% in the communication cost of TR-EDARM as compared to other algorithms. The performance of the algorithms was tested to measure the communication cost of the

Table 9.6   Grocery Dataset

Characteristics of Grocery Dataset
1. Number of items: 60
2. Number of records: 300000
3. Date donated: NA
4. Source Site: http://www.salemmarafi.com/wp-content/uploads/2014/03/ groceries.csv
5. Filename: groceries.csv
6. Area: Computer
7. Relevant Information: A collection of receipts with each line representing 1 receipt and the items purchased. Each line is called a transaction, and each column in a row represents an item.
8. Attribute Information: (name of attribute and type of value domain)
9. The dataset contains transactions made by customers, and each transaction hold records of item(s).

Table 9.7   DS (1,000×8) Dataset

Characteristics of DS (10,000×8) Dataset
1. Number of items: 8
2. Number of records: 10000
3. Source Site: **http://www2.cs.uregina.ca/~dbd/cs831/notes/itemsets/ datasets/original/**
4. Filename: transa.txt
5. Area: Computer
6. Relevant Information: A collection of Boolean values
7. Attribute Information: (name of attribute and type of value domain)
8. dNA

proposed algorithm for the four different datasets. The result shows that all the algorithms exchange a few messages except TR-EDARM algorithm. It is also observed that for all the algorithms, there is considerable improvement in the size of the messages exchanged when the percentage of the minimum threshold is gradually increased. TR-EDARM algorithm performs much better when the threshold value is high, but the performance degrades as threshold value goes on decreasing.

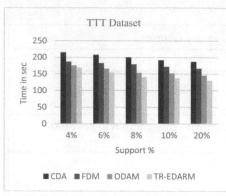
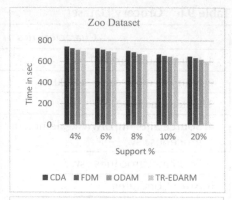
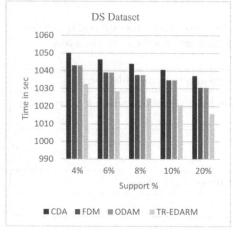
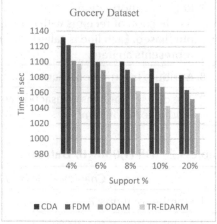

Figure 9.2   TR-EDARM against three benchmark algorithms.

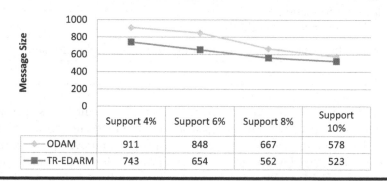

	Support 4%	Support 6%	Support 8%	Support 10%
ODAM	911	848	667	578
TR-EDARM	743	654	562	523

Figure 9.3   Total message size (bytes) for TTT dataset.

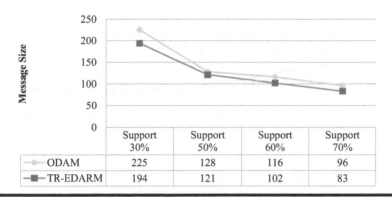

	Support 30%	Support 50%	Support 60%	Support 70%
ODAM	225	128	116	96
TR-EDARM	194	121	102	83

Figure 9.4   Total message size (bytes) for Zoo dataset.

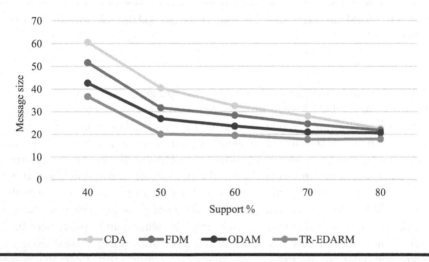

Figure 9.5   Total message size for four different DARM algorithms (DS Dataset).

The number of messages exchange are more for lower values of threshold. From this result, the performance of all the four algorithms improved with the size of messages exchanged with an increase in the minimum support threshold. TR-EDARM has the best performance even at 70% support threshold with a smaller number of messages exchanged. The size of the messages exchanged by TR-EDARM reduces with increase in support threshold.

9.8 Conclusion

The research work identifies the limitations of the DARM algorithm and analyzes it to find the scope of improvements. The algorithms can be improved by reducing the

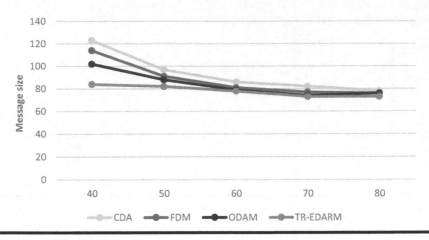

Figure 9.6 Total message size for four different DARM algorithms (Grocery Dataset).

execution time and reducing the number of messages exchanged between the nodes. The performance of DARM algorithms is measured using two parameters, execution time required to execute the algorithm using local and global processing and based on a communication cost in a distributed environment to determine the number of messages exchanged between the nodes. TR-EDARM algorithm is proposed to improve the execution time by reducing the number of transaction scans at each local node, thereby reducing the total execution time to run the entire algorithm. TR-EDARM also focused on reducing the number of messages exchanged between the nodes in a distributed environment, thereby presenting an improvement in the communication cost. The performance of the algorithms was evaluated using four different size datasets, and the improvements concerning various parameters were observed.

The outcome of the research work can be summarized as follows:

- Proposed and implemented TR-EDARM algorithm that showed improvement in execution time up to 20% as compared to existing DARM algorithms.
- Improvement in TR-EDARM algorithm to reduce the message communication cost to 10%– 40% due to the transfer of locally large itemsets across the nodes in a distributed environment.

References

[1] Agrawal, R., Imieliński, T., & Swami, A. (1993). Mining association rules between sets of items in large databases. *Proceeding of SIGMOD '93 Proceedings of the 1993*

ACM SIGMOD International Conference on Management of Data, Washington DC, 25-28 May 1993, 22(2) of SIGMOD Records, 207–216.

[2] Aouad, L. M., Le-Khac, N.-A., & Kechadi, T. M. (2009). Performance Study of Distributed Apriori-Like Frequent Itemsets Mining. *Knowledge and Information Systems*, 23, 55–72.

[3] Jiawei Han, J. P. (2011). *Data Mining: Concepts and Techniques*, 3rd edition. Elsevier, USA.

[4] Chung, S. M. & Luo, C. (2004). Distributed mining of maximal frequent itemsets from databases on a cluster of workstations. *CCGRID '04: Proceedings of the 2004 IEEE International Symposium on Cluster Computing and the Grid*, Chicago, IL, US, 499–507.

[5] Congnan, L. & Chung. S. M. (2008). A scalable algorithm for mining maximal frequent sequences using a sample. *Knowledge and Information Systems*, 15(2), 149–179.

[6] Singh, M. K. (2006). Challenges and research issues in association rule mining. *International Journal of Electronics and Computer Science Engineering (IJECSE)*, 1(2), 767–774.

[7] Agrawal, R. & Shafer, J. C. (1996). Parallel mining of association rules. *IEEE TransKnowledge Data Engineering*, 8(6), 962–969.

[8] Ogunde, A. O. (2011). A review of some issues and challenges in current agent based distributed association rule mining. *Asian Journal of Information Technology*, 10(2), 84–95.

[9] Kotsiantis, S., & Kanellopoulos, D. (2006). Association rules mining: A recent overview. *GESTS International Transactions on Computer Science and Engineering*, 32(1), 71–82.

[10] Jaishree Singh, H. R. (2013). Improving efficiency of apriori algorithm using transaction reduction. *International Journal of Scientific and Research Publications*, 3(1), 1–4.

[11] Kaosar, M. D., Xu, Z., & Yi, X. (2009). Distributed association rule mining with minimum communication overhead. *Proceedings of the 8th Australasian Data Mining Conference (AusDM'09), School of Engineering and Science*. Victoria University, Victoria, Australia.

[12] Lu, H., Feng, L., & Han, J. (2000). Beyond intra-transaction association analysis: Mining multidimensional inter-transaction association rules. *ACM Transactions on Information Systems*, 18(4), 423–454.

[13] Nguyen, S. N. & Orlowska, M. E. (2005). Improvements in the data partitioning approach for frequent itemsets mining. *Proceedings of the 9th European Conference on Principles and Practice of Knowledge Discovery in Databases (PKDD 05)*, Lecture Notes in Computer Science, vol. 3721. Springer, Berlin, Heidelberg 625–633.

[14] Toivonen, H. (1996). Sampling large databases for association rules. *VLDB '96: Proceedings of the 22nd international conference on very large data bases*, Proceedings of the 22nd VLDB Conference Mumbai (Bombay), India.

[15] Abaya, S. A. (2012). Association rule mining based on apriori algorithm in minimizing candidate generation. *International Journal of Scientific & Engineering Research*, 3(7). ISSN 2229-5518.

[16] Vijayalakshmi, V., & Pethalakshmi, A. (2014). A performance based transaction reduction algorithm for discovering frequent patterns. *International Journal of Computer Applications*, 98(4).

[17] Paul, D. (2010). An optimized distributed association rule mining algorithm in parallel and distributed data mining with xml data for improved response time. *International Journal of Computer Science and Information Technology*, 2(2), 88–101.

[18] Karima, H. T. & Lilia, H. T. (2012). Distributed data mining by associated rules: Improvement of the count distribution algorithm. *International Journal of Computer Science Issues*, 9(3).

[19] Sreedevi, M. & Vijay Kumar, G. (2014). Parallel and distributed approach for incremental closed regular pattern mining. *IEEE Explore*.

[20] Chandraker, T. (2012). Incremental mining on association rules. *Research Inventy: International Journal of Engineering and Science*, 1(11), 31–33. ISBN: 2319-6483, ISSN: 2278-4721.

[21] Gharib, T. F., Nassar, H., Taha, M., & Abrahamd, A. (2010). An efficient algorithm for incremental mining of temporal association rules. *Data & Knowledge Engineering*, 69, 800–815.

[22] Assaf Schuster, R. W. (2005). A high-performance distributed algorithm for mining association rules. *Knowledge and Information Systems*, 7, 458–475.

[23] Bache, K. &. (2013). *UCI Machine Learning Repository*. Retrieved from Irvine, CA: University of California, School of Information and Computer Science. http://archive. ics.uci.edu/.

Chapter 10

Identification of Crime-Prone Areas Using Data Mining Techniques

Jainam Rambhia, Bhoomika Valani, Shivam Vora, Chaitanya Kumbar, and Neha Katre

Dwarkadas J. Sanghvi College of Engineering

Contents

DOI: 10.1201/9781003390220-10

10.1 Introduction

Crimes are a significant threat to humanity; numerous crimes occur at regular intervals, and they may be increasing and spreading at an alarming rate. The type of crime can be predicted that will occur in each area using data mining techniques. This work will assist law enforcement agencies in better anticipating and detecting crimes and help them in lowering crime rates. It will also aid people traveling to various locations in understanding the safety and precautions in that area.

The traditional method for analyzing and predicting a given area's crime rate is to look at all the First Information Reports (FIRs) that have been filed in that area. This procedure requires a significant amount of effort and time; even a minor blunder can result in an incorrect outcome. To overcome this problem faced by the police department, the proposed system will help the police department to analyze and predict the crime rate of a particular area using various data mining techniques. The main goal of this research is to predict crimes in a specific location before they occur to increase safety in that area, which will make work easier, reduce time spent on the above, and provide more useful data to the public.

The sections ahead are laid out as follows: In Section 10.2, the related work, previously proposed systems, and methodologies have been discussed. Then, in Section 10.3, the system architecture and work have been explained. It includes details about the dataset and the data pre-processing. Section 10.4 deals with the experimental results, i.e., the model selection and training, brief comparison, and analysis of results. Section 10.5 deals with predicting and visualizing the hotspots of crime-prone areas. Finally, Section 10.6 is the chapter's conclusion.

10.2 Related Work

Data mining is a technique that we use to analyze the trends and patterns in the data obtained. A search engine like Chrome receives millions of queries each day. These queries are nothing but bits of information provided by the users according to his/her needs. These small bits of information may not look useful to the users, but these can be used by the search engine to study the common patterns in these queries and extract the knowledge that cannot be obtained by reading these queries individually. For example, Google's COVID-19 trends use specific search terms as indicators of COVID-19 activities. It found a close relationship between the number of people who search for COVID-related information and the number of people who have COVID. A pattern emerges when all these queries are aggregated. Using this data, these trends can estimate COVID-related activities faster than traditional systems. This example shows how data mining can turn a large collection of data into valuable information that can help meet a current global challenge. One such global issue is the criminal activities that take place frequently. As a result, several researchers have published their research in this area. Studies have been conducted to examine the relationship between criminal activity and various socioeconomic characteristics such as unemployment, income level, and so on.

A researcher like Dr. Pradeep [1] has implemented a system for predicting the likelihood of a crime occurring in a city by analyzing the crime dataset. This research is achieved by using the naive Bayes classifier is used to get the probability of crimes. The model predicts the type of crime, while data visualization aids in data analysis and crime prediction. Puninder et al. [2] focus on the several types of algorithms that can be used to estimate India's crime rate. In this research, complex tools and technologies are elaborated for accurate, efficient, and fast responses.

Shivani et al. [3] propose a mapping- and visualization-based crime prediction tool built-in R with Google maps, googleris, and other R packages. The proposed system employs a variety of visualization approaches to depict crime trends and several methods for predicting crimes using machine learning algorithms. Krishnendu et al. [4] have chosen the elbow method to find the k-value and implement optimized K-means clustering for developing a crime analysis tool that produces an efficient output that improves the accuracy of the final cluster while minimizing the number of iterations. Sunil et al. [5] have implemented the four algorithms i.e. Association Mining (Apriori), clustering (K-means), classification techniques (naive Bayes), and correlation and regression which were executed on the crime dataset with the help of the Weka Tool and R Tool, and the results were visualized graphically for all algorithms. Pratibha et al. [6] have analyzed predicted crimes with the help of various approaches; some of which are K-nearest neighbors (KNN), artificial neural network (ANN), decision trees, extra trees, and support vector machines (SVM). From the results obtained, they compared the training time of the algorithms. Saravanakumar et al. [7] have claimed that Geometric Information System (GIS) is a far more compatible method than current methods. Crime-specific maps of each zone are created to indicate hotspots, crime types, and related information that is not only valuable for police but also vital for the public. Prajakta et al. [8] have compared various techniques like decision tree, random forest, naïve Bayes, and linear model for training their model and have found Random Forest classifier to give more balanced results as compared with other techniques. They have used cross-validation to reduce overfitting and improve the performance of the model. Kim et al. [9] have used KNN and boosted decision tree on Vancouver crime data for analysis and prediction. Their prediction accuracy was between 39% and 44%. Akash et al. [13] have also applied the KNN algorithm for making their predictions. Olta [14] has implemented ANN, naïve Bayes classifier, SVM, and decision tree, of which decision tree gave the highest accuracy of 76%.

Based on the review above, one can see that several data mining techniques have achieved high accuracy in detecting crimes. However, the factors taken into consideration by many previously presented models were limited. Based on these inferences, the proposed approach for the identification of crime-prone areas has taken into account a varied set of attributes primarily affecting the occurrence of crimes. These attributes have been trained and evaluated on various classification and clustering models to give better accuracy.

10.3 Architecture and Working

Predictive modeling is used to predict the type of crime in a particular area based on the given input location and timestamp to identify the type of crime and the prime hotspots of crime. The data is pre-processed to remove null values and cleaned, transformed, integrated, and visualized for better analytical purposes. The crime hotspot predictions are further analyzed using heat maps for a better understanding of the results. The dataset has been tested on various machine learning models like KNN, SVM, K-means clustering, and random forest, out of which the KNN model proves to be the best-fit approach and the proposed system (Figure 10.1).

10.3.1 Data Collection

Data collection is a process of collecting data, i.e., the dataset that must be trained and tested for the identification of crime-prone areas. The dataset is acquired from

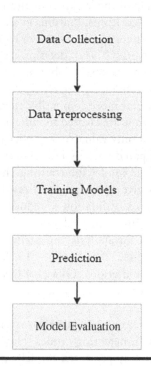

Figure 10.1 Architecture describes the step-by-step process for developing the proposed model.

the crime open-source data of Indore city [11] having 2,090 records and 8 columns. There are different attributes of the dataset. The attributes that are used are:

- **year:** The year in which the crime occurred
- **month:** The month in which the crime occurred
- **day:** The day on which the crime occurred
- **hour:** The hour in which the crime occurred
- **dayofyear:** The day of the year in which the crime occurred
- **week:** The week in which the crime occurred
- **weekofyear:** The week of the year in which the crime occurred
- **dayofweek:** The day of the week in which the crime occurred
- **weekday:** The weekday in which the crime occurred
- **quarter:** The quarter in which the crime occurred
- **act379:** Robbery (Criminal Act)
- **act13:** Gambling (Criminal Act)
- **act279:** Accident (Criminal Act)
- **act323:** Violence (Criminal Act)
- **act363:** Kidnapping (Criminal Act)
- **act302:** Murder (Criminal Act)
- **latitude:** The latitude of the crime location
- **longitude:** The longitude of the crime location

10.3.2 Pre-Processing

Data pre-processing is the process of transforming raw data into useful and efficient data. Initially, the timestamp in the dataset is converted into a standard date–time format and then individual features are extracted from the timestamp. The missing values were filled by the mode of the group by masking to meet the specific conditions belonging to one activity. The correlation matrix is used to select only definite features of timestamps along with the latitude and longitude for predicting a crime. The data is then split into training and testing data, and features were picked for predicting the crime based on the location.

Figures 10.2 and 10.3 show the original data and pre-processed data. Data were pre-processed to fill the empty cells, delete unnecessary data, and add several features.

10.3.3 Model Training and Evaluation Metrics

The dataset is split into train and test data; X_train, X_test comprises the timestamp, latitude, and longitude, and the Y_train, Y_test comprises the type of the crime which is the target value for prediction. Here, basically, four models as mentioned in the methodology were used for training purposes.

	timestamp	act379	act13	act279	act323	act363	act302	latitude	longitude
0	28-02-2018 21:00	1	0	0	0	0	0	22.737260	75.875987
1	28-02-2018 21:15	1	0	0	0	0	0	22.720992	75.876083
2	28-02-2018 10:15	0	0	1	0	0	0	22.736676	75.883168
3	28-02-2018 10:15	0	0	1	0	0	0	22.746527	75.887139
4	28-02-2018 10:30	0	0	1	0	0	0	22.769531	75.888772
...	...	...	...	...	...	...	...	...	...
2085	7/3/2018 3:50	0	0	0	1	0	0	22.712970	75.823580
2086	7/3/2018 21:10	0	0	0	1	0	0	22.693481	75.821483
2087	7/3/2018 12:10	0	0	1	0	0	0	22.531931	75.769126
2088	7/3/2018 10:35	0	0	1	0	0	0	22.719569	75.857726
2089	7/3/2018 23:45	0	0	1	0	0	0	22.686437	76.032055

2090 rows × 9 columns

Figure 10.2   Dataset before pre-processing.

	year	month	day	hour	dayofyear	week	weekofyear	dayofweek	weekday	quarter	act379	act13
0	2018.0	2.0	28.0	21.0	59.0	9.0	9.0	2.0	2.0	1.0	1	0
1	2018.0	2.0	28.0	21.0	59.0	9.0	9.0	2.0	2.0	1.0	1	0
2	2018.0	2.0	28.0	10.0	59.0	9.0	9.0	2.0	2.0	1.0	0	0
3	2018.0	2.0	28.0	10.0	59.0	9.0	9.0	2.0	2.0	1.0	0	0
4	2018.0	2.0	28.0	10.0	59.0	9.0	9.0	2.0	2.0	1.0	0	0
...	...	...	...	...	...	...	...	...	...	...	...	...
2085	2018.0	7.0	3.0	3.0	184.0	27.0	27.0	1.0	1.0	3.0	0	0
2086	2018.0	7.0	3.0	21.0	184.0	27.0	27.0	1.0	1.0	3.0	0	0
2087	2018.0	7.0	3.0	12.0	184.0	27.0	27.0	1.0	1.0	3.0	0	0
2088	2018.0	7.0	3.0	10.0	184.0	27.0	27.0	1.0	1.0	3.0	0	0
2089	2018.0	7.0	3.0	23.0	184.0	27.0	27.0	1.0	1.0	3.0	0	0

2090 rows × 18 columns

Figure 10.3   Dataset after pre-processing.

Cross-Validation Score: Each record is used the same number of times for training and exactly once for testing. To rule out the possibility of overfitting, the method of 10-fold cross-validation is used. The performance metrics used are as follows:

1. **Accuracy**: It is the percentage of test tuples that are correctly classified.

$$\text{Accuracy} = \frac{tp + tn}{tp + tn + fp + fn}$$

2. **Precision and recall:** They are given by

$$\text{Precision} = \frac{tp}{tp + fp} \quad \text{Recall} = \frac{tp}{tp + fn}$$

3. **F1 score:** It is the harmonic mean of precision and recall

10.4 Experimental Results

10.4.1 K-Nearest Neighbor

It's used to identify the correlation between the test and training sets [6]. If the given test set is like the train set, it is given the training set class label. A major limitation emerges when the training set contains fewer data points. This method belongs to the supervised learning category. It's used in data mining, intrusion detection, and pattern recognition. In this, the result is a membership in a class. To categorize an object, a neighbor's mass votes are used with the object being assigned to the most familiar of its KNN.

10.4.1.1 Implementing PCA with the KNN Classifier Model

Principal component analysis (PCA) is a technique for reducing the dimensionality of datasets, increasing interpretability but at the same time minimizing information loss. It does so by creating new uncorrelated variables that successively maximize variance.

The purpose of the pipeline is to assemble several steps that can be cross-validated together while setting different parameters. GridSearchCV is a hyperparameter-tuning function imported from the scikit-learn library which selects the optimum parameters based on the parameters mentioned. This model has specified parameters for several components in PCA; GridSearchCV selects the best hyperparameter based on the default scoring metric accuracy and decides the optimal k-folds of data required to get the best accuracy (Figure 10.4).

The features extracted according to the feature importance scores were:

- **year:** The year in which the crime occurred
- **month:** The month in which the crime occurred
- **day:** The day on which the crime occurred
- **hour:** The hour in which the crime occurred
- **dayofyear:** The day of the year in which the crime occurred
- **week:** The week in which the crime occurred
- **weekofyear:** The week of the year in which the crime occurred

```
            precision    recall  f1-score   support

     1        1.00        1.00      1.00         86
     2        0.82        0.74      0.78         19
     3        0.93        0.98      0.95        147
     4        0.96        0.96      0.96        140
     5        1.00        0.68      0.81         19
     6        1.00        1.00      1.00          3

accuracy                           0.95        414
macro avg     0.95        0.89      0.92        414
weighted avg  0.95        0.95      0.95        414
```

Figure 10.4   Classification report of KNN model.

- **dayofweek:** The day of the week in which the crime occurred
- **weekday:** The weekday in which the crime occurred
- **quarter:** The quarter in which the crime occurred
- **act379:** Robbery (Criminal Act)
- **act13:** Gambling (Criminal Act)
- **act279:** Accident (Criminal Act)
- **act323:** Violence (Criminal Act)
- **act363:** Kidnapping (Criminal Act)
- **act302:** Murder (Criminal Act)
- **latitude:** The latitude of the crime location
- **longitude:** The longitude of the crime location

10.4.2 Support Vector Machine

An SVM performs well for regression, time prediction series, and classification problems [6]. The performance of an SVM can be compared to that of a recurrent neural network. It can make a coherent prototype of nonlinear relations. It is effective at anticipating time series.

The model gave better accuracy when the features were scaled using the StandardScaler method in scikit-learn which standardizes features by removing the mean and scaling to unit variance.

The standard score z of sample x is calculated as:

$$z = \frac{(x - u)}{S}$$

where u is the mean of the training samples and S is the standard deviation of the training samples.

	precision	recall	f1-score	support
0	0.84	1.00	0.91	336
1	1.00	0.21	0.34	82
accuracy			0.84	418
macro avg	0.92	0.60	0.63	418
weighted avg	0.87	0.84	0.80	418

Figure 10.5   Classification report of SVM model.

After transforming the features using the StandardScaler method, the support vector classifier model is used to classify whether the crime occurring is robbery (1) or not (0) (Figure 10.5).

The features extracted according to the feature importance scores were:

- **year:** The year in which the crime occurred
- **month:** The month in which the crime occurred
- **day:** The day on which the crime occurred
- **hour:** The hour in which the crime occurred
- **dayofyear:** The day of the year in which the crime occurred
- **week:** The week in which the crime occurred
- **weekofyear:** The week of the year in which the crime occurred
- **dayofweek:** The day of the week in which the crime occurred
- **weekday:** The weekday in which the crime occurred
- **quarter:** The quarter in which the crime occurred
- **act379:** Robbery (Criminal Act)
- **act13:** Gambling (Criminal Act)
- **act279:** Accident (Criminal Act)
- **act323:** Violence (Criminal Act)
- **act363:** Kidnapping (Criminal Act)
- **act302:** Murder (Criminal Act)
- **latitude:** The latitude of the crime location
- **longitude:** The longitude of the crime location

10.4.3 K-Means Clustering

The K-means clustering algorithm calculates centroids and then repeats the process until the best centroid is discovered [12]. The number of clusters is presumed to be known. The letter 'K' in K-means stands for the number of clusters discovered by the method from data. Using this method, data points are assigned to clusters so that the sum of their squared distances from the centroid is as small as possible (Figure 10.6).

	precision	recall	f1-score	support
0	0.81	0.70	0.75	1672
1	0.19	0.31	0.24	396
accuracy			0.62	2068
macro avg	0.50	0.50	0.49	2068
weighted avg	0.69	0.62	0.65	2068

Figure 10.6 Classification report of K-means clustering model.

	precision	recall	f1-score	support
0	0.81	1.00	0.89	328
1	1.00	0.08	0.15	86
accuracy			0.81	414
macro avg	0.90	0.54	0.52	414
weighted avg	0.85	0.81	0.74	414

Figure 10.7 Classification report of random forest model.

The features extracted according to the feature importance scores were:

- **hour:** The hour in which the crime occurred
- **latitude:** The latitude of the crime location
- **longitude:** The longitude of the crime location

10.4.4 Random Forest

Random forest is a supervised machine learning algorithm that is commonly used to solve classification and regression problems [10]. It uses the majority vote for classification and the average for regression to create decision trees from various samples. The random forest algorithm can handle datasets with both continuous and categorical variables, as in regression and classification. It produces better results for classification problems.

The random forest classifier model makes use of a tree having a maximum depth of level 4 and random state 20 and classifies the location for the criminal activity of robbery. The impurity measure used for constructing trees was the Gini index. Gini index, also known as Gini impurity, calculates the amount of probability of a specific feature that is classified incorrectly when selected randomly. It is another parameter for calculating information gain in decision trees other than entropy (Figure 10.7).

The features extracted according to the feature importance scores were:

- **hour:** The hour in which the crime occurred

- **latitude:** The latitude of the crime location
- **longitude:** The longitude of the crime location

Table 10.1 shows the comparison of the models that have been implemented and evaluated based on the performance metrics selected. KNN had the highest F1 score of 95% as compared to the other trained models.

10.5 Data Analysis & Visualization

The process of getting useful insights from the data is known as data analysis. The act of analyzing data using its graphical representation is known as data visualization.

Figures 10.8 and 10.9 represent the data visualization using kernel distribution estimation plot and bar graph respectively.

Table 10.1 Performance of Various Models during Training

Model	F1 Score (%)	Technique Used
KNN	95	Classification
SVM	84	Classification
Random forest	81	Classification
K-means clustering	62	Clustering

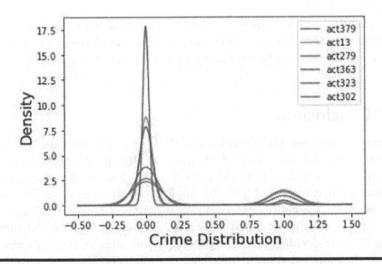

Figure 10.8   Comparison of the relative distribution of different criminal acts.

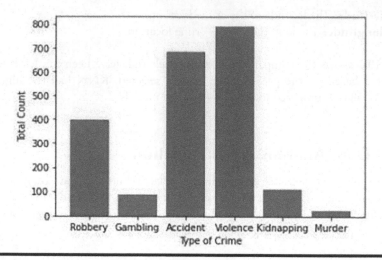

Figure 10.9 Comparison of different crime frequencies using bar charts.

10.5.1 Identification of Crime Hotspots

The predicted data is visualized using heat maps to identify the hotspots for all crimes or any crime. It is a measure of how dangerous a particular area is to devise necessary measures to curb criminal activities.

Figure 10.10 depicts all the crimes committed in the given location taking the latitude and longitude values as input.

The hotspots where robberies have been predominant in the city have been visualized in Figure 10.11.

Figures 10.12 and 10.13 show the heat maps for the identification of areas where robberies have taken place. The observed data comprises 86 rows and the predicted data successfully classifies 80 rows using the K-means clustering model.

10.6 Conclusion

This chapter proposed the identification of crime-prone areas using data mining techniques. The traditional method for analyzing and predicting a given area's crime rate is to look at all the FIRs that have been filed in that area which is tedious and necessitates a significant amount of effort and time. The proposed system will help the police department to analyze and predict the future occurrence of a type of crime in a particular area based on its location and time, thus helping them in devising necessary preventive measures to overcome this problem. For the proposed system, three classification algorithms—K-nearest neighbor, random forest, and SVM—and a clustering algorithm, K-means, were trained

Figure 10.10   Hotspots of all crimes combined.

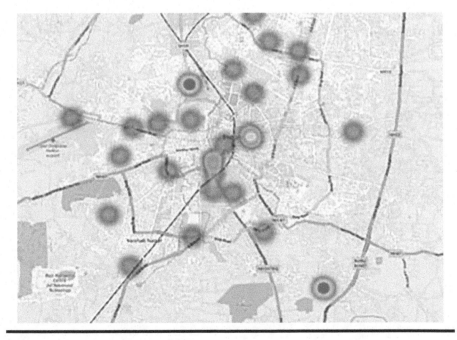

Figure 10.11   Hotspots of robbery.

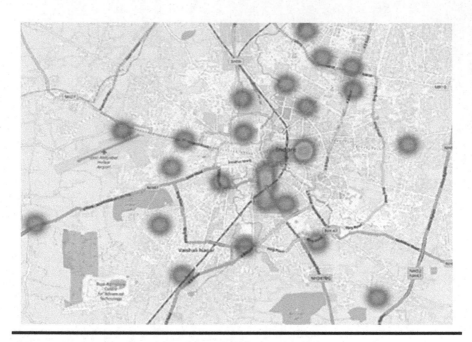

Figure 10.12   Hotspots of test data of robbery.

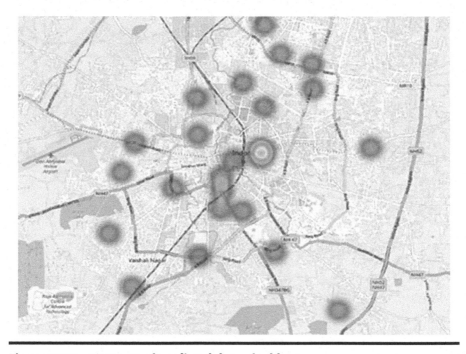

Figure 10.13   Hotspots of predicted data of robbery.

and evaluated for their performance concerning the accuracy, precision, recall, and f-1 score metrics. Of these, KNN gave the best accuracy of 93% among all the other models. Furthermore, the accuracy was improved to 95% with the use of the hyperparameter-tuning function GridSearchCV. It was applied to the model which contributed toward dimensionality reduction and cross-validation which in turn helped to overcome the problem of overfitting. Another advantage of using KNN over others is that it makes use of a multioutput classifier which can be used when there are more than two classification labels. While random forest took multiple trees into account and gave an accuracy of 81%, the tree was, however, built on a limited number of features which accounted for lesser accuracy comparatively. SVM gave an accuracy of 84% as it didn't seem to classify all the data points accurately into the target hyperplane considering all the features. K-means makes use of a distance-based similarity measure and hence doesn't work with a larger number of dimensions leading to a significant reduction in the attributes considered for crime prediction accounting for the least accuracy. Hence, KNN proved to be the best-fit model. Later, the predicted data were visualized using heat maps to identify the crime-prone areas.

References

1. Pradeep BS, "Crime rate analysis and prediction based on locality using machine learning", *Science, Technology and Development*, 316–321, 2021.
2. Puninder K, Geeta R, and Taruna S, "A comparative study to analyze crime threats using data mining and machine learning approach", *2021 International Conference on System, Computation, Automation, and Networking (ICSCAN)*, Puducherry, India, 2021. ISBN 978-1-6654-3986-2.
3. Shivani B and Rushabh D, "Automatic clustering crime region prediction model using statistical method in data mining", *International Journal of Engineering Research & Technology (IJERT)*, 9(04), 697–703, 2020.
4. Krishnendu SG, Lakshmi P, and Nitha L, "Crime analysis and prediction using optimized K-means algorithm", *Fourth International Conference on Computing Methodologies and Communication (ICCMC 2020)*, IEEE Xplore, Erode, India, 2020, Part Number: CFP20K25-ART; ISBN:978-1-7281-4889-2.
5. Sunil Y, Meet T, Ajit Y, Rohit V, and Nikhilesh Y, "Crime pattern detection, analysis & prediction", *International Conference on Electronics, Communication and Aerospace Technology, ICECA*, Coimbatore, India, 2017.
6. Pratibha A, Gahalot, Uprant, Dhiman S, and Chouhan L, "Crime prediction and analysis", *2nd International Conference on Data, Engineering and Applications (IDEA)*, 1–6, 2020. DOI: 10.1109/IDEA49133.2020.9170731.
7. Saravanakumar S and Revathy S, "Crime mapping analysis: A GIS implementation in Madurai city", *International Journal of Science and Research (IJSR)*, 5(3), 2319–7064. ISSN (Online).
8. Dataset.github.com. https://github.com/vikram-bhati/PAASBAAN-crime-prediction/blob/master/data.csv (accessed January 3, 2022).

9. Sharma P, "Understanding K-means clustering in machine learning". analyticsvidhya. com. https://www.analyticsvidhya.com/blog/2021/11/understanding-k-means-clustering-in-machine-learningwith-examples (accessed January 23, 2022).
10. Sruthi ER. "Understanding random forest". analyticsvidhya.com. https://www. analyticsvidhya.com/blog/2021/06/understanding-random-forest/ (accessed January 23, 2022).
11. Prajakta Y., Vaishnavi G., "Predictive modelling of crime dataset using data mining", *International Journal of Data Mining & Knowledge Management Process (IJDKP)*, 7(4), 385–388, 2017.
12. Kim S, Joshi P, Kalsi PS, and Taheri P "Crime analysis through machine learning," *2018 IEEE 9th Annual Information Technology, Electronics and Mobile Communication Conference (IEMCON)*, 415–420, 2018, DOI: 10.1109/IEMCON.2018.8614828.
13. Kumar A, Verma A, Shinde G, Sukhdeve Y, and Lal N "Crime prediction using K-nearest neighboring algorithm," *2020 International Conference on Emerging Trends in Information Technology and Engineering (ic-ETITE)*, 1–4, 2020, DOI: 10.1109/ic-ETITE47903.2020.155.
14. Llaha O "Crime analysis and prediction using machine learning, " *2020 43rd International Convention on Information, Communication and Electronic Technology (MIPRO)*, 496–501, 2020. DOI: 10.23919/MIPRO48935.2020.9245120.

Chapter 11

Smart Baby Cradle for Infant Soothing and Monitoring

Sahil Lunawat, Aditya Adhduk, Vinaya Sawant, and Ritik Sanghvi

Dwarkadas J. Sanghvi College of Engineering

Contents

DOI: 10.1201/9781003390220-11

11.1 Introduction

Lately, many parents are unable to commit sufficient time to their babies due to their work, travel or household chores. Due to this, the need for a smart cradle is constantly rising. A smart cradle is needed that can monitor and ensure the well-being in the absence of the parents.

In this chapter, we have designed a smart cradle that monitors the baby using the Raspberry Pi B+ module, a full-fledged computer the size of a credit card. It is installed with a baby cry detection module that can distinguish between a baby cry and other loud noises, hence accurately detecting the baby cry even in a noisy environment.

11.2 Literature Study

In Infant Care Assistant using machine learning, audio processing, image processing and IoT sensor network [1], the authors have presented a smart infant monitoring and assistance system. It consists of four major units. The infant monitoring unit collects data from various sensors and creates a comfortable environment for the infant by controlling the cradle. The data transfer unit is a medium for the transfer of data between the user, the infant monitoring unit and the data analysis unit. The data analysis unit comprises cry detection, cry analysis and emotion recognition units which determine the emotional state of the infant. The user interface gives the user visual and operational control over the infant monitoring system.

Inside the cradle, a moisture sensor is used to detect whether the infant has wet the cradle bed or not. The mic condenser is a digital sensor used to detect the audio level of the surroundings. Its sensitivity is varied using the on-board potentiometer. When a loud sound is detected, the mic condenser gives a logic HIGH output and subsequently the Raspberry Pi switches on the USB microphone for recording. A USB microphone is connected to the Raspberry Pi. When a loud sound is detected, it records the sounds and cuts it continuously into audio signals of 10s each. These audio signals are then processed for cry detection and cry analysis. For cry detection, librosa library is used to extract all the features such as mel-frequency cepstral coefficients (MFCCs), spectral centroid and Short Term Energy (STE). Based on these feature values, the random forest classifier is used for the classification of baby cry. For emotion detection, the dataset consists of 35,887–4,848 resolution gray scale images. Each image contains a human face and is labeled with one of the seven emotions—angry, disgust, fear, happy, sad, surprise and neutral. A model derived from Xception is used for image classification. All convolutional operations performed are in separable convolutional layers which are followed by batch normalization. A compact form of this architecture known as miniXception is used. The passive infrared sensor (PIR) motion sensor is used to monitor the movement of the infant and inform parents of the same. If the PIR sensor detects motion, data from the camera module is processed to verify whether the infant is awake or not. Raspberry Pi camera module v2 is a high-quality 8-megapixel image sensor. The camera module is mounted to focus directly on the face of the infant. Facial features are extracted from the image and analyzed to determine emotions. All sensor data and results of the Raspberry Pi control system are uploaded to the local database and private cloud interface for storage and also sent to the web application. Raspberry Pi also receives inputs from the user through the web page to control the infant soothing unit and the camera module. Limitation of the system is that the baby cry analysis module has less accuracy of 56% and emotion recognition of 66%. Also, the system accompanies a website instead of an app, which might prove to be slower than an installed app and will not be able to notify users through push notifications.

In Smart Baby Cradle [2], the authors have tried to implement a Smart Baby Cradle-an IoT-based Cradle Management System which consists of wet sensors, microphone and motor which are attached to the cradle along with Arduino Uno board to provide the best suitable environment to the baby. Arduino Uno board is a microcontroller board based on ATmega328P. It has a 16 MHz quartz crystal, USB connection, power jack, and reset button. It collects sensor data and sends it to the baby's parents/guardians via SMS, and for that, a GSM module is used. A GSM module can be used to give a smart cradle the ability to be remotely controlled via GSM communication. It is used to give event feedback to parents, and parents can also control the activities via messaging. A noise sensor is used to detect a baby cry, and when a cry is detected, an immediate alert is sent to parents via SMS and the servo motor starts to swing the cradle. The motor only rotates 180 degrees to and fro in a semicircular motion. Here, cry detection is not done and the protocol is run only when there is noise around the cradle. Limitations of the cradle include the cradle being unable to distinguish between a cry and other loud noises as it uses loudness of the sound to detect cry. Moreover, the connections of the cradle are fragile, and if not handled carefully, the baby may experience electrical shock.

In the development of IoT-based smart baby cradle [3], the authors have developed an IoT-based smart baby cradle. The main circuits attached to the cradle are the PIR sensor, noise sensor, moisture sensor, servo motor and temperature sensor. The PIR sensor is used for the movement of the baby and will make the cradle swing back and forth by sending a signal to the servo motor when required. A digital temperature and humidity sensor is used to measure the temperature and humidity of the cradle. Arduino takes the signal from the Wi-Fi module and sends the data to the Blynk cloud. A Wi-Fi module is used to connect the sensors of the cradle system to the Blynk cloud services via Arduino. The parent will be able to speak to the child through the mobile application which is connected to the camera. The parent will be able to see the child live on the mobile application. The system uses a Blynk cloud for monitoring the baby inside the cradle and measures the body temperature and bed wet condition. Limitations are that the cradle uses the loudness of sound to detect a baby cry, so any loud noise can trigger cradle swinging.

In smart infant cradle with an android application for baby monitoring [4], the authors have developed a smart infant cradle system with an android application for baby monitoring. The system consists of a moisture sensor, methane sensor, sound sensor to swing the cradle when a cry is detected with the help of the servo motor, web camera, and GSM module. Cloud services are used to connect the cradle with the android application. The camera module is used to capture the images. As the baby cries, the baby's image is sent to the parents as a notification in the mobile application. Limitations are that parents are unable to control the cradle using a mobile application and the application only shows images and no other vitals of the baby. The cradle cannot be controlled using a mobile application.

11.3 Proposed Solution

The proposed solution is a smart baby care system that consists of a baby monitoring system, data transfer unit, data analysis unit, and mobile application. The baby monitoring system consists of a data collection unit, controller unit and baby soothing system. Its primary role is to collect data from the cradle sensors and send it to other units of the smart cradle system. The data transfer unit is a channel for data transfer between the user and the cradle. The analysis unit consists of a baby cry detection module. The cry detection module detects when the baby is crying even in a noisy environment. The mobile application empowers the user to control the components of the cradle and get data from the cradle about the baby. The prerequisite of the cradle is that it should be connected to the internet through Wi-Fi at all times.

11.3.1 Baby Monitoring System

11.3.1.1 Data Collection Unit

11.3.1.1.1 Moisture Sensor

Hygiene is important to be maintained in infants and babies, where a lack of attention may lead to infection and skin irritation for the babies. A moisture sensor is used to check the moisture content in the cradle to check if the baby needs a diaper change in case of urination. When it crosses a certain threshold value, it sends an alert to parents via the mobile application (see Figure 11.1).

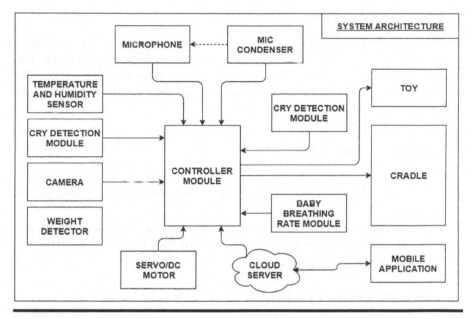

Figure 11.1 **Baby monitoring system—block diagram.**

11.3.1.1.2 Temperature Sensor

A temperature sensor is used to detect the temperature of the baby. Thermal stress and elevated ambient temperature could also cause discomfort to the infant; therefore, a threshold is set for the temperature at higher and lower levels; if the threshold is reached, then an instant alert is sent to parents via mobile application.

11.3.1.1.3 PIR Motion Sensor

PIR motion sensor helps determine if the baby is awake or asleep. Movement signifies the baby is present and awake. If there is no movement and the weight detector detects weight, then the baby is sleeping, during which the camera module takes pictures of the baby's sleeping pattern at regular intervals and stores it in the S3 bucket of Amazon Web Series (AWS) cloud server. These patterns of the baby can be monitored by parents.

11.3.1.1.4 Mic Condenser

A mic condenser is a digital sensor used to detect sounds around the cradle. When a loud sound is detected by the mic condenser, it triggers the Raspberry Pi to switch on the USB microphone for recording the audio and send the real-time audio as the input to the cry detection module to detect if the audio is actually a baby cry or some other loud noises like banging.

11.3.1.1.5 USB Microphone

A USB microphone is placed in the cradle to record sounds and noises for further processing to take place. When a request from the mobile application is received, the sounds from the cradle are recorded and sent to the mobile application. The sounds are also used for processing in the cry detection module, which alerts the parents if the baby is crying.

11.3.1.1.6 Camera Module

A 5 MP Omnivision 5647 camera module is used, which helps the Raspberry Pi to stream the live video of the baby to the mobile application and also allows parents to capture photos of the baby.

The camera module takes pictures at regular intervals. These pictures are presented to the parents via the app. The parents can thus monitor the activities of infant while they are not around.

11.3.1.1.7 Weight (Load cells)

The weight detector module helps monitor the weight of the baby over time. The weight of the baby is recorded after every set time frame and is stored in AWS. By detecting weight, it also helps the microcontroller to check if the baby is present in the cradle or not. All the detection modules and sensors will automatically become dormant if the baby is not present in the cradle.

11.3.1.2 Controller Unit—Raspberry Pi B+

The Raspberry Pi B+ module is used to power the baby cradle to carry out its functions. Sensor data is collected by Raspberry Pi; it analyzes the information and performs certain actions on the basis of given threshold values. Algorithms in Raspberry Pi check the sensor data, and if any threshold value is triggered, then immediately an alert is sent to parents via mobile application. Raspberry Pi also controls the baby soothing system. Whenever a sound is detected, the machine learning algorithm in Raspberry Pi starts processing the sound; if the sound is of a baby cry, then it sends an alert via a mobile application, starts swinging the baby, playing music, and sends a signal for toy rotation. Raspberry Pi also receives information from the mobile application for the execution of tasks such as changing the swinging speed of the cradle, music, ambient light, etc. Information received by Raspberry Pi is stored in the cloud server of AWS. ESP32 module and Arduino Uno are some alternatives that can be used instead of Raspberry Pi.

Raspberry Pi provides high performance compared to Arduino and ESP8266 in terms of storing capacity and processing but at a higher price. Raspberry Pi has inbuilt Wi-Fi and Bluetooth which help it easily connect to the internet and send data to the cloud [5]. These differences make Raspberry Pi a good choice for a smart cradle.

11.3.1.3 Baby Soothing System

The baby soothing system is activated by the controller. If a loud noise is detected by the mic condenser, the cry detection module is triggered and the USB microphone starts recording. The recorded audio is given input to the cry detection module for analysis. If the baby is crying, the cradle will automatically start swinging and playing relaxing music to placate the baby. If the baby does not stop crying for a few minutes, then an alert will be sent to the mobile application notifying the parents to address the baby. The parents can also control the swinging speed of the cradle and can switch it off by turning off the auto-pacifying mode. In this way, auto function of the cradle to automatically swing will stop. Parents can also manually control the baby soothing system as per their preferences, wherein they can set the speed of swinging and time for which it should swing.

Components of the baby soothing system:

11.3.1.3.1 DC Motor

A DC motor is used to swing the cradle. The DC motor starts swinging the cradle whenever the controller sends a signal. Swinging speed can be controlled by parents via the mobile application.

11.3.1.3.2 Music System

A set of speakers is used to play soothing music. A speaker is also used during audio surveillance so that the baby can hear the recorded voice of parents sent from the mobile application. Soothing music is played when a cry is detected. This behavior of the cradle can be changed by the parents from the app. Also, while putting the baby to sleep, parents can play white noise in the cradle which imitates the noise in the womb, thus calming the baby. Parents can also play other soothing music at any time. They can select from a list provided in the mobile application.

11.3.1.3.3 Toy

An overhead toy is attached to the cradle, which helps soothe the baby when he/she is crying. If a crying sound is detected by the cry detection module, Raspberry Pi sends a signal to the toy to start its motion.

11.3.1.3.4 Ambient Light

An overhead ambient light is also attached to control the brightness of the environment in the cradle. The mobile application controls the brightness of the light on a scale of one to ten.

11.3.2 Data Transfer Unit

Message queue telemetry transport (MQTT) protocol is used for communication with the cradle. AWS dynamoDB service stores data sent from the cradle. And subsequently, when the data is requested from the cloud by the user, HTTP protocol is used to send or receive data into the app. For the data heart rate, the data is directly received by the app from the controller. Profile data of the baby along with sleep data, temperature and weight is stored in DynamoDB, and images of the baby are stored in Amazon S3. REST API created and deployed with the help of AWS API Gateway is used to connect the mobile app and AWS.

AWS MQTT IOT core service is used for communication purposes in real time. Both mobile application and cradle act as a publisher and subscriber. Users can publish messages via the mobile application to change the speed of the cradle, swing the cradle or change the music through MQTT. AWS lambda functions are used to control the data flow.

WebSocket protocol is used to communicate with the cradle from the app directly without the integration of AWS. In the case when both the app and the cradle are connected to the same Wi-Fi network and remote monitoring is requested, the data is sent directly from the controller to the app via the Wi-Fi router. This lowers the cost of AWS servers and internet cost incurred by the user for using the cradle and the app.

11.3.3 Data Analysis Unit

The input audio and video frames are received by the data analysis unit from the data transfer unit. The cry detection module is used to predict if the input audio is a cry or not. If a cry is detected by the module, then Raspberry Pi activates the baby soothing system as discussed in the Section 3 of the baby monitoring system.

11.3.3.1 Cry Detection Module

In cry detection analysis, ESC-50 [6] dataset was used which consists of 50 different types of high-quality audios of length 5 seconds each. There are a total of 2,000 audio files in the ESC-50 dataset and approximately 400 audio files were considered relevant, that is, these audios are likely to occur within the vicinity of the cradle. From the ESC-50 dataset, relevant audio files are selected and the modified dataset is formed. The modified dataset has two folders namely cry and no cry, where cry folders consist of baby cry audio files and no cry consists of background noises like clapping, sneezing, footsteps and other types of noise that can be heard in a household environment. The entire flow of the steps used in this module is explained in Figure 11.2.

After organizing the dataset, features of audio files are extracted and a dataset is generated in csv format. Librosa library is used in the process of audio feature extraction. First, the time series and sampling rate of the audio file are extracted.

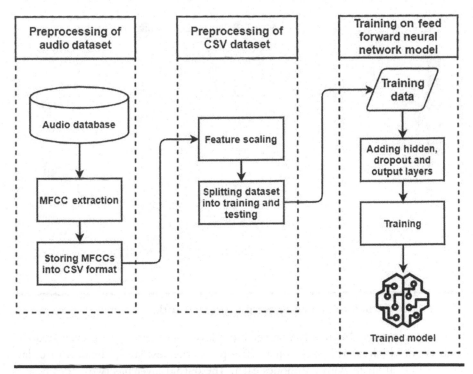

Figure 11.2   Baby cry detection—flow diagram.

Time series is the representation of audio in the form of a NumPy array, and the sampling rate is the number of samples per second taken from a continuous signal to make a discrete signal [7]. The next feature extracted here is MFCC [8]. MFCC is used here because it accurately measures similarities and dissimilarities in audio signals [9]. The time series and sampling rate are then given input to the *mfcc* function provided by the librosa library. Forty different MFCCs are extracted for each audio file in the audio dataset and stored in csv format dataset for further processing.

After generating a csv dataset, preprocessing of data is performed on this dataset. Unwanted columns are discarded, and then independent and dependent variable columns are set. Feature scaling is performed on the MFCC columns for standardization of the data in the columns to prevent the model from being biased toward some variables. The dataset is bifurcated into the training dataset and testing dataset in the ratio of 80:20 respectively. The training dataset is used to train the machine learning model, and after training the model, the testing of the model is to be performed on the testing dataset.

The training of the machine learning model is done using a feed-forward neural network (FFNN) [10]. There are three types of layers in the FFNN classifier—input, output and hidden layers—as shown in Figure 11.3. The data flows only in the forward direction of the neural network from the input layer to the hidden layers and

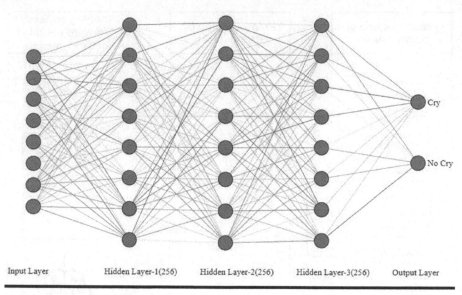

Input Layer Hidden Layer-1(256) Hidden Layer-2(256) Hidden Layer-3(256) Output Layer

Figure 11.3 Structure of feed-forward neural network.

to the output layer. The first layer is the input layer where the input is evaluated and translated, which is then passed on as the input to the next layer. The next three layers are hidden layers with 256 nodes each. The output layer has two nodes here as there are only two possible categories of the output, i.e., cry and no cry. The dropout layer is added in between each layer to avoid model overfitting. The input layer and the hidden layers use the ReLU activation function and the output layer uses a softmax activation function with two nodes for each of the cry and no cry categories to make a prediction. Then, the model is trained on the training dataset.

The model is tested on the testing dataset which received an accuracy of 92.59%. Since the model has high accuracy, it is saved and finally deployed on the Raspberry Pi for its further application on real-time audio. The module takes audio input in the form of 5-second audio clips from the surroundings and processes it to determine if the audio is a baby cry or not.

11.3.4 Mobile Application

A mobile application is created using the Flutter framework and compiled into android and iOS apps to be uploaded onto the Google play store and Apple app store, respectively (Figure 11.4).

11.3.4.1 App Initialization and First Use

On the first installation of the app, it asks the user to connect the app to the cradle by pressing the connect button on the cradle. The app then asks for Service Set

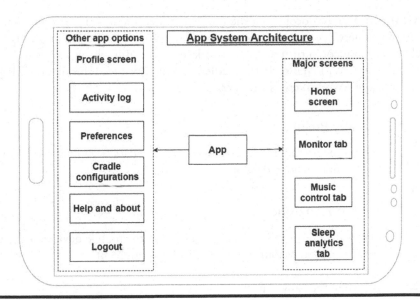

Figure 11.4 Mobile application—System Architecture.

IDentifier and password to the Wi-Fi router it is being connected to. The controller on the cradle responds to it by sending its confirmation and device id to the mobile phone. On completing the Wi-Fi configuration of the cradle, the app asks for details of the baby.

11.3.4.2 Function of the App

11.3.4.2.1 Control of the Cradle

The app controls the function of the components on the cradle, such as the behavior of the swinging motion of the cradle, the ambient light and the rotating of the overhead toy. The user can control the behavior of the cradle by controlling the maximum speed with which the cradle is allowed to swing. The automatic pacifying mode can also be disabled from the app, following which no active actions in the cradle will be undertaken, while passive action, the baby cry detection, continues to notify the parents.

11.3.4.2.2 Monitor Baby On-The-Go

The monitor tab in the app allows users to access the camera and microphone of the cradle. The user can also communicate with the baby by pressing the audio icon in the app to initiate real-time communication with the baby.

The algorithm in the app handles any network scenario—the app can connect to the cradle through the WebSocket protocol directly through the Wi-Fi router or via the MQTT protocol using the internet. When the mobile user is connected to the Wi-Fi network of the cradle, video monitoring can be achieved through the WebSocket protocol in turn saving network resources. But when the mobile user is not on the same Wi-Fi network, the cradle sends the video feed through the MQTT protocol using AWS servers as a broker.

11.3.4.2.3 Baby Profile

The app also lets the user maintain a baby profile. The data stored here is the baby's profile picture, name, gender, date of birth and address.

11.3.4.2.4 Sleep Analytic

The app collects data from the cradle and stores it in the mobile device for the user to view. There are a total of four states that the baby can be in:

■ 'Away', when the baby is not in the cradle,
■ 'Awake', when the baby is awake and inside the cradle,
■ 'Asleep', when the baby is asleep and inside the cradle, and
■ 'Inactive', when the baby is not in the cradle.

The sleep data is recorded with the start and end time of the state along with the state of the baby. This data is sent to AWS and stored in the AWS dynamoDB table. The sleep data can be viewed from the screen analytics tab of the app and categorized into daily and weekly charts.

11.3.4.2.5 Music Control

The user can choose the music being played on the cradle and can seek forward, seek backward, pause and stop the music on the cradle.

11.3.4.2.6 Update Cradle Firmware

The app allows the user to update the firmware software of the cradle whenever an update is required to be installed on the cradle controller.

11.3.4.2.7 Misc

The app provides several other features:

■ Profile page to view and store information about the baby.
■ Activity log displays the activity performed by the user and can be used for analytic purposes.

- Preferences screen allows us to set the notification preferences of the user.
- Help and about screen to view information about the app.
- Logout button to let the user log out of the app.

11.4 Results

11.4.1 Baby Cry Detection

After training the model using FFNN, 92.59% accuracy is achieved on the testing dataset as shown in Figure 11.5 & Figure 11.6. The model is now saved and then tested on real-time audio input from the microphone of the device. It is tested by making a program that takes 5-second input from the microphone for 20 seconds and predicts the output for each audio file. For the first 5 seconds, a random sound (apart from a crying sound of the baby) was given as input via mic, and for the next

```
score = model.evaluate(X_train, y_train, verbose=0)
print("Training Accuracy: {0:.2%}".format(score[1]))
score = model.evaluate(X_test, y_test, verbose=0)
print("Testing Accuracy: {0:.2%}".format(score[1]))
```

```
Training Accuracy: 100.00%
Testing Accuracy: 92.59%
```

Figure 11.5 **Baby cry detection—Accuracy of the trained model.**

```
* recording
Predicted=[[0.0239288 0.9760712 ]]
No cry
-----------------------------
Predicted=[[0.9627882  0.03721176]]
Cry
-----------------------------
Predicted=[[9.9964714e-01 3.5281191e-04]]
Cry
-----------------------------
Predicted=[[0.9977284  0.00227162]]
Cry
-----------------------------
Done!
```

Figure 11.6 **Baby cry detection—Output.**

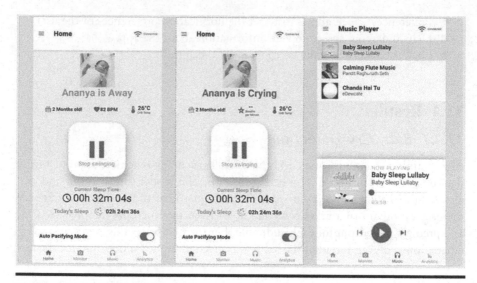

Figure 11.7   User interface of the mobile application.

15 seconds, a baby crying audio outside of the dataset was played and the results are shown in Figure 11.7. Many different audios of baby cries from the internet were tested on this model, and it accurately predicted the correct output.

11.4.2 Mobile Application

The mobile application allows the user to control the cradle. The app is able to connect to the cradle through AWS successfully. The user can see the temperature of the baby in the application. They can either manually control the swinging of the cradle or they can turn on the auto-pacifying mode. In the auto-pacifying mode, the system will continuously detect the crying sounds of the baby; if a crying sound is detected, the system will automatically start swinging of the cradle. The user can also stop automatic swinging of the cradle.

11.5 Conclusion

The proposed idea of a smart cradle is a cheap and easy-to-use system. It can help improve the quality of the care provided to the baby. This system will provide parents with the assurance that their babies are placated in their absence. Constant capturing and monitoring of various biomedical parameters of the baby help parents understand the baby's internal health status. It is a convenient system to monitor the baby from any distance.

11.6 Limitations

If a baby does not stop crying even after swinging the cradle and listening to music or if there is any other emergency, the cradle won't be able to do anything except for raising alerts, and quick response from parents would still be needed. Limited Raspberry Pi computational power affects the overall efficiency of the cradle.

11.7 Future Scope

Reasons for crying should be identified using a machine learning algorithm so that the cradle can be accordingly upgraded to assist parents. Sleep patterns should be analyzed to find the best position in which a baby can sleep for a longer duration of time.

References

[1] C. Lobo, A. Chitrey, P. Gupta, Sarfaraj and A. Chaudhari. Infant care assistant using machine learning, audio processing, Image processing, IoT sensor network. *2020 International Conference on Electronics and Sustainable Communication Systems (ICESC)*, 2–4, 2020.

[2] A. R. Patil, N. J. Patil, A. D. Mishra and Y. D. Mane. Smart baby cradle, *2018 International Conference on Smart City and Emerging Technology (ICSCET)*, Mumbai, India, 2018.

[3] A. B. Tupkar, Prajwal Chahare, Shubham Rade, Rushikesh Wakade and Snehal Bahirseth. Development of IoT based smart baby cradle. *International Advanced Research Journal in Science, Engineering and Technology (IARJSET)*, 7(1), 50–54, 2020.

[4] S. Kavitha, R. R. Neela, K. Harshitha and M. Sowndarya. Smart infant cradle system with an android application for baby monitoring. *IJESC*, 9(5), 22402–22404, 2019.

[5] D. Patnaikuni, A comparative study of Arduino, raspberry Pi and ESP8266 as IoT development board. *2017 International Journal of Advanced Research in Computer Science*, 2350–2352, 2017. DOI: 10.26483/ijarcs.v8i5.3959.

[6] ESC-50. Dataset for environmental sound classification dataset. https://github.com/karolpiczak/ESC-50#esc-50-dataset-for-environmental-sound-classification.

[7] A. Zabidi, W. Mansor, Lee Yoot Khuan, R. Sahak and F. Y. A. Rahman, Mel-frequency cepstrum coefficient analysis of infant cry with hypothyroidism. *2009 5th International Colloquium on Signal Processing & Its Applications*, 204–208, 2009. DOI: 10.1109/CSPA.2009.5069217.

[8] L. Liu, Y. Li and K. Kuo, Infant cry signal detection, pattern extraction and recognition. *2018 International Conference on Information and Computer Technologies (ICICT)*, 159–163, 2018. DOI: 10.1109/INFOCT.2018.8356861.

[9] E. Şaşmaz and F. B. Tek, Animal sound classification using a convolutional neural network. *2018 3rd International Conference on Computer Science and Engineering (UBMK)*, 625–629, 2018. DOI: 10.1109/UBMK.2018.8566449.

[10] K. Manikanta, K. P. Soman and M. S. Manikandan, Deep learning based effective baby crying recognition method under indoor background sound environments. *2019 4th International Conference on Computational Systems and Information Technology for Sustainable Solution (CSITSS)*, 1–6, 2019. DOI: 10.1109/CSITSS47250.2019.903 1058.

Chapter 12

Word-Level Devanagari Text Recognition

Rutwik Shailesh Shah, Harshil Suresh Bhorawat, Hritik Ganesh Sawant, and Vinaya Sawant

Dwarkadas J. Sanghvi College of Engineering

Contents

12.1 Introduction

The process of automatic conversion of a handwritten text into a machine-encoded text is called Handwritten text recognition. It has various real-world applications, and hence, it has been a popular and demanding area of research for many years. Owing to technological advancements, a lot of work has been done in optical character recognition (OCR) and handwritten text recognition of the English language. However, when we consider handwritten text recognition of Indic scripts, not a lot of work has been done in this space. In this work, we address challenges associated with creating an intelligent handwritten text recognizer for the Devanagari script. In India, more than 400 million people use regional scripts for written communication purposes, of which the Devanagari script is the most popular regional script. Twenty-two languages share the Devanagari script and the languages pertaining to it are spread across various regions of India. These languages include Hindi, Marathi, Sanskrit, etc.

The lack of work in the Devanagari script handwritten character recognition (HWCR) is because of multiple reasons. One of the challenges in developing the Devanagari text recognizer is the lack of large publicly available datasets. Modern deep learning architectures consider a huge number of parameters and hence require huge amounts of data for training which is an issue in this scenario. Also, there is no benchmark dataset used in this field, and therefore, it becomes difficult to compare two different methods of character recognition. To tackle these issues, we have used the [1] IIIT-HW-Dev dataset.

More issues arise in Devanagari script recognition because of the vast variations in writing styles and the complexity of the script itself. Devanagari script [2] has 48 letters – 11 vowels and 37 consonants. There is a horizontal line called Shirorekha from which the characters hang. There is no concept of upper and lower case in Devanagari script, unlike Latin script. In Devanagari script, when a consonant is followed by a vowel, the shape of the consonant character is modified and is called a modifier. In addition to these challenges associated with the script, issues also arise in the case of compound characters. The same compound character can be written correctly in two ways; one in which the virama is explicitly written and another where the virama is hidden. A Devanagari script recognizer has to deal with all the stated challenges.

Our aim is to build a model that not only takes into consideration all the stated factors but also recognizes words as a whole without performing character segmentation, which is the case for most of the work done in this domain till now. We are hoping to accomplish this by using a hybrid architecture of deep learning algorithms convolutional neural network (CNN) and recurrent neural network (RNN). We plan to develop an application with a friendly, intuitive and easy-to-use user interface where users can input images that need not be resized to a fixed size, thus avoiding distortion in the aspect ratio, since both convolutional and recurrent layers can operate with variable-size images and feature sequences respectively.

12.2 Literature Review

Optical character recognition (OCR) is the process by which text images are converted into a machine-encoded text. Digitizing text means it can be easily presented, edited, stored and searched, optimizing key administrative tasks. Advancement in

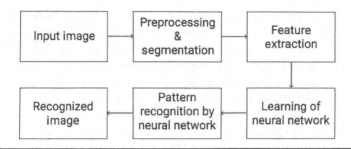

Figure 12.1   Proposed approach by Pankaj Kale.

software technology in the past decade made it possible to implement such capabilities in a software package which gave rise to the second class of sophisticated OCR systems as software. Despite the technological advancements, there is still room for improvement of the handwritten Devanagari character recognition.

Pankaj Kale [3] proposed an artificial neural network (ANN)-based recognition system for handwritten Marathi characters and experiments were performed on 500 characters from 10 different people. The accuracy obtained was 92%. This system's proposed methodology included data collection, pre-processing and segmentation, feature extraction and classification (Figure 12.1).

After this, the data obtained will be an array of segmented characters after removing the shirorekha line. This array is given to the neural network for training. The neural network performs pattern recognition, and the recognized image is obtained as the output. Back-propagation model is used for training the ANN model in this paper. An efficient way of Devanagari character classification would be by using a support vector machine (SVM) classifier. Shalini Puri [4] proposed an approach that involved pre-processing of the scanned image documents, normalization, segmentation using projection profile, removal of the top line, obtaining the shirorekha-less characters and performing feature extraction and finally recognizing the characters by using an SVM classifier. The paper also mentioned the accuracy of the output obtained when the SVM classifier is combined with other classifiers such as K-nearest neighbor (KNN), Fuzzy, hidden Markov models (HMM), RSVM (Reduced Support Vector Machine), etc. The final system took multiple datasets into consideration and achieved an accuracy of 98.35%.

In reference [5], the authors discussed the state-of-the-art of handwritten and machine-printed Devanagari OCR techniques from the 1970s. An effort is made to address the most important results reported so far and it is also tried to bring to light the advantageous directions of the research.

Parul Sahare [6] proposed robust algorithms for character segmentation and recognition for Latin and Devanagari scripts. The three major parts of the approach were pre-processing, segmentation and post-processing. Pre-processing involved binarization, resizing, thinning and skew correction. Primary segmentation paths are obtained by using the structural property. Also, overlapped and joined characters are segmented using the graph distance theory. SVM classifier validates the segmentation results. KNN classifier is used for the recognition of the handwritten input character. The recognition rates are 97.05% for Devanagari script and 97.10% for Latin script, respectively. Deore [7] proposed a system that recognizes the handwritten Devanagari-isolated characters using a group of classifiers. In this, an HWCR system is implemented which is used to recognize 12 vowels and 36 consonants of a Handwritten Devanagari character to isolate unconstrained character images as a complete image. In this approach, the recognition of Devanagari characters was done in three main steps. The first step is pre-processing of the character image which involves resizing and binarization. The second step is feature extraction. For this step, it uses a histogram of oriented gradients as a feature. The third step of this system is classification for which three different classifiers are used. The three classifiers are SVM, KNN and NN. The results obtained from these classifiers are analyzed, combined together and given ahead for classification based on the maximum voting method (Figure 12.2).

The recognition rate achieved by the proposed HWCR system was 88.13%. Bappaditya Chakraborty [8] has implemented CNN architectures of five different depths for recognition of handwritten Devanagari characters. Additional neural architectures have also been implemented by adding two BLSTM (bidirectional long short-term memory) between the convolutional stack. In this system, simulations have been performed on two different databases of handwritten Devanagari characters of 30,408 and 36,172 samples, respectively. The recognition accuracy obtained via this approach was 96.09%.

Devanagari OCR using ANN was proposed by Naveen Malik [9]. The proposed approach stated that at the beginning, sentences, words and characters are segmented. The segmentation accuracy achieved for sentences and words was 100% whereas the segmentation accuracy for characters was 80%. The performance of this OCR depended greatly on the features extracted. Chain code histograms, projection histograms and history of aligned gradients were used for it. The accuracy of the character recognition system obtained was 91.11%. A system that gave the state-of-the-art results on the publicly available Devanagari dataset was the one that

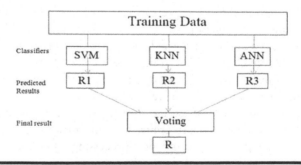

Figure 12.2   Ensembling model of the system made by S. P. Deore.

used RNN which defines the input as a series of feature vectors. The dataset used for this project contained 95,381 samples collected from 12 different individuals. Kartik Dutta's [1] approach was to use a CNN-RNN hybrid network and perform sequence-to-sequence transcription. The output from the CNN-RNN hybrid structure is then modeled using connectionist temporal classification.

Kunal Ravindra Shah proposed an approach that uses Gershgorin's theorem [10] for feature extraction and recognition. This first part of the approach was pre-processing, where noise reduction, gray scaling and binarization were done. The second part was segmentation. After this, for extraction and recognition, they used the Eigen space algorithm using the concept of Gershgorin's theorem. The output is sent to modifiers for recognition and then a digital result is displayed. Prasad Chavan [11] in his paper gave the proposed system where the flow of steps was similar. In pre-processing, the following three steps were involved: binarization (Sauvola's binarization algorithm), skew correction (dilate and thin approach) and Hough transform. Under segmentation, header line, top modifiers, bottom modifiers and fused characters are segmented. The accuracy of the model was less than the one mentioned before.

SVM, ANN and HMM were used for the recognition of handwritten Devanagari script by Aradhana A. Malanker [12]. Before these classification models were used, pre-processing and segmentation were performed. The outputs of the three classifiers are combined using the connectionist scheme. The paper also explained that any character recognition system goes under the following steps, i.e., image acquisition, pre-processing, segmentation, feature extraction, classification and post-processing (Figure 12.3).

The highest recognition accuracy obtained was 95.19%.

Manoj Sonkusare [13] has done a detailed study on the handwritten Devanagari text recognition accuracies obtained when different feature extraction methods and different classifiers are used. The highest accuracy obtained was 98.35% when geometric-based feature extraction and SVM classifier were used. The lowest accuracy was 88.13% when a histogram of oriented gradient was used for feature extraction and a hybrid classifier (consisting of: SVM, K-NN, and NN) was used.

The table below gives a side-by-side comparison of various feature extraction methods used, the various classifiers used and the accuracies obtained by different authors in the handwritten Devanagari text recognition domain (Table 12.1).

12.3 Proposed System

Our proposed system has two main components: Text Recognizer App and Processing Server.

The Processing Server is further divided into two modules: The first module is the pre-processing module, and the second is the feature extraction and recognition module (Figure 12.4).

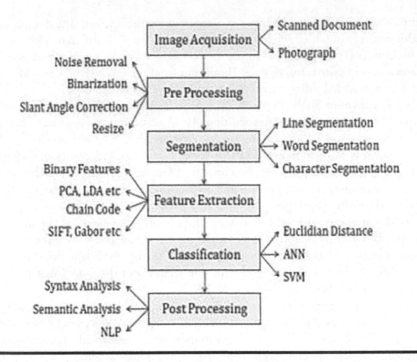

Figure 12.3 Block diagram of Aradhana A. Malanker's character recognition system.

12.3.1 Text Recognizer Application

It is an application that allows users to upload the scanned image of the handwritten text. After processing the scanned image, the digitized text is displayed on the application as output. This digitized Devanagari text can be formatted by the user as required.

12.3.2 Processing Server

The processing server is responsible for converting the scanned input from users into its digitized form. It further consists of two modules: Pre-processing module and Feature Extraction and Recognition module.

12.3.2.1 Pre-Processing

At this stage, the scanned image is pre-processed using various techniques before it is passed on to the processing server for recognition. For a good recognition rate, pre-processing stage is very important. Various techniques used are gray scaling, binarization, noise removal and skew correction.

Table 12.1   Literature Survey

Work	Feature Extraction	Classifier	Accuracy (%)
S. P. Deore	Histogram of oriented gradient	Hybrid classifier (SVM, K-NN and NN)	88.13
Naveen Malik	Chain code histograms, projection histograms, and histogram of aligned gradients	ANN	91.11
Pankaj kale	Array-based feature extraction	ANN	92
Aradhana A Malanker	Binary features	SVM, ANN and HMM	95.19
Bappaditya Chakraborty	Histogram of oriented gradient	CNN	96.09
Parul Sahare	Fixed center distance-based feature, fixed center cut-based feature, neighborhood count- based feature	KNN	97.05
Shalini Puri	Geometry-based features	SVM	98.35

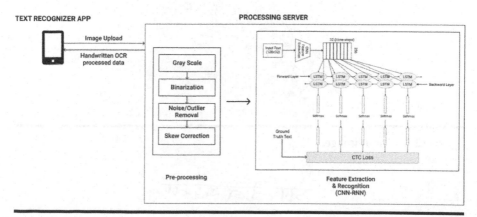

Figure 12.4   Proposed system architecture.

i. **Gray scaling**:

It is the process of converting a colored image from other color spaces like RGB to shades of gray.

ii. **Binarization**:

It is the method of converting the gray-scale image (multitone image) into a black and white image (two-tone image).

iii. **Noise removal**:

It is the process of removing or reducing the noise (for example, noise of a crushed paper) from the image.

iv. **Skew correction**:

It is the process of correcting the alignment of the text in the scanned image so that it appears straight. If skew of the word is in a positive angle, then it is corrected by rotating it in clockwise direction; otherwise, it will be rotated in anti-clockwise direction.

Figures 12.5 and 12.6 depict input and output of a scanned image after pre-processing.

12.3.2.2 Feature Extraction and Recognition

The output image from the pre-processing module is used as input for this module. The input pre-processed image free from noise may decrease the model training time and also increase model inference speed. First, we make use of the

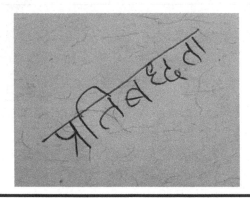

Figure 12.5   Input image.

प्रतिबद्धता

Figure 12.6   Pre-processed image.

convolutional recurrent neural network (C-RNN) to extract the important features from the handwritten line text image of the dataset. The output before CNN FC (fully connected) layer (512×100×8) is passed to the BLSTM which is for sequence dependency and time-sequence operations. Then, CTC (connectionist temporal classification) LOSS [12] is used to train RNN which eliminates the alignment problem in Handwritten since handwritten has a different alignment for every writer. We just gave what is written in the image (ground truth text) and BLSTM output, then it calculates loss; the aim is to minimize the negative maximum likelihood path. Then, CTC finds out the possible paths from the given labels. Finally, CTC decode is used to decode the output during prediction.

12.3.2.2.1 Dataset

For training of the C-RNN model, we make use of the IIIT-HWDev dataset (created by IIIT Hyderabad) [7]. This dataset is annotated using UTF-8, which is the dominant character-encoding scheme across the web. It contains a total of 95,381 word samples collected from 12 different individuals with different educational backgrounds and ages. The writers were free to use pens of their choice and write the words in their natural style. After that, a vocabulary of 9,540 Devanagari words was chosen such that most of the characters present in the dataset are from the UTF-8 Devanagari range. Almost all the words in the vocabulary have the same number of samples in the dataset. On average, each word in the dataset consists of eight basic Unicode characters (Figures 12.7 and 12.8).

12.3.2.2.2 Detailed Workflow C-RNN Model

The input image is passed to the model in batch size. It then passes through five layers of CNN where feature extraction is done. The CNN layers extract 256 feature maps of size 32×1. The extracted features are then passed into the two layers of long short-term memory (LSTM) which form one BLSTM to maintain text

Figure 12.7   Sample images from the IIIT-HWDev dataset.

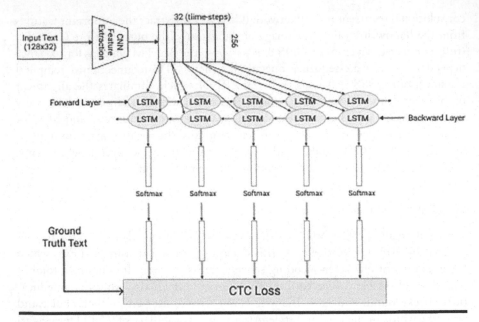

Figure 12.8 Detailed workflow of C-RNN model.

dependencies efficiently from both directions, the output of which is 32×110, i.e. (time-steps $\times$ number_of_classes). Then, CTC loss function is used to train the LSTM without a need for transcription provided the correct spare ground truth texts and numeric value. Finally, CTC decode is used to decode the LSTM output and predict the written text in the scanned image.

12.4 Implementation

After a detailed study of literature and the proposal our approach to build an intelligent Devanagari text recognizer, this chapter will explain the implementation of our system using python (programming language) and TensorFlow. So, the implementation of the system has been divided into four modules namely Dataloader.py, Model.py, and Preprocessor.py, main.py.

- **Dataloader.py:**

    This module is used to load our IIIT-HW-Dev dataset for further training and validation of our models. The dataset folder consists of three folders, i.e., train, test and validate, and each folder is associated with a text file that includes the image path and a corresponding ground truth text. First, we combine the train and validate text files into one file named full.txt and extract all the ground truth texts from it. These ground truth texts are then used to create the character list and store in the charlist.txt file which is further required by CTC. Then, the full.txt file contains only a path of images which is further divided into 90% and 10% for training and validation of the dataset respectively. It also includes various other functions defined for other purposes.

■ **Model.py:**

This module sets up our deep neural networks that are CNN which is used for feature extraction and RNN. It also sets up the CTC loss function to train the RNN. Further, it defines the CTC decoder function to display the digital output.

■ **Preprocessor.py:**

This module is used for pre-processing of the uploaded scanned image as mentioned earlier in the proposed approach. It does the work of noise removal, gray scaling, binarization, skew correction and finally resizing the input to the target size of the image as in the dataset used for better recognition.

■ **Main.py:**

This is the main module which consists of code for training, validation of the dataset and testing of the input from the test folder of the database as well as user-provided scanned handwritten texts.

12.4.1 Training

The training dataset divided from the loaded dataset from Dataloader.py is given as input for training the C-RNN model which is taken from the Model.py module. The model was trained 2–3 times and the one with the best accuracy was finally saved as a snapshot which is taken at defined intervals during the training of the dataset.

12.4.2 Validation

After training of the dataset, validation of the saved model takes place in order to calculate validation error rate of the saved model. In our case, validation error rate was around 13%.

12.4.3 Testing

After we have our trained model saved, we test it for various images to ensure that we get the desired output. Before recognition of text, it is sent to the Preprocessor.py module for pre-processing, and the recognized text is displayed on the terminal.

Table 12.2 shows how the scanned image is processed and the output is provided. Different writing styles, papers, pen colors, backgrounds with varying noise, etc. have been used for testing purposes.

Table 12.2   Testing Output of the Implemented System

Input Image	After Pre-Processing	Recognized Text
ज्ञान	ज्ञान	ज्ञान
जहाज़	जहाज़	जहाज़
विस्की	विस्की	वस्िको
उत्सुकता	उत्सुकता	उत्सुकता
पापा - परी	पापा - परी	पापा-परी
पक्षी	पक्षी	पक्षी
प्राची	प्राची	पुराची
बॉल	बॉल	बॉल
अक्कल	अक्कल	अक्कल
शब्द	शब्द	शब्द
जन्म	जन्म	जन्म
कुत्रा	कुत्रा	कुत्रा
रविंद्र	रविंद्र	रवद्िर
दुष्ट	दुष्ट	दुष्ट
इंग्रजी	इंग्रजी	इंग्रजी

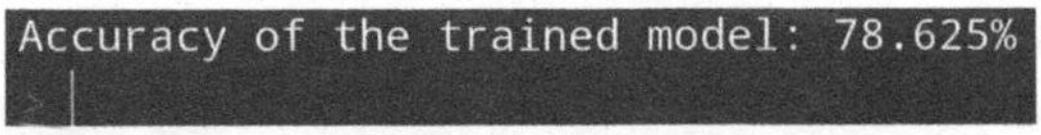

```
Accuracy of the trained model: 78.625%
>|
```

Figure 12.9 Accuracy of the model.

■ **Accuracy:**
   After training the model, the accuracy of the model obtained was
   78.625%. For this, a testing dataset module from IIIT-HWDev dataset was
   used (Figure 12.9).

12.5 Conclusion and Future Scope

A large population of India uses Indic scripts and Devanagari is one such script that
is used on a large scale, especially in rural areas. Digitization of such scripts can aid
in easy storage, editing, searching, optimization and other operations on the given
script. Digitization of such scripts and languages is done by an optical character
recognition system. As the Devanagari script is a complex script unlike the English
language, the variations in the writing of different users have prevented any existing
systems from a great deal of accuracy.

The existing systems in the field of Devanagari text recognition have generally
proposed a three-step solution to the problem.

These systems basically take the image of a handwritten text from the user as
input. Pre-processing is the first step performed on the input. Gray scaling, binarization, skew correction and noise reduction are the most common operations
performed in the pre-processing step. These are performed to minimize any background noise or irregularities in the input to aid the following steps.

The next step is feature extraction which is done by methods like principal component analysis, distance transformation, chain code, etc. The extracted features are
then passed on to a trained classifier. Trained classifiers find out the best matching
class by comparing the stored pattern with input features. Classifiers like CNN,
RNN, KNN and SVM are generally used.

The above process involves character-by-character segmentation of the word.
First, the header line, called the Shirorekha, present in the Devanagari script is
removed. Then, the word is segmented into three zones: the upper zone which is
the portion above the header line, the middle zone and the lower zone which may
contain a vowel or consonant modifier. The issue pertaining to these systems is
that different datasets have been used by different systems. There is no benchmark
dataset to test a given approach. Also, the size of these datasets is not large enough.

The proposed system makes the handwritten Devanagari word recognition possible with deep learning at a word level using convolutional and recurrent neural
networks to recognize the handwritten word without segmentation into individual

characters. This system eliminates the Shirorekha removal and character segmentation steps that have been used in most of the Devanagari text recognition OCRs before this. Our proposed system consists of two major components: the text recognizer application and the processing server. The application lets the users upload a scanned image of the handwritten text. The main part of the handwritten Devanagari character recognition takes place in the processing server which again consists of two sub-parts: the pre-processing unit and the feature extraction and recognition unit. The pre-processing unit is of utmost importance as it helps in achieving good recognition rates. It includes gray scaling, binarization, noise removal and skew correction. Next, the input is passed to the CNN network for feature extraction. Then, the extracted feature vectors are passed to the two layers of LSTM to form one BLSTM to maintain text dependencies efficiently from both directions which is the RNN part of the network. The CTC loss function is used to train the model, and finally, the CTC decode function is used to obtain the output. This approach does not segment the word character by character but recognizes the word as a whole. However, some constraints will affect the accuracy of any such approach. Variations in handwriting styles, blurred images or improperly scanned images can affect the accuracy of the recognition.

In this way, the system performs word recognition without the segmentation process.

The scope of the system can be further expanded. It can be used for line-level script recognition as well. This can be done with the addition of a few layers on the model and a line-level image dataset. If such a dataset is not available, then one can also segment the line into words and then pass the segmented words in a batch of images for prediction and recognition. This can be extended into handwritten text recognition of a few other languages with a condition that a suitable dataset is available for that language.

References

[1] K. Dutta, P. Krishnan, M. Mathew and C. V. Jawahar, "Offline handwriting recognition on devanagari using a new benchmark dataset." *2018 13th IAPR International Workshop on Document Analysis Systems (DAS)*, 25–30, Vienna, Austria, 2018.

[2] Manoj Sonkusare, Roopam Gupta and Asmita Moghe, *A Review on Handwritten Devanagari Character Recognition*, EasyChair Preprints, 2019.

[3] Pankaj Kale, Arti V. Bang, and Devashree Joshi, "Recognition of handwritten Devanagari characters using machine learning approach." *International Journal of Industrial Electronics and Electrical Engineering*, 2015.

[4] S. Puri and S.P. Singh, "An efficient Devanagari character classification in printed and handwritten documents using SVM." *International Conference on Pervasive Computing Advances and Applicationss*, 2019.

[5] R. Jayadevan, S. R. Kolhe, P. M. Patil, and U. Pal. "Offline recognition of Devanagari script: A survey." *IEEE Transactions on Systems, Man, and Cybernetics, Part C (Applications and Reviews)*, 41(6):782–796, 2011.

[6] Parul Sahare and Sanjay B. Dhok, "Multilingual character segmentation and recognition schemes for Indian document images." *IEEE Access*, 2018.

[7] S. P. Deore, and A. Pravin, "Ensembling: Model of histogram of oriented gradient based handwritten Devanagari character recognition system." *International Information and Engineering Technology Association*, 2017.

[8] Bappaditya Chakraborty, Bikash Shaw, Jayanta Aich, Ujjwal Bhattacharya and Swapan Kumar Parui, "Does deeper network lead to better accuracy: A case study on handwritten Devanagari characters." *IEEE*, 2018.

[9] Naveen Malik and Aashdeep Singh, "Character recognition of offline handwritten Devanagari script using artificial neural network." *International Journal of Advanced Computing Research*, 2016.

[10] Kunal Ravindra Shah, "Handwritten Devanagari character recognition." *International Journal of Engineering Research*, 2014.

[11] Prasad Chavan, Suyog Sankpal, Akshay Sonawane, Shahid Shaikh, and Anup Raut, "Handwritten Devnagari optical character recognition", *International Journal of Innovative Research in Computer Science & Technology (IJIRCST)*, 2014.

[12] Aradhana A. Malanker and Mitul M. Patel. *Handwritten Devanagari Script Recognition: A Survey*, IOSR-JEEE, 2014.

[13] Alex Graves, Santiago Fern, Faustino Gomez and Jurgen Schmidhuber, "Connectionist temporal classification: Labelling unsegmented sequence data with recurrent neural networks", *23rd International Conference on Machine Learning*, Pittsburgh, PA, 2006.

Chapter 13

Wall Paint Visualizer Using Panoptic Segmentation

Martin Devasia, Sakshi Shetty, Sheldon Moonjelil, Leander Pereira, and Vaishali Jadhav

St. Francis Institute of Technology

Contents

13.1 Introduction

In architecture and interior design, colour is an important means to modify the visual experience of interiors such that it meets the users' requirements. Apart from the aesthetic impression they create, surface colours of interior space affect

DOI: 10.1201/9781003390220-13

performance as well as emotion and well-being. Surface colour is even supposed to have the power to change the room's perceived layout [1].

Walls are an integral part of the foundation of a room. Walls are something that express a lot about a particular place, and they are usually something that catches the eye first. Wall paints are something that defines the look of the room. While painting, one often comes across the paint catalogue having pages filled with different colours.

As a potent tool of communication, colour has long played an important role in our lives. Colours can have a significant impact on our mental well-being. As a result, picking the proper colour to paint our house is critical. However, not only because of the paradox of choice or conflict of preferences but also because of the inability to imagine multiple colour effects on real walls, the selection process can be overwhelming. The importance of colour design is derived from the significance of colour to the human mind. The colour wheel is an integral tool to find the colours that complement each other in the colour spectrum. Business and corporate offices usually have to adhere to a particular kind of colour scheme that matches their brand. This whole process could end up being very time-consuming.

This book chapter puts forward a system where a user will be able to visualize their wall to be painted from a wide range of colours. It also provides options to suggest colour combinations based on the chosen colour along with extracting the colour palette from an image.

The book chapter is organized as follows: Section 13.2 presents a review of the related work regarding the different methodologies used. Section 13.3 presents the proposed system methodology. Section 13.4 presents the results of the proposed system. Finally, Section 13.5 summarizes the chapter in the conclusion section and includes the further future work needed for the system.

13.2 Related Work

Arbelaez-Estrada et al. [2] developed a system which allowed the user to select a scheme of colours for a product using the natural user interface (NUI) in a 3D environment. The system consisted of a script written in Python that acted as a user interface which allowed the user to control the 3D software with a web camera and a wireless presenter. The system used Blender for the 3D modelling of the product concept and a digital camera for the 3D scanning of the environment. Due to the vibration of the digital camera, the product visualization in the 3D context was sometimes distorted. Also, this system implemented NUI for the designing of conceptual products instead of walls.

Kulshreshtha et al. [3] presented a case study that focussed on the design challenges and evaluation process of the Nippon Paint Colour Visualization application. This case study comprised the iterative designs of the application and these iterative designs were evaluated by several users on the basis of the performance of the tasks like 'painting' the walls using the pictures taken, saving the 'painting' projects for later, buying the actual paint through the app and finally sending the 'painted' screenshots to others, with additional features of layering and masking the walls. In the application, it was required by the users to manually cover the walls that need to be painted. The colour variations after saving the final image were not seen clearly.

Ritter et al. [4] created an interactive texture painting system that allowed users to paint a digital image and used a texture synthesis algorithm to create a texture with natural-looking boundary effects. In order to design an image, the user must first provide a set of example textures that represent a palette. After loading these textures into the system, the user can choose a texture and paint with it on a canvas provided by the application. The system dynamically synthesizes the selected texture in the newly painted region of the canvas as the user moves the virtual brush. This system had difficulty in synthesizing the structured boundaries in a painting.

Martin et al. [5] developed a mapping system for Augmented Reality on a mobile phone that aimed to achieve the real-time requirement and cope with the scale factor and the lack of positioning issue. The process is divided into three stages: Mapping, Augmentation Design and Localization. The responsibility of mapping was to develop a map, which is a cloud of 3D points that will be used as a frame for augmentation design and localization. Each virtual object was placed in the reference frame of the entire map during the augmentation process. This allowed for the monitoring and tracking of augmentations. The end-user used localization to track the map and relocalize itself automatically and manually based on the saved keyframes. In the application, the user had to go through multiple steps to find a preferred colour combination. It did not have the feature to extract colours from any image.

Gonsalves et al. [6] developed an interactive genetic algorithm to generate colour combinations based on user preference. By selecting a colour for each of the four objects as well as the background, the user initiates the interactive process. On the interface, there are several radio buttons. In the next iGA generation, the user can choose whether the colour of a given object and/or the background should be made lighter, darker or more vivid. In the iGA depiction, the user's colour combination options on the interface constitute a 'solution'. The iGA system's goal is to maximize this combination while taking into account the lighter/darker/vividness of the user-selected colours. The system does this by assessing the current solution's fitness. It then generates the next solution based on the user's preferences and a small bit of randomness. The user can choose from the system's suggested colour combinations. The user-iGA interaction cycles continue until the user is happy with the colour combination that the system has proposed. It is a real-time process that does not cause any user fatigue. The application did not have the feature to save multiple colour combinations.

Liu David et al. [7] demonstrated a mobile app for such an application that was developed on the iOS platform. The software uses an iOS device's live camera stream to do three key tasks: (i) it segments off a wall region based on a user-defined seed point; (ii) it monitors the wall region as the camera moves; and (iii) it changes the colour of the wall to a user-selected colour. All of this is done at video frame rates, so when a user looks via the camera on an iOS device, the wall appears to be painted in a new colour. The application is only usable on iOS devices. It requires users to select walls, and in case the walls are partitioned or divided, it misses covering and painting all the wall regions.

Liu Ting et al. [8] developed Magic-wall, a semantic-aware technique for wall colour modification. To create the final visual effect, the user first takes a snapshot of the target room and then feeds the inside scene photograph with a desired hue into the Magic-wall system. The Magic-wall, in particular, is capable of automatically locating wall regions and naturally substituting the desired colour for the current colour of the walls. The entire process of wall colour editing, including wall segmentation and colour replacement, is guided by visual semantics in Magic-wall. Basically, the system uses a state-of-the-art semantic segmentation framework, namely a deep fully convolutional neural network, as the backbone of the proposed Magic-wall for parsing an input image. In the application, if the input image contains a mirror on the wall, it fails to replace the colour on the reflected wall area.

13.3 Methodology

Several methods and algorithms were considered for initial wall detection and selecting the seed point for flood filling. Later, image processing techniques and colour thresholding techniques were applied to replace the walls with a preferred colour, and further processing and colour space conversion were done to give a realistic look to the replaced wall. Since the objective was not to create a real-time application, a slight time delay was admissible but faster and more efficient sub-processes were required for near real-time computation. Figure 13.1 presents the block diagram of the proposed system.

13.3.1 Wall Segmentation

The first process is detection of walls and identifying wall regions in the input image. Panoptic segmentation was performed on the image using the detectron2 model [9], and detected walls are used for further processing. Even though detectron2 successfully detects major wall regions, the segmentation is not extremely accurate as it wrongly labels some other objects as walls. Thus, further processing is needed. Since the model output gives a binary mask of major wall regions, the actual colour of the wall can be identified assuming that the actual regions of the

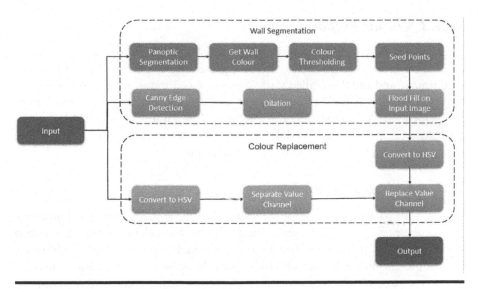

Figure 13.1   System block diagram.

binary wall mask produced by the model contain maximum pixels with the same colour as the wall colour. Thus, the colour with maximum pixels in the binary mask is taken as the wall colour.

On identifying the wall colour, thresholding is used to get a binary mask of the identified wall colour from the model output. Flood fill is performed over the wall area using pixels on the binary mask output of thresholding operation as the seed point. The result of edge detection discussed in the next section is passed into the flood fill operation as an input mask, so that flood filling does not overflow beyond the detected edges. The flood fill function in OpenCV fills a connected component with the specified colour starting from the seed point. The connectivity is determined by the proximity of the neighbour pixels in terms of colour or brightness. It then outputs the logical OR of the original mask and the filled-in regions, so the edges are subtracted out to yield a mask selecting only the wall. The mask is then coloured with the user's preferred colour.

13.3.2 Edge Detection

For edge detection, Canny edge detection algorithm is used. To get better results, edge detection is performed on both the greyscale version and also on the S channel obtained from the hue, saturation and value (HSV) version of the image. Further Gaussian blur is applied on both the previous images with a kernel of size three to smoothen weak edges. Then, Canny edge detection is applied on both lower and upper threshold values of 85 and 255 along with a Sobel kernel of three for calculating a gradient. Both these outputs are then merged and used as a mask for the flood fill algorithm.

13.3.3 Colour Replacement

After flood fill, the wall is replaced with the selected colour. The final step is to give a realistic look to the replaced wall colour-preserving brightness. First, the initial input image and the flood-filled wall colour-replaced image are converted into an HSV format. Then, the V channel of the latter is replaced with the V channel of the former. The V channel contains the brightness value that when added to the replaced wall colour images retains the brightness of each pixel. Finally, the image is converted back into RGB and displayed as output.

13.3.4 Colour Harmonies

In the colour palette generator for the user within the app, the user first chooses the initial colour of choice for the wall. The generator then calculates a tetradic colour scheme based on this colour. The tetradic colour scheme is a colour combination pattern present on the colour wheel where all the colours are at an equal distance from each other, which usually produces good colour combinations, thus giving the user more colour combination ideas for the walls.

13.4 Results and Discussions

The performance of the system was evaluated based on the time taken for each process at each stage. On some specific input images, the limitations of the algorithm were observed which is discussed further. In Table 13.1, the processing time for each of the functions in the system is presented.

Figure 13.2 shows the best case where the input image has a wall colour distinct from all surrounding objects and a good resolution. Here, Canny edge detection gives better results leading to better flood fill, giving an accurately segmented wall with crisp edges and pleasing colour replacement.

As shown in Figure 13.3, where some objects have fairly similar colour as the wall, Canny edge detection misses out some edges near similar-coloured objects and flood

Table 13.1 Processing Time

Process	Time (ms)
Wall segmentation	26,786
Wall colour identification	1,025
Edge detection	23
Thresholding	3
Flood fill	2,697
Colour adjustment	3,317

Figure 13.2   Paint visualization: best case.

Figure 13.3   Paint visualization: average case.

fill slightly bleeds out of wall boundaries into other objects. But even after this limitation, the final output gives quite a pleasing visualization of the replaced wall colour due to the brightness preservation applied in the colour replacement procedure.

In Figure 13.4, where the input is almost a monochromatic image with most objects near the wall having a similar colour, the flood fill operation has more chances of bleeding which gives an unsatisfactory wall colour replacement. But since the brightness is maintained, the final result is quite convincing and visible.

Figure 13.4   Paint visualization: worst case.

Images with good resolution and more distinct wall colours produce the best visualization of paint replacement. This system uses a flood fill algorithm in order to cover the wall regions. The flood fill algorithm starts with a pixel and keeps adding surrounding pixels that have the same colour in a given range or until it reaches the boundary specified in the flood fill mask. The flood fill mask generated using edge detection may sometimes fail to detect all exact edges of the wall since the threshold values passed for Canny edge detection depend on different factors of the image and may differ for different images. Thus, the flood fill may sometimes bleed out of the actual wall regions when the objects around the walls have the same or similar colour as the wall or edge detection fails to detect any edges in the image.

Figure 13.5 shows the application of different wall colours on different given input images.

Figure 13.5   Different wall colours applied on the input image.

13.5 Conclusion

This chapter has presented a Wall Paint Visualizer using Panoptic Segmentation that will help a user virtually visualize a wall paint on the wall before actually painting the wall. To achieve this goal, the detectron2 library has been used for the detection and segmentation of the wall in the given input image. Canny edge detection algorithm has also been used for the edge detection of the walls. Using the flood fill algorithm, the wall is replaced with the selected colour. Finally, for light preservation and realistic paint visualization, HSV format conversion is applied to the input and final images. For user usage, the application was deployed as a web application, where users can visualize different wall colours on the input image with their own colour as well as get wall colour suggestions.

In the future, we would like to implement the system for wall paint visualization on a real-time video input. Also, we would like to use dynamically generated threshold values for Canny edge detection and colour filtering based on the input image, so that more accurate edges can be detected, and better colour filtering can be performed.

References

[1] C. von Castell, H. Hecht, and D. Oberfeld, "Bright paint makes interior-space surfaces appear farther away," *PloS One*, vol. 13, no. 9, p. e0201976, 2018.
[2] J. C. Arbelaez-Estrada and G. Osorio-Gómez, "Natural user interface for color selection in conceptual design phase," *International Journal on Interactive Design and Manufacturing (IJIDeM)*, vol. 11, no. 1, pp. 45–53, 2017.
[3] K. Kulshreshtha, A. I. Niculescu, and B. Wadhwa, "On the design and evaluation of nippon paint color visualizer application–a case study," in *IFIP Conference on Human-Computer Interaction*, Springer, 2017, pp. 372–376.
[4] L. Ritter, W. Li, B. Curless, M. Agrawala, and D. Salesin, "Painting with texture," in *Rendering Techniques*, 2006, pp. 371–376.
[5] P. Martin, E. Marchand, P. Houlier, and I. Marchal, "Decoupled mapping and localization for augmented reality on a mobile phone," in *2014 IEEE Virtual Reality (VR)*. IEEE, 2014, pp. 97–98.
[6] T. Gonsalves and A. Kawai, "User preferred color combination design using interactive genetic algorithm," *Computer Science & Information Technology*, pp. 169–174, 2014.
[7] D. Liu, J. Piersol, and S. Yeung, "Real-time segmentation, tracking, and coloring of walls using iOS,"
[8] T. Liu, Y. Wei, Y. Zhao, S. Liu, and S. Wei, "Magic-wall: Visualizing room decoration by enhanced wall segmentation," *IEEE Transactions on Image Processing*, vol. 28, no. 9, pp. 4219–4232, 2019.
[9] Y. Wu, A. Kirillov, F. Massa, W.-Y. Lo, and R. Girshick, "Detectron2," https://github.com/facebookresearch/detectron2, 2019.

Chapter 14

Fashion Intelligence: An Artificial Intelligence-Based Clothing Fashion Stylist

Pavan Raval, Raj Shah, Vrutik Adani, Lissa Rodrigues, and Vaishali Jadhav
St. Francis Institute of Technology

Contents

DOI: 10.1201/9781003390220-14

14.1 Introduction

Transferring an article of clothing into a product image is a generative task that involves converting the clothing item into a new item, which is then depicted in a separate image used for marketing or sales purposes. With the increased popularity of online shopping, virtually wearing the apparel may enhance a customer's experience by providing a sense of how these products might appear on them. To demonstrate the limits of current Fashion Intelligence approaches, we partition the VITON dataset into three difficulty level subsets based on the human stance in 2D reference photos. The first row in Figure 14.1 shows a simple example from the VITON dataset in which the individual in the image is depicted with a conventional posture, i.e., face forward and hands down. In this scenario, the approaches must simply align the semantic areas of the reference and target pictures. This category includes several ground-breaking synthesis based approaches. The image with the medium-level difficulty from the second row is often with torso posture alterations. Several models have also been proposed in order to maintain the qualities of the garments, such as texture, brand, embroidery, and so on. This is often accomplished by building powerful warping algorithms to match the reference image with clothing deformation [5].

The last row of Figure 14.1 shows a concrete example of postural alterations on both the torso and limbs, resulting in spatial interactions between garment areas and human body components, such as occlusions, disruptions, and deformation. As a result, an adequate algorithm is necessary to comprehend the spatial arrangement of the foreground and background items in the reference image and adaptively keep such an occlusion connection during the Fashion Intelligence procedure. However, content creation and preservation remain unresolved issues in Fashion Intelligence.

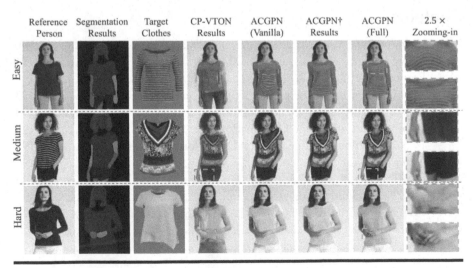

Figure 14.1 Difficulty level of fashion outfits.

To solve the difficulties, we present VITON-HD, a unique high-resolution virtual try-on approach. Specifically, we describe a novel clothing-agnostic human representation that uses position information and segmentation map to completely omit garment information. The segmentation map and clothing item distorted to match the specific human body are then fed into the model. Using this extra data, our innovative ALIgnment-Aware Segment (ALIAS) normalization eliminates information unrelated to the garment texture in misaligned regions and propagates the semantic information across the network. The normalization standardizes the activations related to the misaligned and other areas independently and modulates the standardized activations using the segmentation map. Through multiscale refinement at the feature level, our ALIAS generator synthesizes the human picture wearing the target product while filling the misalignment regions with the clothing texture and keeping the features of the clothing item. To test the performance of our system, we collected a dataset of 1,024×768 pairings of a person and a clothing item for our research. Our results show that VITON-HD outperforms previous approaches in both quantitative and qualitative terms when creating 1,024×768 pictures. We also demonstrate the superiority of our innovative ALIAS normalization module in coping with misaligned regions. We characterize our work as follows:

(i) We provide VITON-HD, a revolutionary image-based virtual try-on technique that, to the best of our knowledge, is the first model to successfully synthesize 1,024×768 pictures. (ii) We offer a clothing-agnostic human representation, which allows our model to be independent of the individual's original clothing item. (iii) To address the mismatch between the warped clothes and the required clothing areas, we offer ALIAS normalization and an ALIAS generator, both of which are successful in preserving clothing features. (iv) We illustrate our method's higher performance by doing tests using baselines on the freshly gathered dataset [5].

14.2 Related Work

Over the past few years, a number of effective recommendation models have been proposed to improve fashion recommendations. To further enhance their performance, this study proposes integrating image semantics by considering the semantic properties of products. Specifically, an interpretable semantic space is defined to extract pre-segmented image regions that correspond to the attributes and interests described by users. In fact, a fashionable image in the above method ignores different user preferences for different parts of the modal image as it is converted into a fixed-length vector. Or, while taking into account the user's customization options for the modal image, ignore the limited visibility of the image and then ignore these invisible options. However, in our model, we derive a large number of user preferences visible and invisible to the target from historical reviews. We're not only improving the performance of our recommendations but also implementing collaborative interpretation of images and texts [3].

Conditional Generative Adversarial Networks (cGANs) use additional information such as class names, texts, and attributes to control the imaging process. However, these methods tend to produce blurry images when dealing with large spatial deformations between the input image and the target image. In this paper, we propose a method that can deal with the spatial deformation of the input image and appropriately generate a 1,024×768 image. Using the misalignment mask as external data, the proposed normalization layer calculates the mean and variance of the misaligned area and other areas in the instance separately.

Although the 3D model-based approach can accurately simulate clothing, it is not widely used because it relies on 3D measurement data. The 2D image-based approach is computationally efficient and suitable for practical use because it does not rely on 3D information. Most existing virtual Fashion Intelligence methods process various aspects of VITON to synthesize a perceptually appealing photorealistic image. Adaptive Content Generating and Preserving Network (ACGPN) predicted that the human analysis card of the person wearing the target's clothing would direct the image composition of Fashion Intelligence [9].

There is no doubt that fashion businesses have invested extensively in embracing AR technology, and to do so, they have partnered with IT behemoths who specialize in it. Snapchat is one of these tech companies that want to differentiate itself from AR technologies that act as a portal for virtual try-ons. Snapchat users may now try on clothing, glasses, purses, and jewelry virtually with enhanced technology that recognizes and reacts to body motions and face measurements. Other new features include voice- and gesture-controlled filters, brand shop and product catalog integrations, virtual storefronts, and the ability for users to search for and purchase photographs or products seen in real life. Unsurprisingly, consumers will not only be able to resolve issues related to size, fit, and appearance but will also be able to explore options, make adjustments, and try on a wider selection of products in less time, resulting in higher conversions and higher costs. Firms can provide more personalization options with virtual try-on, which directly impacts sales and profitability. Customers can use AR to view multiple personalization options to create products that reflect their personality and talent [11].

14.3 Proposed Method

Model overview as explained in Figure 14.2 is $I \in R^{3 \times H \times W}$ for a particular reference image. People and clothes image $c \in R^{3 \times H \times W}$ (H and W indicate the height and width of the image, respectively). The goal of VITON-HD is a composite image $I \in R^{3 \times H \times W}$. Wearing the target clothes c, pose and body shape the details of I and c are retained. During training (I, c, ^I), the model with the trial is simple and the structure is simple; such datasets are costly.

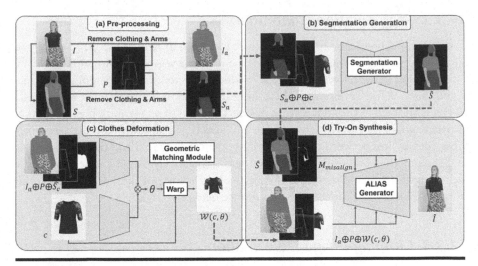

Figure 14.2   Steps for transferring cloth.

Use (I, c, I) instead. The person in the reference photo I'm already wearing c. (I, c, I), direct training can damage the model Ability to generalize during testing, and we configure the first Depiction of a person who is not bound by clothes. Omit Use I's clothing information as input. Our new Expressions that are agnostic to human clothing use both a Map of people to delete and a segmentation map I clothing information. The model generates a segmentation map from a clothing-agnostic representation of a person to support the generation of ^I. Next, transform c to roughly fit the human body. Finally, hit Alignment Aware. Previous Segment (ALIAS) normalization removes misleading information in areas that are not aligned after transformation. c. ALIAS generator fills misaligned areas with clothing Taking care of textures and clothing details.

14.3.1 *Adaptive Content Generating Preserving Network*

The proposed ACGPN is shown in Figure 14.2. First, the Segmentation Generation Module (SGM) gradually creates a mask for body parts Masking distorted clothing areas with semantic segmentation, creating semantic alignment of space Layout. Second, the Clothes Warping Module is designed to target clothing as follows: Warped clothing mask to introduce secondary Difference limits for Thin Plate Splines (TPS) [6] to produce garments that are geometrically consistent but retain their properties Photo. Finally, put steps 3 and 4 into the Content Fusion Module that integrates information adaptively determining the creation or maintenance of each human part in the output composite image from the previous module. The mask repair task takes full advantage of ACGPN's layout adaptability when processing images. Easy, medium, and difficult levels of difficulty.

14.3.2 Segmentation Generation

Considering expressions that are not bound by human clothing (S_a, P) and target garment c, segmentation. The generator GS says the segmentation map $S \in L^{H \times W}$ by the person in the reference image. We educate GS to learn the mapping between S and (S, P, c). The seven original clothing information is complete. It was erased. U-Net is adopted as the architecture of GS. Total loss of segmentation generator LS Written as $L_S = L_{cGAN} + \lambda_{CE} \times L_{CE}$ where L_{CE} and L_{cGAN} represent the pixel-by-pixel cross-entropy loss between the predicted segmentation map $\hat{S}$ and the ground truth map S, and the conditional adversarial loss, respectively. The parameter λ_{CE} is a weighting factor that determines the relative importance of these two losses in the overall LS loss. λ_{CE} is the relative importance between two losses.

14.3.3 Clothing Image Deformation

In this phase, transform the target item of clothing c Match with $\hat{S}$ c; this is the range of $\hat{S}$ clothing. We use the geometric matching module proposed in CP-VTON with clothing-agnostic human representations (I_a, P) and $\hat{S}$. Enter c as input. First, the correlation matrix between the features extracted from (I_a, P) and c is calculated. Using a correlation matrix as input, the regression network predicts TPS transformation parameters θ $R^{2 \times 5 \times 5}$, And c are distorted by θ. In education Phase uses model Sc extracted from S instead of $\hat{S}$ c. The module is distorted with L1 loss. Clothes and clothes Ic were extracted from me. Moreover, the secondary difference condition is adopted. To reduce the apparent distortion of distorted clothing images of transformation. Warp overrides objective function. The clothes that suit the human body are written as follows:

$$L_{warp} = \|I_c - W(c, \theta)\|_{1,1} + \lambda_{const} \times L_{const}$$

where W is a function that transforms c by L_{const}. It is a quadratic difference condition, and const is a hyperparameter of L_{const} [10].

14.3.4 Fashion Intelligence via ALIAS Normalization

Our goal is to generate the final composite image ˆI base about the result of the previous phase. Overall, we Merge expressions of people who are not bound by clothes (I_a, P) And the distorted clothing image W (c, θ) guided by $\hat{S}$. (I_a, P, W (c, θ)) is injected into each layer of the generator. For $\hat{S}$, we propose a new conditional normalization method. It is called ALIAS normalization. ALIAS normalization allows you to use $\hat{S}$ to retain semantic information and remove misleading information from unaligned areas. Masks for these areas. ALIAS normalization has two inputs: (i) the synthetic segmentation map $\hat{S}$; (ii) the misalignment binary mask $M_{misalign}$

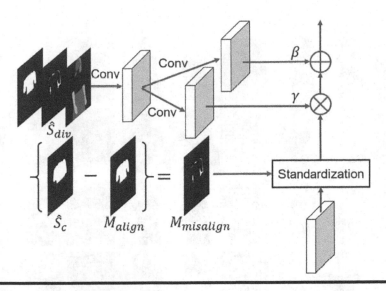

Figure 14.3   ALIAS normalization.

$L^{H \times W}$, which excludes the warped mask of the target clothing image $W(Mc, \theta)$ from $\hat{S}$ c (Mc denotes the target clothing mask), i.e. [7] (Figure 14.3).

$$M_{align} = S_c \cap W(M_c, \theta) \; M_{misalign} = S_c - M_{align}$$

14.4 Experiments

14.4.1 Dataset

Experiments are carried out on the dataset (i.e., the VITON dataset) used in VITON and CP-VITON. It has around 19,000 picture pairings, each with a front-view lady image and a top outfit image. It generates 16,253 pairings after deleting the incorrect picture pairs, which are then divided into a training set of 14,221 pairs and a testing set of 2,032 pairs. ACGPN is pitted against VITON, CP-VTON, and VTNFP. We examine the visual results published in VTNFP's publication and duplicate them for quantitative comparison without using the official VTNFP code. The appendix contains extensive ACGPN try-on findings [5] (Figure 14.4).

14.4.2 Qualitative Analysis

We compare VITON-HD to the publicly accessible codes CP-VTON and ACGPN. Following our model's training and inference procedures, segmentation generators and geometric matching modules of the baselines are trained at 256×192, and their outputs are upscaled to 1,024×768 during inference [9].

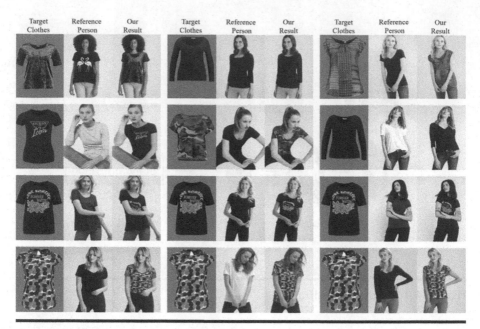

Figure 14.4   Sample input and output.

Figure 14.5   Actual process of fashion intelligence.

14.4.3 Quantitative Analysis

We use Structural SIMilarity (SSIM) to assess the similarity of synthesized pictures to ground truths and Inception Score (IS) to assess the visual quality of generated images. Greater scores on both criteria suggest that the outcomes are of higher quality: the VITON, CP-VTON, VTNFP, and our ACGPN, SSIM, and IS scores. Unsurprisingly, as the difficulty level increases, the SSIM score declines, illustrating the negative link between difficulty level and try-on image quality. Nonetheless, at all difficulty levels, our ACGPN surpasses the other approaches by a wide amount in both criteria. In terms of SSIM, ACGPN outperforms VITON, CP-VTON, and VTNFP by 0.067, 0.101, and 0.044, respectively. The benefits of ACGPN in the middle scenario are 0.062, 0.099, and 0.040, respectively [4] (Figure 14.5).

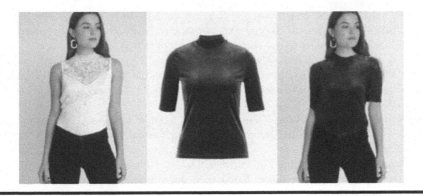

Figure 14.6 Results.

14.5 Conclusion

In this chapter, we introduced a unique adaptive content generating and preserving network (ACGPN) that seeks to provide photorealistic try-on results while maintaining both clothing traits and human identification elements (posture, body parts, and bottom clothes). We showed three carefully built components, namely the Segmentation Generation Module (SGM), the Clothing Image Deformation, and ACGPN. Our ACGPN was tested on the VITON dataset with three levels of try-on difficulty. In terms of quantitative measurements, visual quality, and user studies, the findings clearly demonstrate ACGPN's vast superiority over state-of-the-art approaches [1] (Figure 14.6).

References

[1] H. Joo, T. Simon, and Y. Sheikh, Total capture: A 3d deformation model for tracking faces, hands, and bodies. In: *2018 IEEE/CVF Conference on Computer Vision and Pattern Recognition* (2018), Salt Lake City, UT, USA.

[2] X. Han, Z. Wu, Z. Wu, R. Yu, and L.S. Davis, Viton: An image-based virtual try-on network. In: *The IEEE Conference on Computer Vision and Pattern Recognition (CVPR)* (2018), Salt Lake City, UT, USA.

[3] H. Yang, R. Zhang, X. Guo, W. Liu, W. Zuo, P. Luo. Towards photo-realistic virtual try-on by adaptively generating-preserving image content. In: *IEEE/CVF Conference on Computer Vision and Pattern Recognition (CVPR)* (2020), Seattle, WA, USA.

[4] Q. Wu, P. Zhao, Z. Cui. Visual and textual jointly enhanced interpretable fashion recommendation. *IEEE Access*, (2020), doi: 10.1109/ACCESS.2020.2978272.

[5] H. Lai and S. Lee. The application of artificial intelligence and VR technology in clothing store display design. *IEEE Access*, (2020), doi: 10.1109/ACCESS.2020.3020551.

[6] Chandadevi Giri, Sheenam Jain, Xianyi Zeng and Pascal Bruniaux. A detailed review of artificial intelligence applied in the fashion and apparel industry. *IEEE Access*, (2019), doi: 10.1109/ACCESS.2019.2928979.

[7] M. Tokumaru, N. Muranaka, and S. Imanishi. Virtual stylist project-examination of adapting clothing search system to user's subjectivity with interactive genetic algorithms". *Evolutionary Computation*, 2, 1036–1043 (2003).

[8] Chaitanya Patel, Zhouyingcheng Liao, and Gerard PonsMoll. Tailornet: Predicting clothing in 3d as a function of human pose, shape and garment style. In *Proceedings of the IEEE/CVF Conference on Computer Vision and Pattern Recognition*, 7365–7375 (2020), Seattle, WA, USA, 2020, pp. 7365–7375.

[9] Ruimao Zhang, Wei Yang, Zhanglin Peng, Pengxu Wei, Xiaogang Wang, and Liang Lin. Progressively diffused networks for semantic visual parsing. *Pattern Recognition*, 90, 78–86 (2019).

[10] Amit Raj, Patsorn Sangkloy, Huiwen Chang, James Hays, Duygu Ceylan, and Jingwan Lu. Swapnet: Image based garment transfer. *Lecture Notes in Computer Science*, 11216, 679–695 (2018).

Index